Lecture Notes in Artificial Intelligence   3034

Edited by J. G. Carbonell and J. Siekmann

Subseries of Lecture Notes in Computer Science

Springer
Berlin
Heidelberg
New York
Hong Kong
London
Milan
Paris
Tokyo

Jesus Favela   Ernestina Menasalvas
Edgar Chávez (Eds.)

Advances in
Web Intelligence

Second International
Atlantic Web Intelligence Conference, AWIC 2004
Cancun, Mexico, May 16-19, 2004
Proceedings

 Springer

Series Editors

Jaime G. Carbonell, Carnegie Mellon University, Pittsburgh, PA, USA
Jörg Siekmann, University of Saarland, Saarbrücken, Germany

Volume Editors

Jesus Favela
CICESE, Departmento de Ciencias de la Computación
Km. 107 Carr. Tijuana-Ensenada, Ensenada, B.C. Mexico
E-mail: favela@cicese.mx

Ernestina Menasalvas
Universidad Politécnica de Madrid, Facultad de Informática
Campus de Montegancedo, Boadilla del Monte, 28660 Madrid, Spain
E-mail: emenasalvas@fi.upm.es

Edgar Chávez
Universidad Michoacana de San Nicolás de Hidalgo
Escuela de Ciencias Físico-Matemáticas
Edificio "B", Ciudad Universitaria, Morelia, Michoacan, Mexico
E-mail: elchavez@fismat.umich.mx

Library of Congress Control Number: 2004105252

CR Subject Classification (1998): I.2, H.3, H.4, C.2, H.5, J.1, J.2

ISSN 0302-9743
ISBN 3-540-22009-7 Springer-Verlag Berlin Heidelberg New York

Springer-Verlag is a part of Springer Science+Business Media

springeronline.com

© Springer-Verlag Berlin Heidelberg 2004
Printed in Germany

Typesetting: Camera-ready by author, data conversion by Boller Mediendesign
Printed on acid-free paper   SPIN: 11007968   06/3142   5 4 3 2 1 0

Preface

This volume constitutes the proceedings of the 2nd Atlantic Web Intelligence Conference (AWIC 2004). The conference was held in the city of Cancun, Mexico, a setting that inspired lively discussions and reflections on open issues facing the field of Web intelligence.

The AWIC conferences have been motivated by advances in the field of artificial intelligence and the challenges facing their application to Web-based systems. With this second edition, AWIC provided a forum for specialists from different disciplines of computer science to exchange their experiences and ideas in this growing field of research.

The selection of papers followed a strict, double-blind refereeing process by a renowned international committee. We received 57 contributions, with first authors from 15 different countries, from which 22 papers were selected to be presented and published in this proceedings volume. We thank all members of the Program Committee for their valuable reviews of the papers.

In addition, we were pleased to have as invited speakers Dr. Prabhakar Raghavan, Chief Scientist and Vice President of Emerging Technologies in Verity, Inc. and Consulting Professor of Computer Science at Stanford University, and Prof. C. Lee Giles, Davide Reese Professor of the School of Information Sciences and Technology at The Pennsylvania State University. Abstracts of their lectures are included in these proceedings.

In putting together this conference, we had the pleasure of working with an outstanding group of people. We thank them all for their hard work on behalf of this conference. In particular we would like to thank Manuel Montes y Gómez, Director of the Mexico Research Centre of the Web Intelligence Consortium, Elisa Moran, Marcela Rodríguez, and Jorge Niebla.

We extend a special acknowledgment to our sponsoring organizations: Centro de Investigación Científica y de Educación Superior de Ensenada, B.C., Universidad Michoacana de San Nicolás de Hidalgo, Instituto Nacional de Astrofísica, Óptica y Electrónica, and Sociedad Mexicana de Ciencia de la Computación, in Mexico, and Universidad Politécnica de Madrid, in Spain.

Last, but certainly not least, we thank you for your interest in AWIC 2004, and very much hope you find these conference proceedings to be enriching.

May 2004

Jesus Favela
Ernestina Menasalvas
Edgar Chávez

Conference Organization

Honorary Chair

Lofti A. Zadeh (University of California, USA)

Steering Committee

Janusz Kacprzyk (Polish Academy of Sciences, Poland)
Jiming Liu (Hong Kong Baptist University)
Javier Segovia (Universidad Politécnica de Madrid, Spain)
Piotr Szczepaniak (Technical University of Lodz, Poland)
Ning Zhong (Maebashi Institute of Technology, Japan)

Conference Chairs

Jesus Favela (CICESE, Ensenada, Mexico)
Ernestina Menasalvas (Universidad Politécnica de Madrid, Spain)

Organizing Committee Chair

Edgar Chávez (Universidad Michoacana, Mexico)

Publicity Chair

Manuel Montes y Gómez (INAOE, Mexico)

Program Committee

Ricardo Baeza-Yates (University of Chile, Chile)
Tu Bao Ho (Advanced Institute of Science and Technology, Japan)
Patrick Brézillon (University of Paris VI, Paris, France)
Alex Buchner (University of Ulster, Northern Ireland, UK)
Edgar Chávez (Universidad Michoacana, Mexico)
Pedro A. Da Costa Sousa (Uninova, Portugal)
Dominique Decouchant (LSR-IMAG, Grenoble, France)

Reviewers

R. Baeza-Yates
T. Bao Ho
P. Brézillon
A. Buchner
E. Chávez
P.A. Da Costa Sousa
D. Decouchant
L. Dey
J. Favela
J.A. García-Macías
A. Ghorbani
J. Ghosh
J. Gonzalez
E. Menasalvas
M. Hadjimichael
E. Herrera Viedma
E. Hochzstain
A. Hotho
J. Kacprzyk
S. Kaski
R. Kruse
J. Liu
A. López
A.M. Martínez
O. Marban
O. Mayora
D. Memmi

S. Millan
B. Mobasher
M. Montes y Gómez
B. Motik
A. Nanolopoulos
A. Nuernberger
M. Perez
M. Piattini
P. Quaresma
R. Rastogi
V. Robles
G. Rossi
A. Skowron
M. Spiliopoulou
S. Staab
R. Tadeusiewicz
A. Tchernykh
K. Thornton
M.A. Vila
A. Vizcaino
A. Wasilewska
X. Wu
R. Yager
P.S. Yu
S. Zadrozny
M. Zaki
W. Ziarko

Sponsoring Institutions

Centro de Investigación Científica y de Educación Superior de Ensenada, Mexico
Instituto Nacional de Astrofísica, Óptica y Electrónica, Mexico
Universidad Michoacana de San Nicolás de Hidalgo, Mexico
Universidad Politécnica de Madrid, Spain
Sociedad Mexicana de Ciencia de la Computación, Mexico

Table of Contents

Soft Computing Methods I

Text Processing and Semantic Web

Web Information Retrieval

Categorization and Ranking

Soft Computing Methods II

Social Networks and the Web

Prabhakar Raghavan

Verity, Inc.
892 Ross Drive, Sunnyvale CA 94089, USA
pragh@verity.com

Abstract. Link analysis for web search spawned a surge of interest in mathematical techniques for improving the user experience in information retrieval. Although developed initially to combat the "spamming" of text-based search engines, link analysis has over time become susceptible to innovative forms of "link spam"; the battle continues between web search engines seeking to preserve editorial integrity and their adversaries with strong commercial interests. Such link analysis is but one visible example of the broader area of social network analysis, which originated with the classic experiment from the 60's due to Stanley Milgram, leading to the popular folklore that any two humans have at most "six degrees of separation". Over the last ten years, these ideas from social network analysis have progressed beyond networks of links between people. The divestiture of the telephone monopoly in the United States (and subsequently in other countries) led to the study of networks of phone calls. In the network of emails between users, dense regions are know to form around participants with common topical interests. A new breed of examples comes from so-called *recommendation systems* deployed at eCommerce sites on the web: by analyzing the links between people and the products they purchase or rate, the system recommends to users what products they might be interested in, based on their and other users' past behavior. The simplest incarnation is a recommendation of the form "people who purchased this item also purchased ..." While these examples are promising, much work remains to be done in this nascent area. For instance, what are the models and criteria by which to optimize such systems? How should they be evaluated? How (if at all) should users be compensated for offering their opinions on items, given that the eCommerce site is profiting from these opinions? We describe analytical approaches to these questions drawing from linear algebra and game theory. Recent work has begun exploring so-called *webs of trust*-networks in which a link from one user to another carries a real number denoting how much the first user trusts (or distrusts) the second. Such networks are a critical ingredient at websites such as eBay and epinions. Studies in economics suggest that there is a direct relationship between the trust assigned to a seller and the price that he can charge for a given item. Many computational questions arise in such webs of trust. If A distrusts B and B distrusts C, what does this imply about A's trust for C? If C likes a book, is A likely to? Questions such as these must first be resolved at a philosophical level before being approached mathematically. We describe some recent results in this area that raise a number of questions for further work.

J. Favela et al. (Eds.): AWIC 2004, LNAI 3034, pp. 1-1, 2004.
© Springer-Verlag Berlin Heidelberg 2004

CiteSeer: Past, Present, and Future

Dr. C. Lee Giles

David Reese Professor, School of Information Sciences and Technology
Professor, Computer Science and Engineering
Professor, Supply Chain and Information Systems
Associate Director, eBusiness Research Center
The Pennsylvania State University
University Park, PA
giles@ist.psu.edu

Abstract. CiteSeer, a computer science digital library, has been a radical departure for scientific document access and analysis. With nearly 600,000 documents, it has over a million page views a day making it one of the most popular document access engines in computer and information science. CiteSeer is also portable, having been extended to ebusiness (eBizSearch) and more recently to academic business documents (SMEALSearch). CiteSeer is really based on two features: actively acquiring new documents and automatic tagging and linking of metadata information inherent in an academic document's syntactic structure. We discuss methods for providing new tagged metadata and other data resources such as institutions and acknowledgements.

A Fuzzy Linguistic Multi-agent Model for Information Gathering on the Web Based on Collaborative Filtering Techniques

Enrique Herrera-Viedma, Carlos Porcel, Antonio Gabriel López,
María Dolores Olvera, and Karina Anaya

School of Library Science, Univ. of Granada, Spain

Abstract. Information gathering in Internet is a complex activity. A solution consists in to assist Internet users in their information gathering processes by means of distributed intelligent agents in order to find the fittest information to their information needs. In this paper we describe a fuzzy linguistic multi-agent model that incorporates information filtering techniques in its structure, i.e., a collaborative filtering agent. In such a way, the information filtering possibilities of multi-agent system on the Web are increased and its retrieval results are improved.

1 Introduction

The exponential increase in Web sites and Web documents is contributing to that Internet users not being able to find the information they seek in a simple and timely manner. Users are in need of tools to help them cope with the large amount of information available on the Web [15,16]. Therefore, techniques for searching and mining the Web are becoming increasing vital. Two important techniques that have been addressed in improving the information access on the Web are related to *intelligent agents* and *information filtering*.

Intelligent agents applied on the Web deal with the information gathering process assisting Internet users to find the fittest information to their needs [3,9,14,26]. Usually, several intelligent agents (e.g. interface agent, information discovery agent) organized in distributed architectures take part in the information gathering activity [3,8,9,14,19]. The problem is the design of appropriate communication protocols among the agents. The great variety of representations and evaluations of the information in the Internet is the main obstacle to this communication, and the problem becomes more noticeable when users take part in the process. This reveals the need of more flexibility in the communication among agents and between agents and users [6,25,26,27]. To solve this problem we presented in [6,7,11] different distributed intelligent agent models based on *fuzzy linguistic information* [12,13].

Another promising direction to improve the information access on the Web is related with the filtering techniques. Information filtering is a name used to describe a variety of processes involving the delivery of information to people who need it. Operating in textual domains, *filtering systems* or *recommender*

J. Favela et al. (Eds.): AWIC 2004, LNAI 3034, pp. 3–12, 2004.

systems evaluate and filter the great amount of information available on the Web (usually, stored in HTML or XML documents) to assist people in their search processes [21]. Traditionally, these systems have fallen into two main categories [20]. *Content-based filtering systems* filter and recommend the information by matching user query terms with the index terms used in the representation of documents, ignoring data from other users. These recommender systems tend to fail when little is known about user information needs, e.g. as happens when the query language is poor. *Collaborative filtering systems* use explicit or implicit preferences from many users to filter and recommend documents to a given user, ignoring the representation of documents. These recommender systems tend to fail when little is known about a user, or when he/she has uncommon interests [20]. Several researchers are exploring hybrid content-based and collaborative recommender systems to smooth out the disadvantages of each one of them [1,4,10,20]. Recommender systems employing information filtering techniques often do so through the use of information filtering agents [23]. For example, Amalthaea [19] is a multi-agent system for recommending Web sites.

In this paper, we present a new fuzzy linguistic multi-agent model for information gathering on the Web that use collaborative information filtering techniques to improve retrieval issues. We design it by using a 2-tuple fuzzy linguistic approach [12] as a way to endow the retrieval process with a higher flexibility, uniformity and precision. As we did in [7], the communication of the evaluation of the retrieved information among the agents is carried out by using linguistic information represented by the 2-tuple fuzzy linguistic representation. Users represent their information needs by means of linguistic weighted queries [13] and providing an information need category (medicine, decision making, economy). The weighted queries are composed of terms which are weighted by means of linguistic relative importance weights. To exploit user preferences the multi-agent model incorporates in its architecture a *collaborative filtering agent* that filters and recommends documents related to information need category according to the evaluation judgements previously expressed by other users.

In this paper Section 2 reviews the considered fuzzy linguistic representation. Section 3 presents the new fuzzy linguistic multi-agent model based on collaborative information filtering techniques. Section 4 presents an example for illustrating our proposal. Finally, some concluding remarks are pointed out.

2 The Fuzzy Linguistic Approach

For modelling qualitative information we consider a 2-tuple fuzzy linguistic approach. The 2-tuple fuzzy linguistic approach was introduced in [12] to overcome the problems of loss of information of other fuzzy linguistic approaches [13]. Its main advantage is that the linguistic computational model based on linguistic 2-tuples can carry out processes of computing with words easier and without loss of information.

Let $S = \{s_0, ..., s_g\}$ be a linguistic term set with odd cardinality (g+1 is the cardinality of S and usually is equal to 7 or 9), where the mid term represents an assessment of approximately 0.5 and with the rest of the terms being placed symmetrically around it. We assume that the semantics of labels is given by means of triangular membership functions represented by a 3-tuple (a, b, c) and consider all terms distributed on a scale on which a total order is defined $s_i \leq s_j \Longleftrightarrow i \leq j$. An example may be the following set of seven terms:

$$s_0 = Null(N) = (0, 0, .17) \quad s_1 = VeryLow(VL) == (0, .17, .33)$$
$$s_2 = Low(L) = (.17, .33, .5) \quad s_3 = Medium(M) = (.33, .5, .67)$$
$$s_4 = High(H) = (.5, .67, .83) \quad s_5 = VeryHigh(VH) = (.67, .83, 1)$$
$$s_6 = Perfect(P) = (.83, 1, 1).$$

In this fuzzy linguistic context, if a symbolic method [13] aggregating linguistic information obtains a value $\beta \in [0, g]$, and $\beta \notin \{0, ..., g\}$, then an approximation function is used to express the result in S.

Definition 1. [12] *Let β be the result of an aggregation of the indexes of a set of labels assessed in a linguistic term set S, i.e., the result of a symbolic aggregation operation, $\beta \in [0, g]$. Let $i = round(\beta)$ and $\alpha = \beta - i$ be two values, such that, $i \in [0, g]$ and $\alpha \in [-.5, .5)$ then α is called a Symbolic Translation.*

The 2-tuple fuzzy linguistic approach is developed from the concept of symbolic translation by representing the linguistic information by means of 2-tuples (s_i, α_i), $s_i \in S$ and $\alpha_i \in [-.5, .5)$: i) s_i represents the linguistic label of the information, and ii) α_i is a numerical value expressing the value of the translation from the original result β to the closest index label, i, in the linguistic term set $(s_i \in S)$.

This model defines a set of transformation functions between numeric values and 2-tuples.

Definition 2. [12] *Let $S = \{s_0, ..., s_g\}$ be a linguistic term set and $\beta \in [0, g]$ a value representing the result of a symbolic aggregation operation, then the 2-tuple that expresses the equivalent information to β is obtained with the following function, $\Delta : [0, g] \longrightarrow S \times [-0.5, 0.5)$,*

$$\Delta(\beta) = (s_i, \alpha), \ with \ \begin{cases} s_i & i = round(\beta) \\ \alpha = \beta - i & \alpha \in [-.5, .5) \end{cases}$$

For all Δ there exists Δ^{-1}, defined as $\Delta^{-1}(s_i, \alpha) = i + \alpha$. On the other hand, it is obvious that the conversion of a linguistic term into a linguistic 2-tuple consists of adding a symbolic translation value of 0: $s_i \in S \Longrightarrow (s_i, 0)$.

The 2-tuple linguistic computational model is defined by presenting a negation operator, the comparison of 2-tuples and aggregation operators of 2-tuples:

1. Negation operator of 2-tuples: $Neg((s_i, \alpha)) = \Delta(g - (\Delta^{-1}(s_i, \alpha)))$.

2. Comparison of 2-tuples. The comparison of linguistic information represented by 2-tuples is carried out according to an ordinary lexicographic order. Let (s_k, α_1) and (s_l, α_2) be two 2-tuples, with each one representing a counting of information:

- If $k < l$ then (s_k, α_1) is smaller than (s_l, α_2)
- If $k = l$ then
  1. if $\alpha_1 = \alpha_2$ then (s_k, α_1) and (s_l, α_2) represent the same information,
  2. if $\alpha_1 < \alpha_2$ then (s_k, α_1) is smaller than (s_l, α_2),
  3. if $\alpha_1 > \alpha_2$ then (s_k, α_1) is bigger than (s_l, α_2).

3. Aggregation operators of 2-tuples. The aggregation of information consists of obtaining a value that summarizes a set of values, therefore, the result of the aggregation of a set of 2-tuples must be a 2-tuple. Using functions Δ and Δ^{-1} that transform without loss of information numerical values into linguistic 2-tuples and viceversa, any of the existing aggregation operator can be easily extended for dealing with linguistic 2-tuples. Some examples are:

Definition 3. *Let* $x = \{(r_1, \alpha_1), \ldots, (r_n, \alpha_n)\}$ *be a set of linguistic 2-tuples, the 2-tuple arithmetic mean* $\bar{x}^e$ *is computed as,*

$$\bar{x}^e[(r_1, \alpha_1), \ldots, (r_n, \alpha_n)] = \Delta(\sum_{i=1}^{n} \frac{1}{n} \Delta^{-1}(r_i, \alpha_i)) = \Delta(\frac{1}{n} \sum_{i=1}^{n} \beta_i).$$

Definition 4. *Let* $x = \{(r_1, \alpha_1), \ldots, (r_n, \alpha_n)\}$ *be a set of linguistic 2-tuples and* $W = \{w_1, \ldots, w_n\}$ *be their associated weights. The 2-tuple weighted average* $\bar{x}^w$ *is:*

$$\bar{x}^w[(r_1, \alpha_1), \ldots, (r_n, \alpha_n)] = \Delta(\frac{\sum_{i=1}^{n} \Delta^{-1}(r_i, \alpha_i) \cdot w_i}{\sum_{i=1}^{n} w_i}) = \Delta(\frac{\sum_{i=1}^{n} \beta_i \cdot w_i}{\sum_{i=1}^{n} w_i}).$$

Definition 5. *Let* $x = \{(r_1, \alpha_1), \ldots, (r_n, \alpha_n)\}$ *be a set of linguistic 2-tuples and* $W = \{(w_1, \alpha_1^w), \ldots, (w_n, \alpha_n^w)\}$ *be their linguistic 2-tuple associated weights. The 2-tuple linguistic weighted average* $\bar{x}_l^w$ *is:*

$$\bar{x}_l^w[((r_1, \alpha_1), (w_1, \alpha_1^w))\ldots((r_n, \alpha_n), (w_n, \alpha_n^w))] = \Delta(\frac{\sum_{i=1}^{n} \beta_i \cdot \beta_{W_i}}{\sum_{i=1}^{n} \beta_{W_i}}),$$

with $\beta_i = \Delta^{-1}(r_i, \alpha_i)$ *and* $\beta_{W_i} = \Delta^{-1}(w_i, \alpha_i^w)$.

3 A Fuzzy Linguistic Multi-agent Model Based on Collaborative Filtering Techniques

In this Section we present a new fuzzy linguistic multi-agent model which is developed from the multi-agent model defined in [7]. Basically, we propose to improve the performance of that by incorporating in its architecture collaborative filtering techniques.

3.1 Architecture of Fuzzy Linguistic Multi-agent Model

In [24] a distributed multi-agent model for the information gathering is defined. This model develops the retrieval activity by considering five action levels: *internet users, interface agents, task agents, information agents* and *information sources*. Using this model, in [7] we defined a fuzzy linguistic distributed multi-agent model that uses linguistic 2-tuples to carry out the communication processes among the agents. In such a way, we incorporate in the retrieval process a higher degree of flexibility to carry out the information interchange, but in a precise way.

As it is known, a promising direction to improve the effectiveness of search engines concerns the way in which it is possible to "filter" the great amount of information available across the Internet. As it was said at the beginning, the so-called recommender systems are useful tools to carry out the evaluation and filtering activities on the Web [21]. The combined use of recommender systems together with search multi-agent systems has given very good results on the Web [2,18,19,23].

Then, our proposal consists of applying the use of recommender systems in the multi-agent model presented in [7] to improve its performance. The incorporation of recommender systems in its architecture increases its information filtering possibilities on the Web. To do so, we present a new fuzzy linguistic multi-agent model that integrates in its activity collaborative filtering techniques [20,21], i.e., a new activity level, the level of a *collaborative filtering agent*. Furthermore, the users' expression possibilities are increased. Users specify their information needs by means of both a linguistic weighted query and an information need category. Each term of a user query can be weighted by a relative importance weight. By associating relative importance weights to terms in a query, the user is asking to see all documents whose content represents the concept that is more associated with the most important terms rather than with the least important ones. The relative importance weights are used by the task agent to determinate the number of documents to be retrieved from each information agent. The information need category represents the interest topic of the user's information need, e.g., "information retrieval", "medicine", "decision making",... Previously, a list of information categories available to users must be established. The information need category is used by the collaborative filtering agent to carry out a filtering on documents that are finally retrieved and shown to the users.

This new multi-agent model presents a hierarchical architecture that contains six activity levels (see Fig. 1 in the case of a single user):

1. **Level 1:** *Internet user*, which expresses his/her information needs by means of a linguistic weighted query $\{(t_1, p_1), (t_2, p_2) ..., (t_m, p_m)\}$, $p_i \in S$ and an information need category $A_i \in \{A_1, ..., A_l\}$. He also provides his/her identity $\mathcal{ID}$ (e.g. e-mail address).

2. **Level 2:** *Interface agent* (one for user), that communicates the user query, the information need category and the user identity to the collaborative filtering agent, filters the retrieved documents from collaborative filtering agent to give to the user those that satisfy better his/her needs, and finally, informs the collaborative filtering agent on set of documents used by user to satisfy his/her information needs DU.

3. **Level 3:** *Collaborative filtering agent* (one for interface agent), that communicates the user query to the task agent, receives the more relevant documents chosen by the task agent, retrieves the recommendations on such documents from a collaborative recommendation system using the information need category expressed by the user $RC^{\mathcal{A}_i} = \{RC_1^{\mathcal{A}_i},...,RC_v^{\mathcal{A}_i}\}$ $RC_j^{\mathcal{A}_i} \in Sx[-0.5, 0.5]$), filters the documents by recalculating their relevance using these recommendations, and communicates these documents together with their new relevance degrees to the interface agent. Later, it carries out the tasks to update in the collaborative recommendation system the recommendations on the documents used by the user, i.e., it invites user to provide a recommendation rc_y on each chosen document $d_y^U \in DU$ and this recommendation is stored in the collaborative recommendation system together with the recommendations provided by other users that used d_y^U.

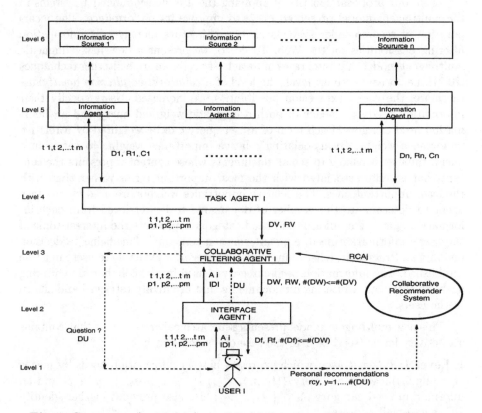

Fig. 1. Structure of a Multi-Agent Model Based on Collaborative Filtering

4. **Level 4:** *Task agent* (one for collaborative filtering agent), that communicates the terms of user query to the information filtering agents, and filters documents provided by information agents by getting those documents from every information agent that fulfill better the weighted query, fusing them and resolving the possible conflicts among the information agents.

5. **Level 5:** *Information agents*, which receive the terms of user query from the task agent and look for the documents in the information sources. Then, task agent receives from each information agent h the set of relevant documents that it found through information sources D^h and their relevance R^h, where every document d_j^h has an associated degree of relevance $r_j^h \in Sx[-0.5, 0.5)$ $(j = 1, ..., \#(D^h))$. It also receives a set of linguistic degrees of satisfaction $C^h = \{c_1^h, c_2^h, ..., c_m^h\}$, $c_i^h \in Sx[-0.5, 0.5)$ of this set of documents D^h with regard to every term of the query t_i.

6. **Level 6:** *Information sources*, consisting of all data sources within the Internet, such as databases and information repositories.

3.2   How Does This Multi-agent Model Work?

The activity of multi-agent model presented in the above Subsection is composed of two phases:

1. Retrieval phase: This first phase coincides with the information gathering process developed by the multi-agent model itself, i.e., this phase begins when a user specifies his/her query and finishes when he/she chooses his/her desired documents among the documents retrieved and provided by the system.

2. Feedback phase: This second phase coincides with the updating process of collaborative recommendations on desired documents existing in the collaborative recommender system, i.e., this phase begins when the *interface agent* informs the documents chosen by the user to the *collaborative filtering agent* and finishes when the recommender system recalculates and updates the recommendations of the desired documents.

The retrieval phase is carried out as follows:

Step 1: An *Internet user* expresses his/her information needs by means of a linguistic weighted query $\{(t_1, p_1), (t_2, p_2), ..., (t_m, p_m)\}$, $p_i \in S$ and an information need category $\mathcal{A}_i$ chosen from a list of information need categories $\{\mathcal{A}_1, ..., \mathcal{A}_l\}$ provided by the system. The system also requires the user's identity $\mathcal{ID}$. All this information is given by the user to the *interface agent*.

Step 2: The *interface agent* gives the query together with the information need category to the *collaborative filtering agent*.

Step 3: The *collaborative filtering agent* gives the query to the *task agent*.

Step 4: The *task agent* communicates the terms of the query $\{t_1, t_2, ..., t_m\}$ to all the *information agents* to which it is connected.

Step 5: All the *information agents* that have received the query, look for the information that better satisfies it in the *information sources*, and retrieve from them the documents. We assume that the documents are represented in the *information sources* using an index term based representation as in vector space model [13,22]. Then, there exists a finite set of index terms $T = \{t_1, ..., t_l\}$ used to represent the documents and each document d_j is represented as a fuzzy subset, $d_j = \{(t_1, F(d_j, t_1)), ..., (t_l, F(d_j, t_l))\}$, $F(d_j, t_i) \in [0, 1]$, where F is any numerical indexing function that weighs index terms according to their significance in describing the content of a document.

Step 6: The *task agent* receives from every *information agent* h a set of documents D^h ordered decreasingly by their relevance R^h. Every document d_j^h has associated a linguistic degree of relevance $r_j^h \in S\mathrm{x}[-0.5, 0.5)$, which is calculated as $r_j^h = \bar{x}^e[\Delta(g \cdot F(d_j^h, t_1)), \ldots, \Delta(g \cdot F(d_j^h, t_m))]$, being g+1 the cardinality of S. The *task agent* also receives a set of linguistic degree of satisfaction $C^h = \{c_1^h, c_2^h, \ldots, c_m^h\}$, $c_i^h \in S\mathrm{x}[-0.5, 0.5)$ of D^h with regard to every term of the query, which is calculated as $c_i^h = \bar{x}^e[\Delta(g \cdot F(d_1^h, t_i)), \ldots, \Delta(g \cdot F(d_{\#(D^h)}^h, t_i))]$. Then, the *task agent* selects the number of documents $k(D^h)$ to be retrieved from each *information agent* h: $k(D^h) = round(\frac{\sum_{i=1}^{n} \#(D^i)}{n} \cdot P_s^h)$, where $P_s^h = \frac{\Delta^{-1}(\lambda^h)}{\sum_{i=1}^{n} \Delta^{-1}(\lambda^h)}$ is the probability of selection of the documents from *information agent* h, and $\lambda^h \in S\mathrm{x}[-0.5, 0.5)$ is the satisfaction degree of *information agent* h which is computed through a 2-tuple linguistic weighted average operator, for example $\bar{x}_l^w$, as $\lambda^h = \bar{x}_l^w[(c_1^h, (p_1, 0)), \ldots, (c_m^h, (p_m, 0))]$.

Step 7: The *collaborative filtering agent* receives from the *task agent* a list of documents $DV = \{d_1^V, \ldots, d_v^V\}$ ordered with respect to their relevance RV, such that, $\#(DV) = v \leq \sum_{i=1}^{n} k(D^i)$. Then, *collaborative filtering agent* filters the documents provided by the *task agent* using the recommendations on such documents provided by other users in previous similar searches which are stored in a *collaborative recommender system*. To do so, the *collaborative recommender system* sends *collaborative filtering agent* the set of recommendations existing on DV associated with the information need category $\mathcal{A}_i$ expressed by the user,

$$RC^{\mathcal{A}_i} = \{RC_1^{\mathcal{A}_i}, \ldots, RC_v^{\mathcal{A}_i}\}\ RC_j^{\mathcal{A}_i} \in S\mathrm{x}[-0.5, 0.5).$$

Then, the *collaborative filtering agent* filters the documents by recalculating their relevance using such recommendations $RC^{\mathcal{A}_i}$. So, for each document $d_j^V \in DV$ a new linguistic relevance degree r_j^{NV} is calculated from r_j^V and $RC_j^{\mathcal{A}_i}$ by means of the 2-tuple weighted operator $\bar{x}^w$ as $r_j^{NV} = \bar{x}^w(r_j^V, RC_j^{\mathcal{A}_i})$, using for example the weighting vector W=[0.6,0.4].

Step 8: The *interface agent* receives from the *collaborative filtering agent* a list of documents $DW = \{d_1^W, \ldots, d_w^W\}$ ordered with respect to their relevance RW, such that $\#(DW) = w \leq v = \#(DV)$. Then, the *interface agent* filters these documents in order to give to the user only those documents that fulfill better his/her needs, which we call Df. For example, it can select a fixed number of documents K and to show the K best documents.

On the other hand, the feedback phase is developed by the *collaborative recommender system* which obtains new recommendations that later can be reused to assist another people in their search processes. In our multi-agent model this feedback activity is developed in the following steps (in Fig. 1 the discontinuous lines symbolize this phase):

Step 1: The *interface agent* gives the user's identity $\mathcal{ID}$ (usually his/her e-mail) together with the set of documents $DU = \{d_1^U, \ldots, d_u^U\}$, $u \leq \#(Df)$ used by the user to the *collaborative filtering agent*.

Step 2: The *collaborative filtering agent* asks user his/her opinion or evaluation judgements about DU, for example by means of an e-mail.

Step 3: The *Internet user* communicates his/her linguistic evaluation judgements to the *collaborative recommender system*, rc_y, $y = 1, ..., \#(DU)$, $rc_y \in S$.
Step 4: The *collaborative recommender system* recalculates the linguistic recommendations of set of documents DU by aggregating again the opinions provided by other users together with those provided by the Internet user. This can be done using the 2-tuple aggregation operator $\bar{x}^e$. Then, given a chosen document $d_y^U \in DU$ that receives a recommendation or evaluation judgement rc_y from the Internet user, and supposing that in the collaborative recommender system there exists a set of stored linguistic recommendations $\{rc_1, ..., rc_M\}, rc_i \in S$ associated with d_y^U for the information need category $\mathcal{A}_i$, which were provided by M different users in previous searches, then a new value of recommendation of d_y^U is obtained as $RC_y^{\mathcal{A}_i} = \bar{x}^e[(rc_1, 0), ..., (rc_M, 0), (rc_y, 0)]$.

4   Concluding Remarks

We have presented a fuzzy linguistic multi-agent model based on collaborative filtering techniques which improves the search processes on the Web and increases the users' satisfaction degrees.

In the future, we want to study proposals that allow users to express better both their information needs, for example, by using multi-weighted queries [13].

Acknowledgements
This work has been supported by the Research Project TIC2003-07977.

References

1. Basu, C. Hirsh, H. Cohen, W.: Recommendation as classification: Using social and content-based information in recommendation. *Proc. of the Fifteenth National Conference on Artificial Intelligence.* (1998) 714-720.
2. Boone, G.: Concept features in RE: Agent, an intelligent email agent. *Proc. of Autonomous Agents.* (1998) 141-148.
3. Brenner, W. Zarnekow, R., Witting, H.: *Intelligent Software Agent, Foundations and Applications.* Berlin Heidelberg: Springer-Verlag. (1998).
4. Claypool, M., Gokhale, A., Miranda, T.: Combining content-based and collaborative filters in an online newpaper. *Proc. of the ACM SIGIR Workshop on Recommender Systems-Implementation and Evaluation.*
5. Chau, M., Zeng, D., Chen, H., Huang, M., Hendriawan, D.: Design and evaluation of a multi-agent collaborative Web mining system. Decision Support Syst. **35** (2003) 167-183.
6. Delgado, M., Herrera, F., Herrera-Viedma, E., Martín-Bautista, M.J., Vila., M.A.: Combining linguistic information in a distributed intelligent agent model for information gathering on the Internet. In Wang, P.P. (Ed.), *Computing with Words.* John Wiley & Son. (2001) 251-276.
7. Delgado, M., Herrera, F., Herrera-Viedma, E., Martín-Bautista, M.J., Martínez, L., Vila., M.A.: A communication model based on the 2-tuple fuzzy linguistic representation for a distributed intelligent agent system on Internet. Soft Computing. **6** (2002) 320-328.

8. Fazlollahi, B., Vahidov, R.M., Aliev, R.A.: Multi-agent distributed intelligent system based on fuzzy decision making. Int. J. of Intelligent Syst. **15** (2000) 849-858.
9. Ferber, J.: *Multi-Agent Systems: An Introduction to Distributed Artificial Intelligence.* New York: Addison-Wesley Longman. (1999).
10. Good, N., Shafer, J.B., Konstan, J.A., Borchers, A., Sarwar, B.M., Herlocker, J.L., Riedl, J.: Combining collaborative filtering with personal agents for better recommendations. *Proc. of the Sixteenth National Conf. on Artificial Intelligence.* (1999), 439-446.
11. Herrera, F., Herrera-Viedma, E., Martínez, L., Porcel C.: Information gathering on the internet using a distributed intelligent agent model with multi-granular linguistic information. In: Loia, V. (Ed.), *Fuzzy Logic and The Internet.* Physica-Verlag. Springer. 2003. In press.
12. Herrera, F. Martínez, L.: A 2-tuple fuzzy linguistic representation model for computing with words.IEEE Trans. on Fuzzy Syst. **8** (6) (2000) 746-752.
13. Herrera-Viedma, E.: Modeling the retrieval process for an information retrieval system using an ordinal fuzzy linguistic approach. J. of the Ame. Soc. for Inf. Sci. and Tech. **52**(6) (2001) 460-475.
14. Jennings, N., Sycara, K., Wooldridge, M.: A roadmap of agent research and development. Autonomous Agents and Multi-Agents Syst. **1** (1998) 7-38.
15. Kobayashi, M., Takeda, K.: Information retrieval on the web. ACM Computing Surveys. **32**(2) (2000) 144-173.
16. Lawrence, S., Giles, C.: Searching the web: General and scientific information access. IEEE Comm. Mag. **37**(1) (1998) 116-122.
17. Lieberman, H.: Personal assistants for the Web: A MIT perspective. In Klusch, M. (Ed.), *Intelligent Information Agents.* Springer-Verlag. (1999) 279-292.
18. Maes, P.: Agents that reduce work and information overload. Comm. of the ACM. **37** (1994) 31-40.
19. Moukas, A., Zacharia, G., Maes, P.: Amalthaea and Histos: Multiagent systems for WWW sites and representation recommendations. In Klusch, M. (Ed.), *Intelligent Information Agents.* Springer-Verlag. (1999) 293-322.
20. Popescul, A., Ungar, L.H., Pennock, D.M., Lawrence, S.: Probabilistic models for unified collaborative and content-based recommendation in sparce-data environments. In *Proc. of the Seventeenth Conf. on Uncertainty in Artificial Intelligence (UAI).* San Francisco, (2001) 437-444.
21. Reisnick, P., Varian, H. R.: Special issue on recommender systems. Comm. of the ACM. **40**(3) (1997).
22. Salton, G., McGill, M.G.: *Introduction to Modern Information Retrieval.* McGraw-Hill. 1983.
23. Schafer, J.B., Konstan, J.A., Riedl, J.: E-Commerce recommendation applications. Data Min. and Know. Disc. **5** (1/2) (2001) 115-153.
24. Sycara, K., Pannu, A., Williamson, M., Zeng, D.: Distributed intelligent agents. IEEE Expert (1996) 36-46.
25. Yager, R.R.: Protocol for negotiations among multiple intelligent agents. In: Kacprzyk, J., Nurmi, H., M. Fedrizzi, M. (Eds.), *Consensus Under Fuzziness.* Kluwer Academic Publishers. (1996) 165-174.
26. Yager, R.R.: Intelligent agents for World Wide Web advertising decisions. Int. J. of Intelligent Syst. **12** (1997) 379-390.
27. Yager, R.R.: Fusion of multi-agent preference orderings. Fuzzy Sets and Syst. **112** (2001) 1-12.

Case-Based Reasoning as a Prediction Strategy for Hybrid Recommender Systems

Mark van Setten[1], Mettina Veenstra[1], Anton Nijholt[2], Betsy van Dijk[2]

[1] Telematica Instituut, P.O. Box 589, 7500 AN, Enschede, The Netherlands
{Mark.vanSetten, Mettina.Veenstra}@telin.nl
[2] University of Twente, P.O. Box 217, 7500 AE, Enschede, The Netherlands
{anijholt, bvdijk}@cs.utwente.nl

Abstract. Hybrid recommender systems are capable of providing better recommendations than non-hybrid ones. Our approach to hybrid recommenders is
the use of prediction strategies that determine which prediction technique(s)
should be used at the moment an actual prediction is required. In this paper, we
determine whether case-based reasoning can provide more accurate prediction
strategies than rule-based predictions strategies created manually by experts.
Experiments show that case-based reasoning can indeed be used to create prediction strategies; it can even increase the accuracy of the recommender in systems where the accuracy of the used prediction techniques is highly spread.

1 Introduction

Recommender systems are intelligent systems that are capable of helping people to
quickly and easily find their way through large amounts of information by determining what is interesting and what is not interesting to a user. Recommenders employ
prediction techniques to determine what is and what is not interesting by learning
from the user and sometimes other users. Examples of such techniques are information filtering [3], social filtering [6] [12], genre-based recommendations [15], case-
based reasoning (CBR) [13], and item-item filtering [7]. Current recommender research focuses on using a mixture of prediction techniques. Such hybrid recommenders are capable of providing better recommendations than individual techniques [1]
[4] [5] [16] [17]. Our hybrid recommender approach uses prediction strategies that determine which prediction technique(s) should be used at the moment an actual prediction is required. Initially we used manually created rule-based strategies. Creating
these manual strategies requires expert knowledge; because this is a major drawback,
we now focus on strategies that teach themselves when to use which techniques.

This paper determines whether CBR can provide more accurate prediction strategies than manually created rule-based predictions strategies. We first describe hybrid
recommenders in general and our hybrid recommender approach in particular. We
then explain how we use CBR as a prediction strategy. This is followed by a description of the experiments in which CBR as a prediction strategy is compared with
manually created rule-based strategies. We then present and discuss the results of the
experiments and conclude this paper on using CBR as a prediction strategy.

J. Favela et al. (Eds.): AWIC 2004, LNAI 3034, pp. 13-22, 2004.
© Springer-Verlag Berlin Heidelberg 2004

2 Hybrid Recommenders and Prediction Strategies

Burke [5] describes seven different types of hybridization methods for recommender systems: weighted, mixing, switching, feature combination, cascade, feature augmentation, and meta-level. He also provides an example of a cascade hybrid recommender system called EntreeC that recommends restaurants to users using both CBR and social filtering as prediction techniques.

Buczak, Zimmerman and Kurapati describe a weighted hybrid TV recommender that combines three prediction techniques [4]: two techniques that analyze implicitly gathered viewing data using Bayesian learning and Decision Tree learning, and one technique that contains explicitly provided interests about the user for different aspects of TV programs, such as times, channel and genres. Predictions of these three techniques are fused with an artificial neural network.

Another example of a weighted hybrid TV recommender is described by Ardissono, Gena, Torasso, Bellifemine, Chiarotto, Difino and Negro [1]. In this system, three prediction techniques are combined: a stereotype-based technique, a technique based on explicitly provided interests from the user, and a technique that employs a Bayesian belief network that learns from implicitly gathered user behavior data. The weights used to combine the predictions are based on confidence scores provided by the individual techniques.

Our approach employs switching hybridization by deciding which prediction technique is most suitable to provide a prediction. The decision is based on the most up-to-date knowledge about the current user, other users, the information for which a prediction is requested, other information items and the system itself [16] [17]. Such a hybrid is called a prediction strategy. Where prediction techniques actually generate predictions, strategies only choose one or more predictors that generate predictions on their behalf. Predictors are either prediction techniques or other prediction strategies.

The way prediction strategies retrieve information for their decision is similar to the ensemble method approach used in visual analysis [14] and text classification [2]. Each prediction technique exposes a set of reliability or validity indicators providing information that can be used to decide whether to use the technique or not. Two examples of validity indicators are 'the number of similar users that rated the information' for social filtering and 'the number of similar rated items by the user' for CBR.

Prediction strategies can use one of several decision techniques to make a decision based on the validity indicators; examples of such decision techniques are decision rules, neural networks, Bayesian networks and CBR. In [16] [17] we have shown that prediction strategies indeed provide more accurate predictions when using manually created decision rules. These rules were created using expert knowledge on the different prediction techniques and the two domains for which the prediction strategies were created: a TV recommender and a movie recommender.

As the need for expert knowledge is a drawback of manually created rule-based strategies, we have been investigating the possibility to create prediction strategies that teach themselves when to use which prediction techniques. Several machine learning algorithms can be used as a decision technique, including neural and Bayesian networks. However, due to the nature of prediction strategies, specifically the usage of validity indicators, CBR is the most promising and hence investigated in this paper. The other algorithms are topics for future research.

3   Case-Based Reasoning Based Strategy

CBR is a method to solve new problems by adapting solutions that were used to solve past problems [10]. With CBR, one searches for past cases that are analogous to the current case; the solutions of the most analogous past cases are then used to create a solution for the current case. Because all prediction strategies try to determine which prediction technique can best provide a prediction for a specific prediction request, a prediction strategy using CBR must consequently do so. A prediction strategy can only learn how well the different prediction techniques performed when feedback has been received from the user. This feedback represents the actual interest of the user, which the strategy can compare with the predictions of the individual techniques in order to determine which technique retrospectively predicted best. For this reason, when using CBR as a prediction strategy, a case represents a specific prediction request for which feedback of the user has been received. As validity indicators provide information that can be used to decide whether to employ a technique or not, these indicators can also be used by CBR to describe the case of a prediction request. E.g. the three validity indicators of the CBR prediction technique are: number of similar items rated by the user where sim > 0.5, where sim > 0.7 and where sim > 0.9.

For prediction strategies, it is best to use a case-base per prediction technique instead of a global case-base with all validity indicators of all techniques. In a global case-base problems arise when techniques are added to, changed within or removed from a strategy; all old cases become invalid as they are based on a set of techniques that no longer exists. With a case-base per technique, only for the new or changed technique must the case-base be rebuilt. Furthermore, with a global case-base, a larger case-base is necessary before accurate decisions can be made: the probability that a similar set of validity indicators occurs for one technique is higher than the probability that a similar set of indicators occurs for many techniques at the same time.

The outcome of a prediction technique is a score indicating the predicted interest of the user; the outcome of the decision within a strategy is not the prediction but an indication which prediction technique can best be used to provide the prediction. In order to keep the set of techniques flexible, a case solution is needed that not only reflects the performance of a technique, but that is also independent of the other techniques. When using an indication such as a rank that relates different techniques to each other, any change to the set of techniques would render every case-base invalid. We use the prediction error of techniques as the score. The prediction error is the absolute difference between the prediction and the feedback of the user; the lower the error the more suitable that technique was, in retrospect, to generate the prediction.

For every prediction request, the goal of the CBR-based strategy is twofold. First, determine the expected error of each prediction technique using those stored cases that have similar validity indicators as the current situation. Second, choose the technique with the lowest expected error as the one that should provide the prediction.

3.1   Determining Analogous Cases

The key element of CBR is determining which old cases are analogies of the current prediction request [18]. Traditional CBR systems calculate the distance between two cases; old cases with the least distance from the current case are retrieved to determine the outcome for the current case. The closer a case is to the current situation, the more important that case should be in determining the outcome for the current request; the importance should be used as a weight.

The four most frequently used distance measures in CBR are [8]: unweighted Euclidean distance (ued), weighted Euclidean distance (wed), maximum measure (mms) and mean squared difference (msd). We also explored an information retrieval measure that calculates similarity instead of distance, namely cosine similarity (cs) [11]. With cosine similarity, the similarity between two cases is determined by the cosine of the angle between two vectors containing the values of the case attributes.

Using distances as weights is difficult due to the non-fixed upper level of distance; the maximum possible distance is unknown or may differ per distance measure. However, similarity measures are in the range of [0, 1] [18], one means that two cases are exactly the same and zero means that two cases are completely different. As traditional CBR systems use distances, it is necessary to convert distances into similarities. We explored three types of conversion functions for the conversion of distance to similarity: linear functions, sigmoidal functions and the inverted function. The linear function *linear(d, m)* converts the distance d to similarity s linear over the distance from 0 to m. Distances equal to or larger than m all have a similarity of 0. Sigmoidal functions are often used in machine learning for smooth transitions [9]. The sigmoidal function *sigmoidal(d, k, m)* has a tuning parameter k, which is used to determine the flatness of the smoothing function. The sigmoidal function, including transformations to place it in the distance domain of [0, m] and in the similarity range of [0, 1] is:

$$s = \frac{1}{1 + e^{k(d - \frac{1}{2}m)}} \tag{1}$$

Using $0.5m$ assures that similarity is halfway between zero distance and the maximum affordable distance m; in our experiments we choose this midpoint in order to determine the smoothening effects of a sigmoidal function compared to linear functions that also have a midpoint at $0.5m$. However, the inverted function *inverted(d)* does not have its similarity midpoint at $0.5m$. The function used is the inverted function, transposed to have a value of 1 at a distance of 0:

$$s = \frac{1}{(d + 1)} \tag{2}$$

3.2 Limiting Case-Base Size

One of the drawbacks of using CBR as a prediction strategy is the scalability issue of CBR: the larger the case-base, the more time it takes to make a decision; for every prediction request, similarity has to be calculated between the current request and all cases in the case-bases. For this reason, we also experimented with limiting the size of the case-bases using the first-in/first-out method, which allows the system to keep learning from recent situations. Recent situations have a higher probability of resembling future prediction requests than much older cases.

However, removing old cases from the case-bases has a risk: some of the removed cases may represent situations that, although they do not occur often, they do occur every now and then; e.g. a new user registering system. If the case-base is too small, the cases representing such an event may have been removed by the time such an event reoccurs. Because the frequency in which special situations occur differs per system, the optimal size of the case-bases also differs per system; the more frequently special situations occur, the smaller the necessary case-base size. For this reason, it is necessary to experiment with case-base sizes in order to determine the optimal size: optimal with regard to both accuracy and speed.

4 Experiments

In order to determine how well CBR-based strategies perform compared to manually rule-based prediction strategies, we performed experiments on two datasets:
- The TiV dataset [17]. This dataset contains 31,368 ratings of 24 people for 40,539 broadcasts from four weeks of TV programs from Dutch television.
- The 1 million ratings MovieLens dataset. This is the publicly available dataset from the movie recommendation system developed at the University of Minnesota (http://www.grouplens.org). The dataset contains 1,000,000 ratings by 6,040 users for 3,592 movies. We only used the first 160,000 ratings in this experiment.

Both the rule-based and the CBR-based prediction strategies use the same set of prediction techniques. For details on the used techniques and the rule-based strategies, we refer to [17] for the TiV dataset and to [16] for the MovieLens set.

4.1 Accuracy Measure

As a measure for the accuracy of the different prediction strategies, we use the accuracy of the resulting predictions; better prediction strategies result in better predictions. As an accuracy measure we use a combination of the often-used mean absolute error (mae) and coverage. Herlocker [6] compared mae, coverage and other possible accuracy measures for recommender systems, including measures like precision, recall and ROC curves, and concludes that mae is a good choice for systems that generate predictions per item, like our hybrid recommender systems.

We combine mae and coverage because in many systems, such as TV systems, it is not only important that a good prediction can be made, measured by mae, it is also important that a prediction can actually be made, measured by coverage. Most TV programs are only available at the moment of broadcast. For this reason, we combine both measures into the global mean absolute error (gmae); it is the same as mae, but when a prediction technique or strategy cannot make a prediction the default value zero is assumed as the prediction. The lower the gmae the better the accuracy[1].

---

[1] Accuracy presented in this paper is based on a rating scale from -1 to +1, where -1 indicates a very strong negative interest and +1 a very strong positive interest; 0 indicates a neutral or indifferent interest.

To evaluate the accuracy of the prediction strategies throughout the usage period of the systems, we divided the set of ratings in each dataset into different sets. Set A consisted of the first set of ratings (in time), set B of the next set of ratings, etc. When testing each set, the ratings of all previous sets were used for training. At the end also the overall accuracy over the whole dataset was calculated. The TiV dataset was divided into four sets, one set per week (with 8867, 8843, 6890, and 6768 ratings respectively). Since there is no logical unit to divide MovieLens, like the weeks in TiV, the MovieLens dataset was divided into 16 sets of 10,000 ratings each. X-validation was chosen over randomly drawn train and test sets as x-validation represents the order in which users actually accessed and rated the information.

4.2 Performed Experiments

First, the TiV dataset was used to experiment with different combinations of distance measures, distance to similarity conversion functions and case selection functions. We used all four distance measures, ued, wed, mms and msd, in combination with the three different distance to similarity functions, linear, sigmoidal and inverted, using different parameter values. We also experimented with the cosine similarity function. As case selection functions we used: all cases, only the most similar two, only the most similar three, the eldest most similar case, the newest most similar case, cases with similarity > 0.30, cases with similarity > 0.50, and cases with similarity > 0.70.

While exploring different similarity functions, we quickly discovered that steeply descending similarity functions provide the best results, e.g. *inverted, linear(d, m)* and *sigmoidal(d, k, m)* where $m < 4$. With such small distance ranges, especially when combined with a threshold value, both inverted and sigmoidal functions can easily be approximated by computationally simpler linear functions. Of all distance measures, ued is always one of the best, no matter what distance to similarity functions we use. Of the different distance to similarity conversion functions, a linear function with a low value for *m* performs best. In order to determine what value to use for *m*, we ran several other simulations resulting in $m = 2$ and sim > 0.50 providing the best results.

This best combination was then used in the CBR-based prediction strategy that was compared with the manually created rule-based prediction strategy. Furthermore, we examined the impact of using limited case-base sizes on the accuracy of the CBR-based strategy. Finally, the results were cross-validated with the MovieLens dataset.

5 Results

To determine whether CBR-based prediction strategies can provide more accurate predictions than manually created rule-based strategies we compared the results of both strategies. The rule-based strategy used was the best performing strategy determined in previous experiments [17]. The CBR-based strategy used the best performing combination of distance measure, distance to similarity function and case selection method: ued, *linear(d, 2)* and sim > 0.50. The results are listed in Table 1.

The results show that the CBR-based prediction strategy outperforms the manually created rule-based strategy, except in the first week. This is caused by the fact that

CBR needs time to build up case-bases; without enough cases, the strategy has too little data to make good decisions. But even in the first week, the CBR-based strategy still outperforms the best individual prediction technique. The increased accuracy is statistically significant (using a paired samples T-test and 95% confidence).

Table 1. Results of CBR-based versus rule-based strategy (bold indicates the best predictor)

	Week 1	Week 2	Week 3	Week 4
Rules-Based Strategy	**0.2935**	0.1774	0.1934	0.1602
CBR-Based Strategy	0.3031	**0.1710**	**0.1861**	**0.1535**
Best Technique	0.3530	0.1899	0.2171	0.1693

5.1 Impact of Limiting Case-Base Size

In order to determine the impact of limiting the size of the case-bases, which improves the speed and scalability of a CBR-based strategy, we experimented with several sizes. The results are shown in Table 2.

Table 2. Results of limiting the case-base size (bold indicates better predictions than no limit)

Case-base size	Week 1	Week 2	Week 3	Week 4
No limit	0.3031	0.1710	0.1861	0.1535
1000	0.3056	0.1784	0.1965	0.1593
2500	0.3047	0.1772	0.1917	0.1614
5000	**0.3029**	0.1743	0.1881	0.1568
7500	0.3043	0.1728	**0.1842**	0.1535
10000	0.3043	0.1720	**0.1831**	**0.1523**
12500	0.3043	**0.1708**	**0.1830**	**0.1506**
15000	0.3043	0.1713	**0.1841**	**0.1502**
17500	0.3043	0.1712	**0.1853**	**0.1501**

These results show that using a limited case-base can further improve the accuracy. We hypothesize that the removal of old cases made the strategy more accurate, since these cases represented old situations that did not occur again in the system. Furthermore, some prediction techniques behave differently early on in a system than they do later on, even under the same conditions according to the validity indicators. For example, in two situations A and B, a validity indicator of social filtering indicates that there are 40 similar users that have rated the item for which a prediction is necessary; however, in situation A, early in the system, the similarity of these 40 users is based on less rated items by each user than in the later situation B; hence the probability that social filtering provides an accurate prediction is higher in situation B than in A.

However, the improved effect of limited case-base sizes may also be influenced by the time-based characteristic of TiV. Because all users started using TiV at the beginning of week 1, no special situations like a new user occurred in later weeks. On the other hand, there is one special occasion between week 2 and 3: at that time almost all channels changed their programming drastically because at that time the new TV season started; this makes existing users similar to new users. The limited case-base size did not have any negative effects on the accuracy, on the contrary, accuracy increased more with limited case-base sizes after the second week than with unlimited sizes.

5.2 Cross-Validation

Cross-validation in the MovieLens dataset (see Table 3) shows that the CBR-based strategy does perform well in MovieLens, although not as well as in the TiV dataset. Sometimes, the rule-based strategy still out-performs the CBR-based strategy; however, even in those situations the CBR-based strategy is still better than the best individual prediction technique, making it an adequate prediction strategy.

Table 3. Results of the cross-validation of CBR-based versus rule–based strategy in the MovieLens dataset (bold indicates the best predictor in that set)

Set	10000	20000	30000	40000	50000	60000	70000	80000
Rule-Based	**0.3830**	**0.3953**	0.3880	0.4006	**0.3889**	**0.3803**	0.3973	0.3667
CBR-Based	0.3887	0.3968	**0.3830**	**0.3904**	0.3912	0.3815	**0.3954**	**0.3638**
Best Technique	0.3835	0.4050	0.3911	0.3966	0.3932	0.3820	0.4033	0.3678
Set	90000	100000	110000	120000	130000	140000	150000	160000
Rule-Based	0.3786	0.3737	**0.3688**	**0.3943**	**0.3924**	0.3787	0.3670	**0.3591**
CBR-Based	**0.3780**	**0.3721**	0.3714	0.3961	0.3963	**0.3782**	**0.3668**	0.3625
Best Technique	0.3826	0.3782	0.3715	0.3970	0.3950	0.3835	0.3713	0.3622

We have formulated two hypotheses for the lesser performance of the CBR-based strategy in MovieLens. The first is that the rule-based strategy created for the TiV dataset was not as good as the rule-based strategy created for the MovieLens dataset. Because both rule-based strategies have been designed by the same experts and several tuning experiments have been performed to optimize the rule sets in both strategies, we believe this hypothesis to be invalid.

Table 4. Results of the cross validation of limiting the case-base size in the MovieLens dataset (bold indicates better predictions than no limit)

Set	10000	20000	30000	40000	50000	60000	70000	80000
No limit	0.3887	0.3968	0.3830	0.3904	0.3912	0.3815	0.3954	0.3638
CB Size 12500	0.3887	**0.3963**	**0.3829**	0.3904	0.3944	0.3822	0.3964	0.3669
CB Size 25000	0.4057	0.4235	**0.3827**	0.3917	0.3924	0.3823	0.3963	0.3650
CBSize 50000	0.3887	0.3968	0.3830	0.3904	0.3912	0.3815	**0.3951**	**0.3634**
CB Size 100000	0.3887	0.3968	0.3830	0.3904	0.3912	0.3815	0.3954	0.3638
Set	90000	100000	110000	120000	130000	140000	150000	160000
No limit	0.3780	0.3721	0.3714	0.3961	0.3963	0.3782	0.3668	0.3625
CB Size 12500	0.3799	0.3778	0.3728	0.3997	0.3990	0.3813	0.3719	0.3667
CB Size 25000	0.3790	0.3747	0.3715	0.3966	0.3972	0.3789	0.3701	0.3668
CB Size 50000	0.3784	0.3729	0.3717	0.3967	**0.3961**	0.3790	0.3673	0.3648
CB Size 100000	0.3780	0.3721	0.3716	0.3964	0.3965	0.3785	0.3669	0.3630

The second hypothesis has to do with the observation that the prediction techniques for the TiV dataset have a much higher spread in their accuracy than the techniques for the MovieLens dataset. Spread is defined as the difference between the accuracy of the best performing technique and the accuracy of the worst performing technique. The average spread over the 16 validation sets in MovieLens is 0.0666, while the average spread over the four weeks in TiV is 0.3076. This means that the expected errors calculated by the CBR-based prediction strategy in the MovieLens dataset tend to be situated close together, making the probability of a wrong decision larger as the decisions are based on these expected errors. Since the spread is higher in the TiV dataset, the probability of a wrong decision is smaller.

Limiting the size of the case-base in MovieLens resulted in a decreased accuracy for the CBR-based prediction strategy (see Table 4). Only in a few situations did accuracy improve slightly, for example when using a size of 50000; in other subsets using the same case-base size accuracy decreases again.

We believe that the small spread of accuracy in the prediction techniques of MovieLens is also the reason why limiting the case-base size results in such different results. In order to confirm the influence of the spread of accuracy in prediction techniques, additional research is necessary; either experimenting with two different datasets and prediction strategies that show similar spread patterns or by developing one or two prediction techniques for MovieLens that increases the spread in accuracy.

6 Conclusions

In this paper, we determined whether CBR could provide more accurate prediction strategies than manually created rule-based prediction strategies. Experiments have shown that in systems where prediction techniques have a large spread in accuracy, CBR can indeed provide more accurate prediction strategies. However, in systems where the prediction techniques have a small spread in accuracy, the accuracy of a CBR-based strategy becomes more unreliable; sometimes accuracy is better than the rule-based strategy, sometimes worse. However, even with a small spread, a CBR-based strategy still outperforms the best individual prediction technique.

One of the main benefits of using CBR instead of the manually created rules in rule-based prediction strategies is that no expert knowledge is required to create the prediction strategies. A downside of using CBR as a prediction strategy is the performance and scalability penalty of CBR. Rule-based systems are very fast and scalable because they are model based. Since CBR is memory based, the speed of CBR-based strategies depends on the size of the case-bases.

In some systems, limiting the size of the case-bases not only improves speed and makes the system more scalable, it can also improve the accuracy of a CBR-based prediction strategy. However, more research is needed to determine under which conditions improved accuracy can be expected with limited case-base sizes.

All things considered, we conclude that CBR can indeed be used to create prediction strategies for hybrid recommender systems. However, one must be aware of the conditions under which CBR will increase accuracy over manually created rule-based prediction strategies.

Acknowledgments

This research is part of the PhD project Duine (http://duine.telin.nl) at the Telematica Instituut (http://www.telin.nl) and the Freeband projects Xhome and WASP (http://www.freeband.nl). The authors like to thank Mannes Poel and Erik Boertjes for their comments, support and help in this research. Also thanks to the researchers at the university of Minnesota for making the MovieLens datasets publicly available.

References

1. Ardissono, L., Gena, C., Torasso, P., Bellifemine, F., Chiarotto, A., Difino, A., Negro, B.: User Modeling and Recommendation Techniques for Personalized Electronic Program Guides. In: Ardissono, L., Maybury, M. T., Kobsa, A. (eds.): Personalization and User-Adaptive Interaction in Digital TV. Kluwer (to appear)
2. Bennett, P. N., Dumais, S. T., Horvitz, E.: Probabilistic Combination of Text Classifiers Using Reliability Indicators: Models and Results. In: Proceedings of SIGIR'02 (Tampere, Finland). ACM (2002) 207-214
3. Billsus, D., Pazzani, M. J., Chen, J.: A Learning Agent for Wireless News Access. In: Proceedings of IUI 2000 (New Orleans, USA). ACM (2000) 33-36
4. Buczak, A. L., Zimmerman, J., Kurapati, K.: Personalization: Improving Ease-of-Use, Trust and Accuracy of a TV Show Recommender. In: Proceedings of the Workshop Personalization in Future TV'02 (Malaga, Spain). 3-12
5. Burke, R.: Hybrid Recommender Systems: Survey and Experiments. User Modeling and User-Adapted Interaction 12, 4 (2002) 331-370
6. Herlocker, J.: Understanding and Improving Automated Collaborative Filtering Systems. University of Minnesota (2000)
7. Herlocker, J., Konstan, J. A.: Content-Independent Task-Focused Recommendation. IEEE Internet Computing 5, 6 (2001) 40-47
8. Mendes, E., Mosley, N., Watson, I.: A Comparison of CBR Approaches to Web Hypermedia Project Cost Estimation. In: Proceedings of WWW2002 (Honolulu, Hawaii, USA). ACM (2002) 272-280
9. Mitchell, T. M.: Machine learning. McGraw-Hill, New York, USA (1997)
10. Riesbeck, C. K., Schank, R.: Inside CBR. Lawrence Erlbaum Associates, Northvale, NJ, USA (1989)
11. Salton, G., McGill, M.: Introduction to Modern Information Retrieval. McGraw-Hill, New York, USA (1983)
12. Shardanand, U., Maes, P.: Social information filtering: algorithms for automated "Word of Mouth". In: Proceedings of Human factors in computing systems 1995 (New York, USA). ACM (1995) 210-217
13. Smyth, B., Cotter, P.: A personalised TV listings service for the digital TV age. Knowledge-Based Systems 13, 2-3 (2000) 53-59
14. Toyama, K., Horvitz, E.: Bayesian Modality Fusion: Probabilistic Integration of Multiple Vision Algorithms for Head Tracking. In: Proceedings of ACCV 2000, Fourth Asian Conference on Computer Vision (2000)
15. Van Setten, M.: Experiments with a recommendation technique that learns category interests. In: Proceedings of IADIS WWW/Internet 2002 (Lisabon, Portugal). 722-725
16. Van Setten, M., Veenstra, M., Nijholt, A.: Prediction Strategies: Combining Prediction Techniques to Optimize Personalisation. In: Proceedings of the Workshop Personalization in Future TV'02 (Malaga, Spain). 23-32
17. Van Setten, M., Veenstra, M., Nijholt, A., van Dijk, B.: Prediction Strategies in a TV Recommender System: Framework and Experiments. In: Proceedings of IADIS WWW/Internet 2003 (Algarve, Portugal). 203-210
18. Watson, I. D.: Applying CBR: Techniques for Enterprise Systems. Morgan Kaufmann Publishers Inc., San Francisco, CA, USA (1997)

Facing Environment Discontinuity through User Location

Rosa Alarcón and David A. Fuller

Computer Science Department, Pontificia Universidad Católica de Chile,
Vicuña Mackenna 4860, Santiago 6904411, Chile
{ralarcon, dfuller}@ing.puc.cl

Abstract. Web communities are an important current trend in the Web. Unlike web "surfers", their members share common interests and gathers for long periods. One of their key needs is interactivity among members, nevertheless, web applications are discontinuous and passive in the sense that users must login constantly into their applications to know the last events. As users are more mobile, distributed or belongs to various communities, this feature could overwhelm them and hinder interactivity. Our aim is to provide web applications with a proactive approach, where users can be reached through different devices *seamlessly*. In order to do so, it is important to determine events relevance and users availability preferences for multiple contexts. The proposal is enabled as a multi-agent system (MAS) where agents reason based on ontologies and direct event notification trough different channels or devices.

1 Introduction

Nowadays web technology has become one of the most important infrastructures for supporting diverse communities; it may be because the Web allows ubiquitous access in a simple way thanks to the HTTP protocol and its addressing scheme [1], which in turn had foster its growth and had make possible the emergence of web communities.

Although there is not a consensual definition of the "web community" concept, it can be seen as a place where, unlike "web surfers", people gather for a shared purpose or interest, get to know each other over time, and develop personal relationships [2].

This place would be virtual and composed of documents representing community's interests (i.e. html pages, chat logs, e-mail threads, etc.). There are two characteristics that seem to be fundamental for their success: the lack of control (as members actions and interest shapes the community) and the interactivity and communication among their members (people interests become the content).

In addition, web standards have proven to be flexible, simple and small enough to be supported in different devices (such as PDAs, laptops, etc.), enriching web content and services (streaming audio and video conferences, cell phone ring tones, personal agendas with preprogrammed alarms, e-commerce, etc).

However, the web communication model (URLs requested by users), delegates on them the responsibility of keeping updated on the state of the community. So that, members must typically login and logout constantly from a community portal in order to keep informed of the changes occurred since their last session. In this sense web

J. Favela et al. (Eds.): AWIC 2004, LNAI 3034, pp. 23-32, 2004.

applications for support web communities are passive and discontinuous. As these users can belong to various communities[1] at a time, this could impose on them work and cognitive overload resulting from making many different tasks simultaneously and from its interruption (it forces users to make changes on their mental context) [3].

It is very interesting that users needs are already begin to be addressed in some popular platforms that mainly support users by providing structure to shared data (i.e. Yahoo Groups, MSN Groups, MSN Share Point, etc.) or opportunities for rendezvous (i.e. ICQ, MSN Messenger, Yahoo Messenger, etc.).

In the former case, in addition to data structure support there are additional tools that exploit users' mail systems and even their cellular telephones to deliver sensitive information (i.e. meeting remainders, messages from the group, etc.), so that users do not need to check their group site constantly (or remember constantly that they need to check) but keep confident on be properly disturbed trough those media.

In the second case, sharing support is basic (i.e. chat), but user communication is fostered: users availability and status is showed (available, busy, on the phone, etc.), privacy is addressed as well (users can hide themselves or banish another).

Nevertheless, as users engage in several communities (i.e. work, research, etc.), it will be very complex to keep updated of its status and changes without being overwhelmed by the additional effort required (log into the community, solve compatibility issues, etc.). Communication channels and protocols heterogeneity (peer-to-peer and wireless applications, web-based services, proprietary protocols, etc), make it hard to send messages trough different devices automatically. But, as more devices and applications are providing web access, the Web becomes a promising media to enable a seamless transition between different devices.

We want to face web applications discontinuity and passiveness by allowing the virtual space to reach users proactively through some device. As the number of communities a user can be related to increases, so does the number of changes that he or she could be informed about. But these changes have different degrees of relevance for each user depending on his or her situation or user context (i.e. at the office, at home, eating, etc.) and interests (i.e. a medical emergency of a close relative could be more important than a boss message for some users).

In this paper a model to represent users' multiple contexts and relevance is presented. A multi-agent architecture and the ontology[2] used to deliver content under this restriction are presented as well (User Context Ontology).

The strategy and the proposal draw from previous experiences in the subject. Although our current approach is more complex and flexible, it required few extensions to the former server and ontologies (User Context), which suggested us that the architecture is pretty stable.

Section 2 discusses other approaches to the problem. Section 3 introduces MAS architecture, while section 4 presents the user context ontology and multiple context relevance inference strategy. Finally, section 6 presents our conclusions.

---

[1] A Business Week/Harris Poll on online communities (1997) reports that 42% engage in work related activity, 35% in socializing and 18% in hobbies. 39% surfs the web, while 57% used to visit the same places (http://www.businessweek.com/bwdaily/dnflash/april/nf70424b.htm).

[2] An ontology is a *specification of a conceptualization*. That is, is a formal description based on concepts and relationships that can exist for an agent or a community of agents [4]

2 Discontinuity and Seamless Transition

A web communities example are virtual work groups, which are small and auto-regulated groups of people that perform specific tasks, share decisions, responsibilities and goals; but are separated in terms of space, time and cultures, so they must maintain their connections through communication technologies [5].

They could be in different countries, follow different regulations and be in different time zones (being forced to communicate asynchronously) or they can be closer: they may be part of a building construction project where engineers, architects, shareholders and builders staffs are located in different places in the same country, city or region. Moreover, the distance can be variable if they move from place to place or among different offices in the same building (nomadic workers).

This community is usually supported trough web portals that allow them to share data and services (i.e. Scout Portal Toolkit, WebSphere Portal, Oracle9iAS Portal) or provides additional support such as a recommended task structure or policies and roles (i.e. MS SharePoint). Although portal's changes are marked, users must remember their previous interaction and interpret this changes in relation to his or her actual goals (i.e. recall previous messages to remember current task's restrictions).

To diminish this dependence mail-based notifications systems, allow users to specify interesting events and notifies them about its occurrence (i.e. MS SharePoint or Yahoo Agenda). As well, mail-based applications allow users to react to particular events (i.e. confirm an invitation to a meeting) following a protocol-based interaction.

But users must log into their e-mail systems to get notifications on time; otherwise, they would be useless (i.e. meetings remainders). Moreover, the more mobile users are, the more unlikely is the probability that they are logged in e-mail systems for long periods, so the probability of having out-dated messages increases.

Attempts to perform a more immediate contact exploit peer-to-peer networks and web servers to deliver notifications (i.e. ICQ, Mp3, SMS, Voice/Video–Conferencing, Instant Messaging, etc). Based on this technology, web portals can be more proactive (i.e. Yahoo Agenda sends message alerts through the user's cell phone). The drawback is that it could happen that the usage of different channels simultaneously can overwhelm users (i.e. an alert for the approximation of a meeting can arrive as cell phone SMS ring tone, an e-mail pop-up, and an ICQ pop-up at the same time!).

In addition, as these are proprietary services we cannot keep track of users reaction so that an important message would not arrive on time (i.e. if a message sent to ICQ has not been seen; it could be interesting to wait for some time and then, automatically, send it to a cell phone); or it can arrive when the originator event has already changed (i.e. an alert for a canceled meeting), which could lead to misunderstandings or be simply annoying.

In contrast, CoolTown [6] exploits web technology, wireless networks and portable devices to support "web presence" for people, places and things. That is, physical objects like printers, paintings or cars hold a device (a beacon or a tag) that relates the object with a web page that describes it. People and places are also represented as web pages and objects physically close are represented in the same page.

This way, users can access seamlessly the virtual space from the physical world by pointing things' tags (i.e. updating web information about a car location) and the physical world from the virtual space (i.e. turn off the lights). But, although virtual space is enriched, again the interaction responsibility is on the side of the user.

In a former experience [5], we develop a multi-agent system (AwServer) that was able to deliver information trough different media based on Internet services *proactively*, so users were contacted through e-mail, private messaging systems, cellular phone or interface widgets depending on the relevance of the information. Additionally, users could specify their availability preferences (from 8:00 to 19.00).

All these media were seen as different interfaces of a unique web space spread over multiple devices. This space was structured in terms of a work ontology from which user actions' relevance was inferred. A case study involving 3 small groups members (one of them was a control group) was conducted.

What we observed from the experience was that members of the control group reported a lack of acknowledge, felt isolated and visited almost daily the site in order to find out what has happened. Groups supported by proactive applications reported a higher sense of group belonging, as they were able to perceive that something was occurring in the group site as well as the actions of their partners.

On the other hand, without taking into consideration information relevance and users' current situation, proactive environments could increase the risk of information overload (spam).

3 Agent Architecture

We built a FIPA [7] compliant multi-agent system (AwServer) that manages the delivery of messages informing about events occurred in a virtual space through different devices. In addition, user context was taken into account; in this paper, it represents user preferences to be disturbed as well as his or her communicational resources (which are personal and heterogeneous) [5], [8].

AwServer is composed of agencies (a set of agents that delivers a single service), one associated to each user. Agencies are composed of a User Context Agent (UCA) and one agent for each kind of community to which the user belongs.

For example, in figure 1, we can see that user 1 (represented by a laptop) belongs to a work community (WCom); then his agency is composed of a Work Context Agent (WCA) and a UCA agent. User 2 (represented by a desktop computer) and user 3 (represented by a palm and a cellular phone), belong to WCom and TCom (Thematic Community) communities, so their agencies are composed of a Thematic Context Agent (TCA), a WCA, and UCA agents.

As well, a Proxy Agent (PA) in conjunction with a component (AgentListener servlet, represented by the small boxes) behaves as an interface between web applications (WCom and TCom) and agencies. For the sake of clarity in figure 1, there is a PA associated to each agency although this is not strictly necessary.

PA redirects events generated in each community to WCA or TCA agents (solid arrows for WCom and dotted arrows for TCom). All communication among agents occurs at the knowledge level following FIPA ACL standard [9].

Each agent has its own knowledge base and reacts to changes in their environment based not only on external events but also on their memory and inferences.

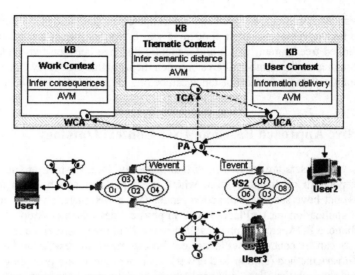

Fig 1. System architecture. *WCA* agent infers relevance of virtual space 1 events (*VS1*). *UCA* agent infers the *user willingness* to perceive this information. *TCA* agent infers relevance of virtual space 2 events (*VS2*). *PA* agent collects virtual space events trough the *AgentListener* component (shadow boxes in the border of ovals) and routes them to the *agencies*

3.1 Relevance Inference

In order to deal with potential spam, our first experience with AwServer estimates events relevance based on an interpretation context (Work Context), which is an ontology that specifies, at a high level, the interactions in a work related environment.

It can be argued that interaction in some web communities (i.e. research, health, gardening, etc.) can hardly be structured in order to infer user actions' relevance. In order to face this concern we built a discussion forum and realized that although users' interaction can be modeled, they are very specific to the task at hand (create topics, answer them, etc.), but at a high level, user's actions were similar to those occurring in a work community: users basically add, modify and delete objects (work activities, web pages, user profiles, topics, object 1, object 2, etc.).

These transforming operations (add, modify, delete) occur also in users' context: they add, modify and delete their vPlaces (which is discussed in the next section).

These operations are asymmetric (Asymmetric Virtual Manipulation or AVM) in the sense that as users expect to perform successful operations, a message confirming this status has *low* or *none* relevance for the performer, but it is very important for other community members as for them it is unexpected (i.e. a topic was erased) [5].

This strategy for inferring relevance is the basic reasoning layer of WCA, TCA and UCA agents. In addition, consequences of users' actions in a work environment can be specified because the environment has some structure: there are responsibilities, preconditions to execute activities and consequences or post-conditions from its execution, among others [8]; but a more relaxed interaction (i.e. a discussion forum) could take less advantage from this strategy (lurkers have no responsibilities).

However, as communities' interests are reflected in the content of their virtual space, we take advantage of their content structure. So that, topics are arranged in a doubled linked tree (parent, child) and semantic distance between two nodes of the tree is calculated as the number of arcs between them. In this case relevance is inverse to the semantic distance (a short distance can belong to "high" relevance scale).

4 Proactive Approach Based on User Context Ontology

We can say that users are located in virtual places (vPlaces), which are abstractions that correspond to applications from where users perform actions (transformation operations) but have specific interaction modes (i.e. a web page, an SMS account, a MS Word application, etc). vPlaces *reside* in physical devices (a desktop computer, a cellular phone, a PDA, etc.). A physical *device* can hold many virtual places.

For users can be contacted, vPlaces need an electronic address (*e_address*) and a *content delivery* method (similar to a driver). As more devices are providing a way to be accessed through the Web, it is very simple to deliver messages to these devices just by writing an appropriate method (i.e. java mail, java socket support, etc.).

vPlaces can be *portable* and *perturb* users in different degrees: a "new mail" ring tone through a cell phone could be more disturbing than a web based mail system that lacks of push technology and is not portable.

Some examples of vPlaces (arranged according to their perturbation degree) could be: *eMailPlace, WebPlace, collabAppPlace, privMessagingPlace, cellular_MailPlace* and *cellular_SMSPlace* (fig. 2).

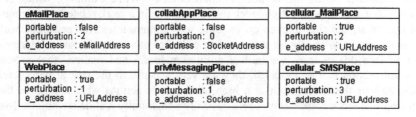

Fig. 2. Examples of vPlaces ordered by their *perturbation index*

User context is formally described and designed as an ontology written in DAML + OIL syntax (DARPA Agent Markup Language and Ontology Inference Layer) [10]. For the sake of simplicity, fig. 2 presents the ontology in a graphic format.

User context is described in terms of concepts, slots, individuals (objects) and restricted relationships: has, instance_of, superclase, one_of and cardinality. A user is a *Person* that owns a set of *vPlaces* and is *located* at some of them, we capture their movement across locations trough the login/logout functions, but it could be possible to perform this task through sensors.

Users action (*transformation operations*) and relevance (*urgency*) estimated by WCA or TCA are sent to UCA as *events*. In both cases, urgency is represented as discrete values (low, medium, high, sure) although it could be a continuous function.

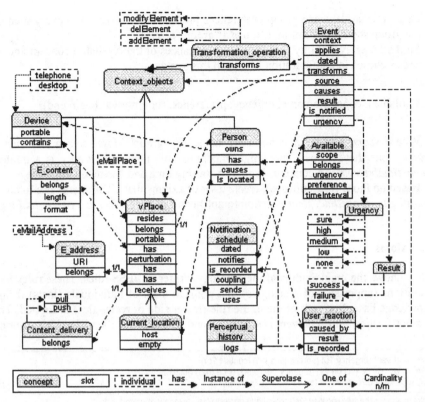

Fig 2. UContext ontology. A *vPlace resides* in a *device*, has *content*, an *electronic address* and a *content delivery method*. *vPlaces belongs* to a *person*. A *person is located* at a *vPlace*. WCA infers event *urgency*. Based on *user location* (*coupling*) and *availability* preferences (*time*) a *notification* is *scheduled*. User *reaction* is *recorded* in a *perceptual log*

Events include information about the vPlace where it was originated and its kind of community (*context*) that is, a WCom or a TCom event. Taking into account users' *current location*, we can prescribe a coupling level: the interaction is coupled if the user "is" in the place where events are generated (it could be that the user originates the events) or it can be uncoupled if he or she "is not" located at the vPlace where events are generated (it could be that another member of the community generated the event or the user has left the vPlace).

4.1 Users' Availability Preferences

It makes sense that users availability preferences are specific for each community (scope): for example, a user would like to be available from 8:00 to 19:00 hours in his or her work community while in the discussion forum he or she maybe would like to be available from 19:00 to 21:00 hours and the whole day for his family community.

To our surprise, in a previous experience with AwServer, some users claimed that in order to trust the commitment of their partners (i.e. a member could choose to be not available at all) some group preferences profile should exists, and every member of the group should commit to it (it has a "group" scope).

So that, user availability preferences are instances of the Available concept and are stored as entries in configuration files with this syntax:

Available (scope, username, urgency, preference, timeInterval(begin end))   **(1)**

Where *scope* can be a community name or "group", *username* a user name, *urgency* one these values: sure, high, medium, low, none. *Preference* is a boolean value, *timeInterval* is a concept, *begin* is a starting time and *end* an ending time.

Based on those restrictions we create a set of axioms that UCA agents use to create a *notification schedule. User reaction* to notifications is recorded in a *perceptual log*.

4.2 Axioms

Fig. 3 shows the main axioms of the ontology written as JESS rules. These rules have conditions (upper side of rectangles) that point to a set of individuals (facts) from a knowledge base. For each of them, the rule (lower side of rectangles) is applied. That is, a notification for each event is scheduled and *sent* to a specific *vPlace* or *location*.

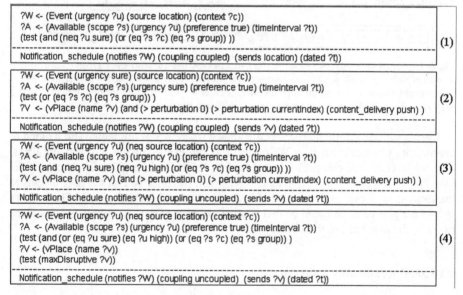

Fig. 3. vPlace and time selection. Users engage in *coupled* (1, 2) or *uncoupled* interaction (3, 4). *Events* have *low* (1, 3), *medium* (1, 3), *high* (1, 4) or *sure* (4, 2) urgency. User *availability* preferences *scope* is considered: preferences can be applied to a whole *group,* or on a personal basis, in this case user preferences for each community (*context*) is applied

When a coupled event occurs, the chosen vPlace is the same where the event was originated (Fig.3.1). A more perturbing behavior is implemented for urgent events: an exception is considered for events with the highest relevance level (sure); in this case, the next vPlace in the perturbation order that resides in the same device will be chosen: in the example, *privMessagingPlace* (a popup window), would appear (Fig.3.2).

For uncoupled events, messages will be directed to asynchronous vPlaces, represented by negative perturbation indexes that support push technology (i.e. e-mail systems). In the example, *WebPlace* is the first asynchronous vPlace, but is a regular Web site without support for push capability. For this reason, it is not eligible and the selected vPlace must be the *eMailPlace* (Fig.3.3).

In the case of events with higher relevance (high) the chosen vPlace has a higher perturbation index (*cellular_MailPlace*) and for the highest urgency, the vPlace with the highest perturbation index is chosen (*cellular_SMSPlace* respectively) (Fig.3.4).

When events are the result of inference processes (created by WCA agent or UCA agent) we assume that the event source is the current user location.

Once a vPlace is chosen, for synchronous interaction, the *chosen* time is the closest to the actual (now), while for asynchronous interaction, the time is chosen according to user availability preferences (1): preferences that have a "group" scope will be applied to users of that group; otherwise they will be applied on a personal basis, that is, user preferences specified with a community scope (or event context) are applied

As preferences are set in terms of time intervals, notifications are scheduled as soon as possible within the interval.

When more than one event is scheduled to a vPlace, their precedence order is determined by their arrival order. When the user acknowledges the notification, the event is stored in the Perceptual History log, and the User Reaction is recorded in order to correct or reinforce agents' assumptions. That is, UCA agents wait for user acknowledgment through a PA's *Waiting* behavior (a thread suspension execution).

5 Conclusions

Our objective was to provide web communities with the capability of reach users proactively in order to foster interactivity among their members and sense of group belonging, as previous experiences suggested [5], [8]. Three concerns are related to this objective: user devices heterogeneity, cognitive overloading (spam) and users belonging to multiple web communities at a time.

The strategy, based on a User Context Ontology, has proven to solve the first concern. Regarding the second one, a previous approach seam to be useful to infer events relevance provided that these communities follow certain well established norms (work practice). However, interaction among members of most web communities, lack of such degree of structure: their member can remain silent (lurkers) but actively engaged or can be very productive but visit the community from time to time and although we can model their behavior from a work perspective (with very relaxed restrictions), no significative advantages come out from this approach.

However it is possible to model their interactions in a higher level of abstraction (somebody adds, deletes or modifies something) and even so obtain significative results that serve as a basis for relevance criteria.

Of course these relevance will be enriched if specific rules are defined: activities consequences in a work context or semantic proximity in a discussion forum.

Users' availability preferences scope needs to be specified for users that belong to multiple communities at a time, which is something that already occurs. As well group scope policies need to be provided.

We addressed those needs by extending slightly the User Context Ontology, however the high degree of modularity provided by multi-agent technology made possible that no changes were required on AwServer code. The inclusion of a new kind of agent was eased as well. TCA agent is structurally similar to WCA agent, but in addition, it maintains a tree structure that organizes forum topics and allows the agent to estimate the semantic proximity of a new topic to a former topic that he or she specifies as "interesting". We found this approach promising, because interesting topics could be identified as users navigate trough the tree (or pages of a courseware), then, users with similar interests could be detected and interaction among them facilitated (opportunistic group formation).

References

1. Dix, A.: Challenges for Cooperative Work on the Web: An analytical approach. Groupware and the World Wide Web. Bentley, R., Busbach, U., Kerr, D., and Sikkel, K., (eds). Dordrecht, Kluwer (1997).
2. Hof, R. D., Browder, S. and Elstrom, P.: Internet communities. In Business Week (European Edition), May 5, (1997), Pp. 39-47.
3. Speier, C., Valacich, J. and Vessey, I.: The Influence of Task Interruption on Individual Decision Making: An Information Overload Perspective. Decision Sciences, (1999) 30 (2), 337-360.
4. Gruber, T.R.: A translation approach to portable ontology specification. Knowledge Acquisition. Vol. 5 (1993) 199-220.
5. Alarcón, R., Fuller, D.: Intelligent Awareness in Support of Collaborative Virtual Work Groups. Lecture Notes in Computer Science. Haake, J., Pino, J. A. (eds.), Springer-Verlag Berlin (2002) 2440, 168-188.
6. Kindberg, T., Barton, J., Morgan, J., Becker, G., Caswell, D., Debaty, P., Gopal, G., Frid, M., Krishnan, V., Morris, H., Schettino, J., Serra, B., Spasojevic, M.: People, places, things: web presence for the real world. In ACM Journal Mobile Networks and Applications (MONET). (2002), 7 (5), 365-376.
7. Burg, B.: Foundation for Intelligent Physical Agents. Official FIPA presentation, Lausanne, February 2002. See http://www.fipa.org for further details.
8. Alarcón, R., Fuller, D.: Application design based on work ontology and an agent based awareness server. Lecture Notes in Computer Science, Decouchant, D., Favela, J., (eds) , Springer-Verlag Berlin (2003).
9. Bellifemine, F., Pitt, J.: A Protocol-Based Semantics for FIPA '97 ACL and its implementation in JADE. Proceedings of VI Congress of the Italian Association for Artificial Intelligence (AI*IA), 1999.
10. Horrocks, I.: DAML+OIL: a description logic for the semantic web. Bull. of the IEEE Computer Society Technical Committee on Data Engineering, (2002) 25(1):4-9.

Adaptive Resource Management in the PIÑAS Web Cooperative Environment

Sonia Mendoza[1], Dominique Decouchant[1],
Ana María Martínez Enríquez[2], and Alberto L. Morán[1,3]

[1] Laboratoire "Logiciels, Systèmes, Réseaux", Grenoble, France
Sonia.Mendoza@imag.fr, Dominique.Decouchant@imag.fr, Alberto.Moran@imag.fr
[2] Depto. de Ingeniería Eléctrica, CINVESTAV-IPN, D.F., México
ammartin@mail.cinvestav.mx
[3] Facultad de Ciencias UABC, Ensenada, B.C., México

Abstract. The PIÑAS Web cooperative environment allows distributed authors working together to produce shared documents in a consistent way. The management of shared resources in such an environment raises important technical issues due to the constraints imposed by Web technology. An elaborated group awareness function is provided that allows each author notifying his contributions to other authors, and controlling the way by which other contributions are integrated into his/her environment. In order to support this function, essential to every groupware application, we designed a self-adaptive cooperative environment. We propose a new way of structuring Web documents to be considered as independent resource containers with their corresponding management context. This representation of information simplifies the design of mechanisms to share, modify and update documents and their resources in a consistent and controlled way. Scenarios are used to motivate the need for robust mechanisms for the management of shared Web documents and to illustrate how the extensions presented address these issues.

Keywords: Web document, shared resource, self-adaptive cooperative environment, PIÑAS platform, replication and updating.

1 Introduction

Working in the Web distributed environment, users can only consult and/or produce independent resources (e.g. text, images, audio, video, CGI scripts, applets, etc.) that are mainly accessible from HTML pages stored on local or remote servers. As all resources are completely independent, their management is performed following a per resource modification procedure that can generate undesirable effects, such as references to non-existent resources, duplication of (possibly costly) resources, unused obsolete resources and incomplete Web pages, among others. These well known problems come from the fact that it does not exist a real notion of Web document that keeps together a set of referring and

J. Favela et al. (Eds.): AWIC 2004, LNAI 3034, pp. 33–43, 2004.
© Springer-Verlag Berlin Heidelberg 2004

referred resources. Consequently, each time a new Web page is created or modified to be (re)published, many efforts are required by the concerned user (e.g. webmaster) to manually obtain the correctness of the resource set.

Web document management becomes more complicated when resources are also referred from documents managed by other users. In fact, links among documents and resources are unidirectional. This Web characteristic makes impossible, by examining a resource, to know how many local or remote documents are using it, and consequently to decide if it is still used or if it can be reclaimed or conserved for later use. The effects of this lacking information can produce as possible results the "Error 404: Object not found!" for "direct" inaccessible documents (e.g. HTML pages) or broken representations of them when referring to renamed, moved or deleted resources (e.g. a GIF image).

Considering these limitations and the problems that arise due to them, this work aims to propose some mechanisms for providing to a distributed authoring group a self-adaptive cooperative environment for managing shared Web documents and their resources. We start this paper by discussing related work. Section 3 presents the foundation of this work: the PIÑAS platform. Section 4 introduces the principles underlying our self-adaptive cooperative environment. Afterwards, Section 5 describes our notion of Web document entity, while Section 6 uses scenarios to illustrate some mechanisms for the management of such an entity.

2   Related Work

Previous work (e.g. [8]) have highlighted the issue of information structuring on the Web. Nowadays, Web technology allows only one level of structure: a whole page. However, Web-based cooperative applications incorporate additional levels, which come from those that recognize directory hierarchies to others that identify portions of Web pages.

The WebDAV [4] protocol provides basic support for hierarchical organizations of resources called collections. However, it does not define mechanisms for sharing resources among multiple collections nor atomic operations on collections. Current work of the WebDAV group is extending the basic collection functionality to cover up those disadvantages. Nevertheless, the advanced collection functionality does not support resource sharing among collections stored on different Web sites. By contrast, PIÑAS relies on resource and relationship replication to allow such a facility.

The ContentSpec [5] project is a document management protocol for use in combination with Open Hypermedia Systems. Like PIÑAS, it decomposes Web documents into fragments. An important difference between these two approaches is that ContentSpec manages individual portions, rather than whole documents, as its main goal is to address the problem of spending time on downloading a large multimedia document, when the user is interested in a few fragments. In contrast with this approach, PIÑAS supports integrated cooperative authoring of fragmented Web documents.

Lotus Notes [7] is a distributed document-base system that can work on both a LAN and the Internet. The key data element is known as *note* that contains a list of items. A note refers to another by means of a *notelink*, which identifies the target note and the database that stores it. In contrast to the PIÑAS approach, a note may have several sons, but at most one father in a note hierarchy.

3   The PIÑAS Platform

The PIÑAS platform [6] aims at providing support for the development of cooperative applications on the Web. More specifically, it has been designed to provide support for the cooperative authoring of documents on the Web. It provides a set of services for the identification, naming and management of authors, documents, resources, sessions, projects, applications and events. These services are available to cooperative applications through standard interfaces (e.g. HTTP protocol) and through more specialized interfaces (e.g. proprietary extensions and conventions to standard protocols). On one hand, "PIÑAS-aware" applications are capable of requesting these services, thus gaining access to the features (e.g. richer contents) of the platform that they are capable to handle. On the other hand, "non-PIÑAS-aware" applications are capable of requesting services using standard interfaces, thus allowing the user to gain access to specific features, while avoiding sending them information (e.g. proprietary formatting information) they will not be able to deal with.

3.1   Requirements

For the design of the PIÑAS platform, we identified the following requirements: the need for pertinent document and resource *sharing*, *availability* and *consistency*. We also identified additional issues that need to be resolved: the need for *author, document* and *resource identification*, development of specific *access mechanisms*, *access moment specification* and *access site specification*.

To achieve these requirements, we define and use the following mechanisms: *fragmentation, access control, concurrency control, replication, automatic updating* and *virtual naming* of documents and resources. These mechanisms are developed and mapped into the system architecture of the PIÑAS platform, which is further discussed in the following subsection.

3.2   Architecture

The architecture of the PIÑAS platform is based on a three layer distributed model that integrates key components to provide support for cooperative authoring on the Web (see Fig. 1). The upper layer shows that cooperative applications are built on the top of it. Based on their functional requirements, these applications use the features provided by this middleware. In the bottom layer, we can see a set of key basic entities for supporting cooperative authoring. They are managed by extensible services located in the middle layer.

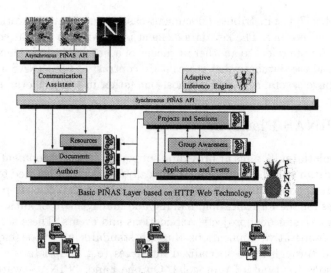

Fig. 1. The PIÑAS Platform Architecture

Fig. 1 also shows that a further decomposition of each layer brings up individual components for managing each one of the following entities: Authors, Documents and their Resources, Sessions, Projects, Events, Applications and Group Awareness [6]. In this paper, we focus on the components for document and resource management.

4   A Self-adaptive Cooperative Environment

In a previous work [2], we presented the first principles of a self-adaptive cooperative environment, taking into account the entity space manipulated by the authors and the set of actions applied to it. In this paper, we propose additional principles, so that the system is able to analyze the actions of each author, to discover some related points of interest and to determine both individual and common goals. The system is designed as an autonomous Group Awareness Agent (GAA) to allow authors to work more efficiently and productively.

In order to update the author's self-adaptive cooperative environment, the GAA periodically evaluates the entity space in parallel with the actions applied by the author (see Fig. 2). This evaluation is completed by both statistic measures and analysis of the concurrent interactions. Thus, based on the author's access rights on the entity space, the GAA can install dedicated tools in his environment and make them available according to his/her current activities (e.g. if *George* is playing the role of *reviewer* on document *report*, the GAA enables an annotation tool).

The GAA also guides and dynamically adapts the author environment according to individual preferences. Thus, the author is able to easily export his contributions and to integrate other author contributions in a comfortable and

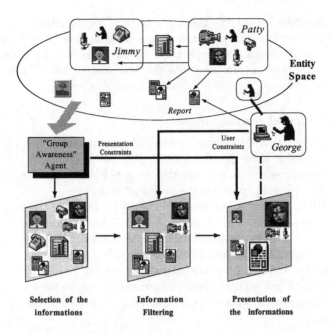

Fig. 2. The Self-Adaptive Cooperative Environment Principle

simple way. To notify an outgoing event [3], the GAA inspects the author's preferences to know if it has to be notified and, if so, when (e.g. immediately). Symmetrically, before notifying an incoming event, the GAA verifies if the author is on-line. If so, the GAA inspects the author's preferences to determine if the event has to be notified and, if so, when (e.g. as soon as the author is on-line).

Before presenting how the GAA updates the author's environment according to these principles, we present our notion of Web document entity.

5   Towards a New Web Document Entity

Because the GAA is interested in the evolution of the different interrelated entities that compose the author's self-adaptive cooperative environment, the management of them constitutes an unavoidable endeavor. Thus, we propose an elaborated notion of Web document entity that can be considered as a closure and a container of resources. This notion is designed to satisfy the following GAA's requirements:

Containment consistency- a Web document entity should be treated as a container of all resources needed and used by the document. In this way, elaborated operations should allow to correctly share, modify, copy, move, rename or delete it, or its component resources.

Resource sharing- a (possibly costly) resource should be shared among several Web documents stored on the same site or on different Web sites.

Relationship integrity- the correctness of relationships among Web documents and their shared resources should be guaranteed. For example, when performing a document copy operation on the same site or between different sites, the user should be ensured that the new created Web document is immediately accessible.

5.1   The Virtual Naming Space

To well manage the Web document entity, we define a virtual naming space which is fully compatible with the well known URL based system [1]. Thus, existing standard Web browsers as well as other targeted Web cooperative applications are able to transparently access the proposed entity.

The author, document and resource names, provided by the user to designate them, are logical names (e.g. "Jimmy", "Report" and "Diagram01.gif" in Fig. 3). A logical name does not contain information allowing to locate the associated entity in the storage Web base. Thus, correspondences between logical and physical names are managed by a virtual naming system that is responsible for: 1) the allocation of new virtual identifiers corresponding to the logical names, and 2) the organization of the associated entities in a hierarchical structure.

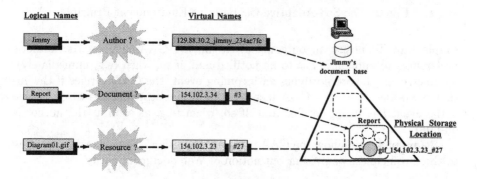

Fig. 3. Virtual Naming Spaces

Each document then defines a virtual naming space in which all its resources are organized and stored. For example, the resource logically named "Diagram01.gif" corresponds to the entity virtually named "154.102.3.23_#27" and stored in the file "gif_154.102.3.23_#27". Each virtual identifier is unique, not re-allocable and valid for the entity's life. The correspondances between logical, virtual and physical names are dynamic and user transparent.

5.2   The Document Composition

A self-adaptive environment should allow distributed authors to cooperatively and independently produce local replicas of shared Web documents even in temporary disconnected mode. In order to support this kind of cooperative work, we propose to base the document naming and management on the definition of a Document Naming Table (DNT) that can be modified on each working site in an autonomous way:

Adding/Deleting DNT resources- authors can add/delete resources to/from a shared document using a role-based access control strategy.

Modifying DNT resources- several authors can modify different resources on the same document following a master/slave policy [6].

Thus, after validation of independently performed modifications, an unification principle is followed to obtain a global state of the DNT. For example, the insertion of the image "Diagram01.gif" in the document "Report" (c.f. Fig. 4), must be integrated to the local DNT replica as well as to all remote (possibly modified) DNT replicas. To achieve consistency, an updating mechanism ensures modification diffusion and merging of DNT replicas.

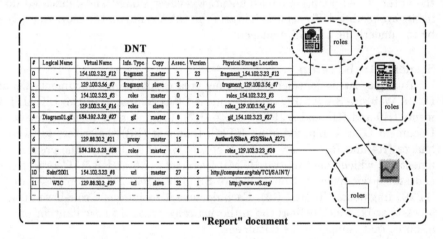

DNT

#	Logical Name	Virtual Name	Info. Type	Copy	Assoc.	Version	Physical Storage Location
0	-	154.102.3.23_#12	fragment	master	2	23	fragment_154.102.3.23_#12
1	-	129.100.3.56_#7	fragment	slave	3	7	fragment_129.100.3.56_#7
2	-	154.102.3.23_#3	roles	master	0	1	roles_154.102.3.23_#3
3	-	129.100.3.56_#16	roles	slave	1	2	roles_129.100.3.56_#16
4	Diagram01.gif	154.102.3.23_#27	gif	master	8	2	gif_154.102.3.23_#27
5	-	-	-	-	-	-	-
6	-	129.88.30.2_#21	proxy	master	15	1	Author1/SiteA_#33/SiteA_#271
8	-	154.102.3.23_#28	roles	master	4	1	roles_129.102.3.23_#28
9	-	-	-	-	-	-	-
10	Saint'2001	154.102.3.23_#8	url	master	27	5	http://computer.org/tab/TCI/SAINT/
11	W3C	129.88.30.2_#39	url	slave	32	1	http://www.w3.org/
...		...	...	...	...	...	...

"Report" document

Fig. 4. DNT Based Document Composition

5.3   The PIÑAS Document Manager

A key service for the GAA is the PIÑAS Document Manager. To manage document's components, it uses the services provided by the Resource Manager, the Proxy Manager and the Relationship Manager. The semantics of operations to be applied on documents and resources have been defined in terms of containment [9].

The *Resource Manager* allows to insert/delete a resource into/from a document and to copy/move a resource from a document to another. Also, it is in charge of creating the resource descriptor in the DNT.

The *Proxy Manager* is in charge of creating/deleting a resource's proxy and moving a proxy from a document to another. A proxy represents an actual resource contained in other document that is created when inserting that resource into a document. Thus, the notion of proxy allows for saving storage space and achieving location and attribute independency.

The *Relationship Manager* allows to create/delete relationships between two resources, between a proxy and the actual resource it represents, and between a proxy and the resource that refers to it. This manager implements first-class relationships as the format for many resources does not have native support for embedded references.

6   The Group Awareness Agent

After presenting our notion of Web document entity, this section aims at motivating the need for robust mechanisms for the management of such an entity in a cooperative work context. We use scenarios to illustrate how the GAA updates the author's self-adaptive environment, whenever shared and replicated documents are modified. To achieve its task, the GAA relies on the services provided by the underlying PIÑAS managers.

Scenario 1: the setup

To begin, let us consider that Jimmy creates and stores documents D0 and D1 on Web site SA (cf. Fig. 5). Document D0 is composed of two HTML fragments (R0 and R1) and a JPEG image (R2). Fragment R1 refers to image R2. Document D1 is composed of an HTML fragment (R3) that refers to two GIF images (R4 and R5). Patty shares Web site SA with Jimmy. She creates document D2 which contains two HTML fragments (R6 and R7). George creates and stores document D3 on Web site SB. Document D3 is composed of two HTML fragments (R8 and R9). Each document maintains a role-based control access matrix, which defines the authoring roles granted to each author on each resource that composes the document.

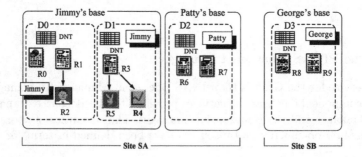

Fig. 5. Jimmy, Patty and George authoring independently

Scenario 2: sharing a resource using a single Web site

The present scenario shows how document D1 is shared between Jimmy and Patty, whose bases are centralized on site SA.

Let us suppose that Jimmy grants Patty authoring roles on document D1: she can annotate fragment R3 and modify images R4 and R5. In order to update Patty's self-adaptive environment, the Document Manager requests the corresponding managers to create a proxy P0D1 in Patty's base and to establish a relationship between document D1 and proxy P0D1. Document D1 is not replicated as Jimmy and Patty bases are stored on the same Web site. Then, the Document Manager notifies the GAA of such an event, which is put in a queue. At the moment the event has to be notified, the GAA verifies if Patty is on-line. Supposing that she is off-line, the GAA stores the event to notify it later.

Next time Patty enters to her self-adaptive environment, the GAA informs her that Jimmy invites her to contribute to document D1. Sometime later, Patty inserts image R4 (document D1) into fragment R7 (document D2) and finally saves document D2. Consequently, the Document Manager requests the corresponding managers to create a proxy P0R4 in the DNT of document D2 and to establish two relationships: 1) one between resource R7 and proxy P0R4, and 2) other between proxy P0R4 and resource R4 (cf. Fig. 6).

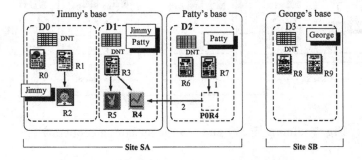

Fig. 6. Patty shares Jimmy's resource R4

Thus, the self-adaptive cooperative environment allows Jimmy to grant Patty authoring roles on document D1 while protecting the rest of his base (e.g. document D0 and its resources R0, R1 and R2). Likewise, document closure allows him to share some resources (e.g. R3, R4 and R5) and to deny others. Moreover, documents D1 and D2, which respectively contain the actual resource R4 and the proxy P0R4, can be manipulated in a uniform way as the GAA makes the use of proxies invisible to authors.

Scenario 3: sharing a resource among Web sites

This scenario illustrates how document D1 is shared among Jimmy, Patty and George, whose bases are distributed on Web sites SA and SB.

Let us consider that Jimmy grants George authoring roles on document D1: he can annotate fragment R3 and images R4 and R5. In order to update George's self-adaptive environment, the Document Manager creates a partial replica of Jimmy's base in site SB, which at least contains document D1. Then, the Document Manager notifies the GAA of such an event, which is put in a queue. When the event has to be notified, the GAA verifies if George is on-line. Considering that he is on-line, the GAA inspects George's preferences to determine at which moment event must be notified. Supposing that he specified to be notified as soon as possible, the GAA informs him that Jimmy and Patty invite him to work together on document D1.

Later, George inserts image R4 (document D1) into fragments R8 and R9 (document D3) and finally saves document D3. Thus, the Document Manager requests the corresponding managers to create a proxy P1R4 in the DNT of document D3 and to establish three relationships: 1) between resource R8 and proxy P1R4, 2) between resource R9 and proxy P1R4, and 3) between proxy P1R4 and resource R4 (cf. Fig. 7).

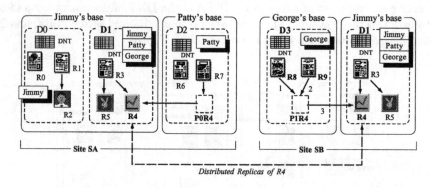

Fig. 7. Jimmy, Patty and George authoring cooperatively

Because Jimmy's document D1 is replicated on site SB, an up to date replica of resource R4 will be always available at George's site. The Document Manager automatically maintains consistency between replicas of document D1 stored on sites SA and SB. All sites are autonomous as direct references to remote resources never exist.

7   Discussion and Conclusion

In this paper, we proposed some basic mechanisms for providing to distributed authors a self-adaptive cooperative environment for managing shared Web documents and their resources. An elaborated group awareness function is achieved by the GAA, which allows each author notifying his contribution to other authors and controlling the way by which other contributions are integrated into his environment. To keep such an environment up to date, the GAA relies on the services provided by the underlying PIÑAS platform.

As the management of shared Web documents raises important technical issues due to the constraints imposed by Web technology, we presented our notion of Web Document entity to overcome them. Such an entity is modeled as a closure and a container of related resources, on which elaborated functions can be applied to correctly share, copy, move, rename or delete them. In order to support these functions, we designed and implemented the PIÑAS Document Manager, which constitutes a key service for the GAA.

Acknowledgments

This work is supported by: ECOS/ANUIES project M03M01, CONACyT projects 29729-A and 33067-A, CNRS/CONACyT projects 12411/J200-845 and 15051/J200-1159, and CONACyT and SEP-SESIC/UABC with scholarships 118380 and grant P/PROMEP: UABC-2000-08 respectively provided to the first and forth authors.

References

1. T. Bernes-Lee, R. Cailliau, A. Luotonen, H. Frystyk Nielsen and A. Secret, *The World Wide Web*, Communications of the ACM 37(8), pp. 76-82, August 1994.
2. D. Decouchant and A. M. Martínez, *A Cooperative, Deductive, and Self-Adaptive Web Authoring Environment*, In Proc. of MICAI'2000: Advances in Artificial Intelligence, The Mexican International. Conference on Artificial Intelligence, pp. 443-457, Lecture Notes in Artificial Intelligence, no 1793, Springer Verlag, Acapulco (Mexico), 11-14 April 2000.
3. D. Decouchant, A. M. Martínez, J. Favela, A. L. Morán, S. Mendoza and S. Jafar, *A Distributed Event Service for Adaptive Group Awareness*, In Proc. of MICAI'2002: Advances in Artificial Intelligence, The Mexican International Conference on Artificial Intelligence, pp. 506-515, Lecture Notes in Artificial Intelligence, no 2313, Springer Verlag, Merida (Mexico), 22-26 April 2002.
4. Y. Y. Goland, E. J. Whitehead Jr., A. Faizi, S. R. Carter and D. Jensen, *HTTP Extensions for Distributed Authoring - WebDAV*, RFC 2518, Microsoft, U. C. Irvine, Netscape and Novel, February 1999.
5. J. Griffiths, S. Reich and H. C. Davis, *The ContentSpec Protocol: Providing Document Management Services for OHP*, In Proc. of the 5th Workshop on Open Hypermedia Systems, ACM Hypertext'99 Conference, pp. 29-33, Darmstadt (Germany), 21-25 February 1999.
6. A. L. Morán, D. Decouchant, J. Favela, A. M. Martínez, B. Gonzalez Beltrán and S. Mendoza, *PIÑAS: Supporting a Community of Co-Authors on the Web*, In Proc. of DCW'2002 The Fourth International Conference on Distributed Communities on the Web, pp. 114-125, Lecture Notes in Computer Science, no 2468, SpringerVerlag, Sydney (Australia), 3-5 April 2002.
7. A. S. Tanenbaum and M. van Steen, *Distributed Systems: Principles and Paradigms*, Prentice Hall, New Jersey (USA), pp. 678-691, 2002.
8. D. Ramduny and A. Dix, *Why, What, Where, When: Architectures for Cooperative Work on the WWW*, In Proc. of HCI'97, the 7th Human Computer Interface Conference, pp. 283-301, Bristol (UK), 21-25 February 1997.
9. E. J. Whitehead Jr., *Uniform Comparison of Data Models Using Containment Modeling*, In Proc. of The Thirteenth ACM Conference on Hypertext and Hypermedia, pp. 182-191, ACM Press, Maryland (USA), 11-15 June 2002.

A Fuzzy Multi-agent System for Secure Remote Control of a Mobile Guard Robot[1]

Luis Mengual[*], Jesús Bobadilla[**], Gracián Triviño[*]

[*] DLSIIS, Facultad de Informática, U.P.M. Campus de Montegancedo s/n 28660,
Boadilla del Monte (Madrid) Spain
{lmengual, gtrivino}@fi.upm.es
[**] IA, Escuela Universitaria de Informática, U.P.M. Complejo Politécnico de Vallecas
Km.7 de la Carretera de Valencia, 28031, Madrid Spain
jbobi@eui.upm.es

Abstract. This paper presents a secure multi-agent architecture running on a Web environment. It is directed at monitoring mobile robots used for surveillance in sensitive environments (nuclear plants, military grounds) and domotic applications in smart buildings. Our Guard Robots are semi-autonomous mobile robots providing video streams encrypted via wireless to existing watchguard systems on Internet. In our Web system the robot movement must be controlled in real time using a joystick while the robot's position is obtained using a Webcam carried by the robot. The problem arises because the used network is not time deterministic and the bandwidth is limited and evolves dynamically. Although the best image quality is desired, a low-resolution image can be enough to navigate and avoid obstacles. We suggest a solution focused on a multi-agent architecture in which agents have fuzzy controllers and provide the best image quality for the available bandwidth, CPU power, video size and cipher engine.

1 Introduction

Multimedia applications development is growing rapidly at present. The growth of the Internet has caused a tremendous increase of multimedia traffic but nowadays the Internet does not offer a guarantee of quality of service for multimedia applications. Multimedia services such as video-on-demand, video-conferencing, video-telephony, distant learning, distributed games, multimedia communications among military transports, electronic news and e-commerce impose new QoS (quality of service) requirements such as a bandwidth guarantee (end-to-end and at network level), low delay-jitter and acceptable loss rate to avoid re-transmissions.

In addition, the problem of secure communications over the Internet (e-commerce, billing systems, access to bank information, etc) has extended to real-time communications. The necessity to protect multimedia data distributed over the

---

[1] This work is supported partially by *Science and Technology Ministry* of *Spain* under the projects: *"A Multi-Agent System Architecture for the automatic and dynamic Implementation of security protocols (TIC2001-3376)"* and "Open System of Multimedia Digital Presentation in Real Time *(TIC2000-1734-C03-02)"*

J. Favela et al. (Eds.): AWIC 2004, LNAI 3034, pp. 44-53, 2004.
© Springer-Verlag Berlin Heidelberg 2004

Internet makes encrypting audio/video flows necessary. The objective is to allow such resulting flows to be transmitted and later reproduced in real time.

It is therefore essential to choose a specific place for the cipher engine in the *code* of our multimedia application and to choose an encryption algorithm fast enough to allow real time communications. Providing Quality of Service (QoS) and security services for multimedia streaming has been a difficult and challenging problem.

Over the past years there has been a considerable amount of research within the field of quality-of-service (QoS) support for distributed multimedia systems [1,..,5]. According to [1], adaptive control schemes presented in the literature can be generally classified into three categories: sender-driven, receiver-driven and transcoder-based.

Sender-driven adaptive schemes, which will be discussed in this paper, fall into two strategies: buffer-based or loss-based. Buffer-based adaptive schemes use the occupancy of a buffer on the transmission path as a measure of congestion. Loss-based adaptation schemes adjust the rate based on the packet loss and bandwidth experienced by the receivers. Video conferencing, and multimedia streaming generally use UDP and Real-time Transport Protocol (RTP) [6] as their transport protocol. Some rate control mechanisms utilize the RTP Control Protocol (RTCP) [6] to obtain feedback information from receivers. RTCP is used along with RTP to provide quality information on the corresponding RTP media stream as well as some user-specific information.

The Internet Engineering Task Force (IETF) has proposed many service models and mechanisms to meet the demand for QoS. Notably among them are the integrated Services/Resource reservation protocol (RSVP) [7] model, constrained-based routing, traffic management and scheduling. Integrated services (IntServ) [8] and Differentiated services (DiffServ) [9] are the two existing models that provide varying QoS in the Internet.

The agents are autonomous programs situated within an environment and whose aim is to sense it and act upon it, using its knowledge base, and to learn in order to act in future. Multi-agent systems have been used in multimedia environments to optimize the different communication parameters such as bandwidth, quality of service and different multimedia communication parameters [10, 11, 12]. The Integrated Services (IntServ) model acknowledges precisely how agents are used for resource reservation (reservation Setup Agent).

In addition, multi-agent systems have been used widely in the security field to warn and protect communications or have been used for the smart and automatic implementation of security protocols. The usual security solutions (symmetric or asymmetrical cryptography) for the messages exchanged between agents or flexible solutions based on formal description techniques were implemented [13, .. ,17].

The present paper introduces a multi-agent architecture directed at optimizing encrypted and codified JPEG video transmission for the control via Internet of WIFI-technology mobile robots. The Java Media Framework (JMF) [18] is the basis of the development of a versatile application-programming interface (API) for incorporating time-based media into Java applications and, therefore, is portable and independent from the underlying hardware. To include the Blowfish cipher engine in the video conferencing application in JMF, the Cryptix open source cryptographic software library [19] was used.

2 Multi-agent Structure

The structure proposed is a multi-agent system with security and multimedia services. The security layer of the agents establishes a secure path over the Internet between a video server agent placed in a mobile robot (which detects a video signal from a Webcam) and a video client agent in the Internet. Subsequently the agents multimedia layer allows transmission of encrypted Video/Audio JPEG-GSM flows via Internet.

The JPEG Video quality is adapted dynamically to changes of the bandwidth in the network. We suggest an adaptive control scheme, sender-driven, and based on the data provided by RTCP reports from the receiver on the current bandwidth. A fuzzy controller of the agent's multimedia layer determines the optimum quality of JPEG flows depending on the bandwidth, CPU power or cipher engine.

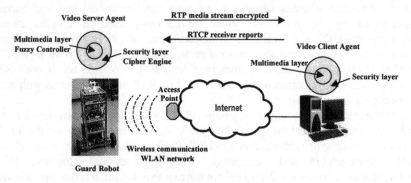

Fig. 1. Structure of the Web System

The system provides, for instance, the guard of a building the means to control remotely a mobile robot equipped with a Webcam [20, 21, 22], and offers more options than the fixed cameras used by most of the buildings for security purposes.

This type of systems will evolve as the number and quality of the sensors installed in the robot increase and the robot becomes more autonomous and, overall, a more intelligent assistant with more features.

One of the main obstacles we have overcome is the wireless communication between the operator and the robot. For the sake of making a general approach we suggested using a public network and, therefore, subject to problems such as variable bandwidth and security attacks.

2.1 Security Layer

This layer allows a secure communication between the agents. It was developed in Java ("1.3.0" version- Java 2 Runtime Environment, SE) and we were able to set up an infrastructure on which the security protocol was implemented dynamically from formal protocol specifications. These security protocols will distribute session keys. This security layer is fitted with a cipher engine run by the Cryptix library (Cryptix open source cryptographic software library v1.2) and is based on the Blowfish algorithm.

Blowfish is a symmetric block cipher that takes a variable-length key, from 32 bits to 448 bits. Blowfish was designed in 1993 by Bruce Schneier and is a fast, free alternative to existing encryption algorithms. Since then it has been studied considerably [23], and it is slowly gaining acceptance as a strong encryption algorithm. Blowfish is unpatented and license-free, and is available free for use. In order to test the ciphering speed in the memory we reached a speed of 5Mbytes/s (Pentium II-400Mhz), which is capable of transmitting encrypted video recordings in real time. The aim of the cipher engine is to cipher the payload of RTP packets that carry the video/audio data captured. Likewise, RTP packets will be encapsulated in UDP datagrams, and finally in IP packets (see Fig. 1).

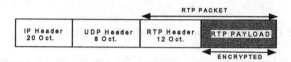

Fig. 2. How encrypting is incorporated in a *video streaming with RTP*

2.2 Multimedia Layer

This layer is responsible for the transmission of encrypted audio/video flows, which are sent from the mobile robot and received remotely by the agents over the Internet. The code of the layer was developed on a Java Media Framework 2.1.1c platform (Sun Windows Performance Pack). JMF [18] enables to capture audio/video signals by using a microphone and a Webcam, data coding and to transmit/receive audio/video flows in real time with the RTP/RTCP protocol. We implemented it by developing a Codec JPEG with the cipher engine for the agent's security layer, in particular, the *"...packetizer/...depacketizer"* types.

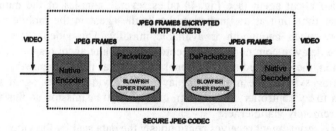

Fig. 3. Secure JPEG Codec in JMF

"....Packetizer" class is an implementation of the *"BasicCodec" interface* inside the architecture of JMF classes and interfaces. This class encapsulates the JPEG data in RTP packets that will be sent over the network. The class *"...Depacketizer"* is used in the receiver. This class receives in a buffer RTP packets and depacketizes it to obtain a complete frame in JPEG format. Our solution consists in encrypting the video/audio data before it is included in the RTP packets (see Fig. 2 and 3).

3 Adaptive Control

A multi-agent system approach was proposed for dynamic bandwidth allocation to obtain the best JPEG quality in Video Transmission. The aim is that reaching a network congestion level (and its corresponding bandwidth reduction) we can keep up remote control with the robot. In our system the available bandwidth is reported by the most recent RTCP sender report from the client multimedia agent. The video server agent in the guard robot has a fuzzy controller that dynamically evaluates the best JPEG quality transmission based on the current CPU power, video size, current bandwidth and the cipher engine selected.

3.1 Dynamic Optimizing Algorithm with JPEG Quality

Initially, the video server agent assesses the bandwidth by transmitting non-stop streams of bits to the receiving agent into the MTU (Maximum Transfer Unit) of the wireless network that belongs to the mobile robot. The MTU is the largest size of IP datagram, which may be transferred using a specific data link connection. In a wireless data link the size of MTU is 2,346 octets with 30 header octets and 32-bit cyclic redundancy check (CRC). Thus, taking into consideration the IP/UDP headers, the maximum amount of data user bytes per WLAN frame is 2,284 bytes (see Fig. 4).

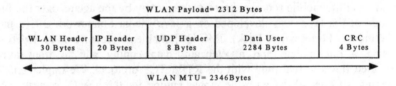

Fig. 4. MTU in a wireless network

The video client agent (see Fig. 1) takes several samples of the number of bits received per time unit at destination and tells the agent in the mobile robot (video server) how much bandwidth is available initially. The video server agent also assesses the delay in communication according to remote agent response. Taking into consideration, the estimated and additional data such as the CPU power, window size and operating system, the multimedia layer of the video server agent assesses by means of a fuzzy controller the optimum quality for transmission so that the robot is controlled remotely via Internet.

The video server agent receives continuously the data sent by the video client agent through RTCP reports about the available bandwidth (W). These data is evaluated to detect a relevant variation and in this case the fuzzy controller reassesses the current optimum quality depending on the changes of W (see Fig. 5). This could happen when the network is congested.

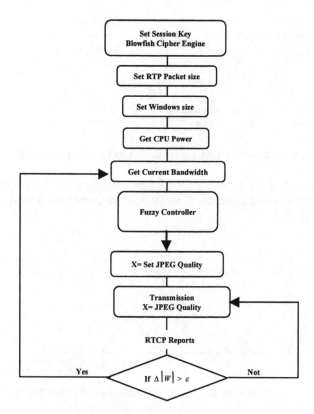

Fig. 5. Adaptive Control algorithm

3.2 Fuzzy Controller

We propose in this sub-heading to create fuzzy controllers with different qualities, operating systems, transmission technology and bandwidth, based on the test of performance of encrypted video transmission and unencrypted JPEG. Here, we present the fuzzy controller in the agents' multimedia layer that is responsible for adjusting in the mobile robot the optimum video transmission quality of encrypted JPEG. It uses the Blowfish algorithm, Linux Suse 8.1 operating system, a 352x288-window size, a packet size of 1024 bytes and a propagation delay estimated below 0.5s.

The variables to be considered for the transmission of coded video JPEG are CPU power of our agent's system and available bandwidth. This information is obtained dynamically by the video server agent from the video client agent through RTCP reports). As regards the bandwidth (see Fig. 6) we define the following membership functions with linguistic variables/labels: Low (0-500Mbps), Medium-Low (0-1Gbps), Medium-High (500-2Gbps), High (1Gbps--). We define the following functions for CPU power (see Fig. 6): membership functions with linguistic variables/labels: Low (400Mhz-1Ghz), Medium (400Mhz-2Ghz), High (1Ghz--).

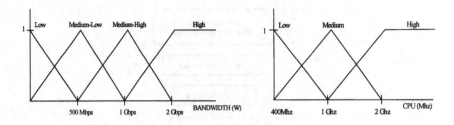

Fig. 6. Membership functions for fuzzy set of bandwith and CPU Power

We finally define the following membership functions for JPEG Quality (see Fig. 7), with linguistic variables/labels: Low (0-0,3), Medium-Low (0-0,5), Medium-High (0,3-0,7), High (0,5--).

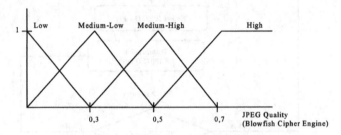

Fig. 7. Membership functions for fuzzy set of JPEG Quality

The rules of the fuzzy group, which are the knowledge base, are described on table 1. In this table, 12 fuzzy rules were defined to govern the controller's decisions.

Table 1. Fuzzy Rules

1. If (Bandwidth is Low) and (CPUpower is Low) then (JPEGquality is Low)
2. If (Bandwidth is Medium-Low) and (CPUpower is Low) then (JPEGquality is M-Low)
3. If (Bandwidth is Medium-High) and (CPUpower is Low) then (JPEGquality is M-High)
4. If (Bandwidth is High) and (CPUpower is Low) then (JPEGquality is M- High)
5. If (Bandwidth is Low) and (CPUpower is Medium) then (JPEGquality is Low)
6. If (Bandwidth is Medium-Low) and (CPUpower is Medium) then (JPEGquality is M-Low)
7. If (Bandwidth is Medium-High) and (CPUpower is Medium) then (JPEGquality is M-High)
8. If (Bandwidth is High) and (CPUpower is Medium) then (JPEGquality is M-High)
9. If (Bandwidth is Low) and (CPUpower is High) then (JPEGquality is Low)
10.If (Bandwidth is Medium-Low) and (CPUpower is High) then (JPEGquality is M-Low)
11.If (Bandwidth is Medium-High) and (CPUpower is High) then (JPEGquality is M-High)
12.If (Bandwidth is High) and (CPUpower is High) then (JPEGquality is High)

A Mandani fuzzy controller has been used: AND has been implemented as MIN; OR has been implemented as MAX; Aggregation has been implemented as MAX; Defuzzification has been implemented as centroid. Figure 8 shows the controller surface obtained:

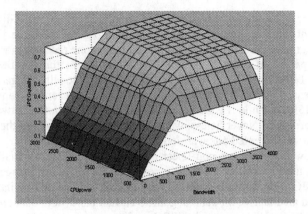

Fig. 8. Control surface obtained

4 Experimental Results

About 500 tests were carried out to prove the features of the implementation. The tests evaluated the performance of real time video transmission with JPEG code in JMF. The transmission was analyzed by evaluating the incorporation of a Blowfish cipher engine and by using different Network technologies: Local Area Networks (LAN) 10/100 Mbps, Wireless Local Area Networks (WLAN) 11 Mbps and Frame Relay 2 Mbps.

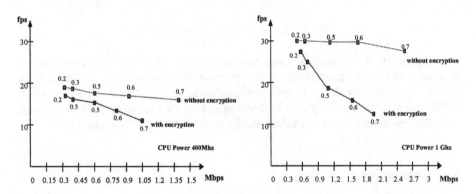

Fig. 9. Effects of the cipher engine. Laboratory test CPU power 400Mhz-1Ghz without fuzzy controller

Some of the most relevant results are shown in figures 9 and 10. We analyzed the effect of the cipher engine in the transmission without fuzzy controllers and used Linux Suse 8.1 operating system and different CPU powers. The figures show that by using the cipher engine the number of frames per second suffer a steep non-linear fall due to the increase of the number of bits that go into cipher engine. This behaviour is not so frequent without the cipher engine. In addition, the more the CPU power is increased the greater the fall. In this case the cipher engine receives more information in the same period of time; this leads to a reduction in the number of fps, and therefore the effects on the communication are proportionally bigger. If the CPU power is increased by 1 Ghz (see Fig. 9) there is a fall that ranges from 27-12 fps (a reduction of 15fps). While if CPU power is 400Mhz there is a fall between 18-10 fps (a reduction of 8 fps). Nevertheless, when CPU power was doubled the transmission of encrypted or unencrypted bits was doubled

Results show that there is a non-linear behaviour, according to variable bandwidth parameters in the network and the CPU power of the video server agent during the encrypted JPEG video transmission. Owing to this we decided to introduce fuzzy controllers and an adaptive model that gathers current bandwidth data on the available bandwidth continuously to assess the JPEG quality.

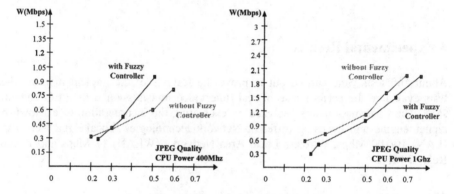

Fig. 10. Results of the Fuzzy controller

In figure 10 we compared some results from the empirical test performed in laboratory with the results when a fuzzy controller was used to optimize JPEG quality. We used for this purpose a multimedia server agent with a CPU power of 400Mhz and 1Ghz. From figure 10 we can infer that for a given bandwidth the fuzzy controller recommends an equivalent quality to the obtained in laboratory tests.

5   Conclusions

This paper describes a practical solution of remote-controlled mobile robots in real time by using fuzzy logic to assess and select the best quality of JPEG video transmission. Using fuzzy logic was necessary due to the non-linear behaviour of the cipher engine when the video transmission flows via Internet were encrypted. The fuzzy controller is included in a video server agent with a dynamically adaptive control based on RTCP reports, which give information about the available bandwidth of the video client agent. The outcome achieved by the fuzzy controller we developed is the same as the results from the robot testing.

References

1. Wang, X., Schulzrinne, H."Comparison of Adaptive Internet Multimedia Applications". IEICE Transactions on Communications June (1999).
2. Kumar, R., Rao, J.S., Chattopadhyay, S. and Rao, G. K. "A Protocol to Support QoS for Multimedia Traffic over Internet with Transcoding". Trusted Internet Workshop 2002. December 18, 2002, Taj Residency, Bangalore, India
3. Shu-Ching Chen, Mei-Ling Shyu, Gray, I., Hongli Luo; "An adaptive multimedia transmission protocol for distributed multimedia applications". 23rd International Conference on Distributed Computing Systems Workshops, 2003. Proceedings., 2003.
4. Malik, M.A.; Gondal, I.; "Optimized routing for efficient mobility over IP networks for multimedia transmission". International Conference on Information Technology: Coding and Computing [Computers and Communications], 2003. Proceedings. ITCC 2003., April 28-30, 2003 Page(s): 244 –247.
5. Dumitrescu, S., Xiaolin Wu. "Optimal variable rate multiplexing of scalable code streams". Data Compression Conference, 2003. Proceedings. DCC 2003 , 25-27 March 2003.Page(s): 424
6. RFC 1889. RTP: A Transport Protocol for Real-Time Applications.
7. RFC 2205.Resource ReSerVation Protocol (RSVP)
8. RFC 1633. Integrated Services in the Internet Architecture
9. RFC 2474. Definition of the Differentiated Services Field in the IPv4 and IPv6 Headers
10. Gang Wei; Petrushin, V.A.; Gershman, A.V.; "The Community of Multimedia Agents project ".IEEE International Conference on Multimedia and Expo, 2002. ICME '02. Proceedings. , Volume: 2 , 26-29 Aug. 2002. Page(s): 289 -292 vol.2.
11. Manvi, S.S.; Venkataram, P.; "Adaptive bandwidth reservation scheme for multimedia traffic using mobile agents ". 5th IEEE International Conference on High Speed Networks and Multimedia Communications, 3-5 July 2002. Page(s): 370 –374.
12. Yoshimura, T.; Ohya, T.; Kawahara, T.; Etoh, M.; "Rate and robustness control with RTP monitoring agent for mobile multimedia streaming ". IEEE International Conference on Communications. ICC 2002. Volume: 4 , 28 April-2 May 2002. Page(s): 2513 -2517 vol.4
13. Mengual, L., García, J. "Security Architecture For Agents Communication". Upgrade. Volumen III, Nº6, Págs 52-58, 2002
14. Boudaoud, K.; McCathieNevile, C. "An intelligent agent-based model for security management". Seventh International Symposium on Computers and Communications, 2002. Proceedings. ISCC 2002. Taormina, Italy. Page(s): 877 –882.
15. Gorodetski, V.; Kotenko, I. "The multi-agent systems for computer network security assurance: frameworks and case studies". IEEE International Conference on Artificial Intelligence Systems, 2002. (ICAIS 2002), Divnomorskoe, Russia. Page(s): 297 –302.
16. Mengual L, de la Puente C "Secure intelligent agents based on formal description techniques". Lectures Notes in Artificial Intelligent (LNAI 2663). Page(s): 134-141. 2003
17. Borselius, N.; Hur, N.; Kaprynski, M.; Mitchell, C.J. "A security architecture for agent-based mobile systems". Third International Conference on 3G Mobile Communication Technologies, 2002 (Conf. Publ. No. 489), London, UK. Page(s): 312 –318.
18. http://java.sun.com/products/java-media/jmf/.
19 http://www.cryptix.com/
20. Birk, A. and Kenn,H., "RoboGuard,a Teleoperated Mobile Security Robot". Control Engineering Practice,volume 10, no. 11, pp. 1259-1264, Elsevier, 2002
21. Borenstein, J., Koren, Y.,"Real-time Obstacle Avoidance for Fast Mobile Robots". IEEE Transactions on Systems, Man, and Cybernetics, Vol.19, No5, Sep/Oct. 1989
22. A security guard robot(Secom): http://www.robotslife.com/news/034.shtml
23 S. Vaudenay. "On the weak keys of Blowfish. Fast Software Encryption, Vol. 1039 of Lecture Notes in Computer Science, pages 27--32, 1996. Springer Verlag.

Implementation of an Ontology Sharing Mechanism for Multiagent Systems Based on Web Services

Leonid Sheremetov[1], Miguel Contreras[1], Alexander Smirnov[2]

[1]Instituto Mexicano del Petroleo,
Eje Central Cardenas N 152, Col. San Bartolo Atepehuacán Mexico, D. F. 07730
{sher, mcontrer}@imp.mx
[2]St.Petersburg Institute for Informatics and Automation of the Russian Academy of Sciences
39, 14th Line, St. Petersburg, 199178, Russia
smir@.iias.spb.su

Abstract. Development of dynamic open service environment for web based systems integration becomes a time challenge. In this paper, an approach based on the integration of agent technology with the functionality of Web Services (WS) is proposed. An interface allowing to expose the functionality of the multiagent system to web based systems and vice versa is implemented as a component of the CAPNET agent platform (AP) allowing to consume the services of an agent or group of agents residing on a FIPA compliant AP in a service oriented (non-agent like) way. Ontologies constitute the centrepiece of the knowledge retrieval, sharing and reuse mechanisms either on the web or among agents. In the case study, a web enabling Ontology Agent and a bridge WS have been implemented over the CAPNET to facilitate knowledge sharing within the KSNet framework. Implementation details are discussed.

1. Introduction

One of the major constraints to wide acceptance of e-business communities is the difficulty of collectively bringing together many disparate industry competitors, non-industry players, and other participants or units, and ensuring a common level of knowledge, understanding, and commitment. To be efficient, e-Business communities require cooperation and an open exchange of information among all participants. Within the enterprise, information infrastructure as the mean to bring together different software applications (existing legacy applications and one developed in a current framework) is the key component to enable this cooperation, information and knowledge exchange in an open distributed environment. Moreover, the trends in the software development indicate that the next technological innovation in this field should integrate connected organizations and multiple platforms for the applications through Dynamic Service Environments (DSE).

Today, WS are believed to be the crucial technology for web based business communities [1]. WS can be seen as high-level interfaces through which partners can conduct business operations. A current trend is to WS-enable legacy applications allowing XML-based data exchange between a legacy application and a software

J. Favela et al. (Eds.): AWIC 2004, LNAI 3034, pp. 54-63, 2004.

client [2]. Existing frameworks facilitate this effort by offering 'wrapping' services. For example, the business methods offered via the legacy application's EJB extension can be automatically exposed as individual Simple Object Access Protocol (SOAP) services [3]. Today, most of the software clients that access WS are non-agent applications.

On the other hand, software agents' technology also is looking for the development of open, stable, scalable and reliable network architecture that allows standards compliant agents to discover each other, communicate and offer services to one another [4]. For example, within the AgentCities effort, a 5th Framework IST project funded by the European Commission, a distributed test-bed to explore and validate the potential of agent technology for dynamic service environments is currently under development [5].

Recently a few works have been published devoted to the integration of the both approaches looking for solutions permitting software agents to offer their specific services as WS to general software clients and vice versa [6, 7]. As more application software is developed using agents as component building blocks [8, 9], a need to expose various functional parts of such applications as services is likely to increase.

In [10], a Component Agent Platform (CAP) as an agglutinating centre for the implementation of the enterprise information infrastructure was described. FIPA Reference Model [11] was chosen for the definition of agents' properties and functions since it provides standards for heterogeneous interacting agents and agent-based systems, and specifies ontologies and negotiation protocols. In this paper, we extend the proposed approach to Web applications. For this, a WS based interface allowing to expose the functionality of the Multiagent System (MAS) to other web based systems and also to consume external services is proposed. This interface is integrated as a component of the CAPNET (a new version of the CAP agent platform developed over the .NET framework) allowing consuming the services provided by agents residing on a FIPA compliant AP in a service oriented (non-agent like) way.

In the rest of the paper, a framework based on two models for WS and MAS integration is presented. Implementation of the framework through Agent Dispatcher WS and WS Proxy Agent is described. In the case study, a web enabled Ontology Agent and a bridge WS have been implemented over the CAPNET to facilitate knowledge sharing within the KSNet framework. Finally, discussion of the obtained results and conclusions are presented.

2. Multiagent Systems and Web Services Integration

In the WS – MAS integration scenario it is easy to see the need for some mechanism that allows agents to use the functionality provided by systems based on WS either in- or outside of the organization and to allow those services to use the ones that agents in a MAS implement. The framework for the WS – MAS integration developed in this paper is depicted in fig. 1 (with the Message Transport Service not shown for clarity of the interactions) and described below for two different scenarios.

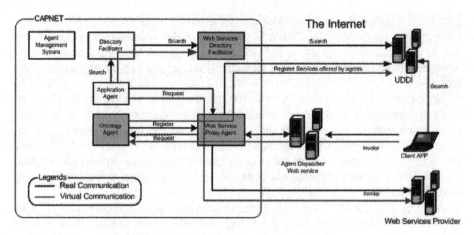

Figure 1. WS-MAS Integration Framework architecture

2.1 Agents Consuming Web Services

To consume WS, a special directory facilitator (DF) agent was designed. This agent, called WSDF registers himself as a DF in one or more platforms and will refuse every attempt to register on it for application agents that doesn't expose the functionality of a WS Proxy Agent (WSPA) described below. Additionally it would store information pertaining to WS such as the WSDLs and accounts needed to access those services if necessary, and previously known. When a search for a service is requested to this agent, it makes a search in its internal repository and in the UDDI performing a translation from DFAgentDescription to WSDL and back to a DFAgentDescription. Then, the WSDF generates a set of DFAgentDescriptions, specifying (i) the WSPAs registered with the WSDF as service providers (according to the specified search constraints) and (ii) all the necessary information allowing the application agent to invoke the WS from some WSPA as service properties. This way, when the application agent requests the service from the WSPA it provides all the service properties; thus the need for the WSPA to make another search on the WSDF is eliminated. Once an agent has the DFAgentDescription that tells him from whom to request the service (a WSPA in this case) it requests the service from the WSPA that will invoke the corresponding WS and return back the results.

Up to this point it should be clear, how the searching and invocation is performed starting from the search on a WSDF. But the missing part is how to integrate the WSDF within the overall architecture of a FIPA compliant AP. To achieve this, the WSDF registers himself with one or more DFs in the AP. It allows him to receive requests when a federated search is requested from a "normal" DF. This makes transparent to the application agents the fact that they are getting results from resources outside the AP. Also both the possibility to directly request the WS invocation with a known WSDL and the way to contact a WSPA are open. Additionally agents can be aware of the presence of WSDF in their AP, if they perform a search for the WSDF service in the ordinary DFs.

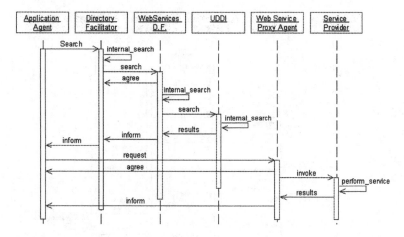

Figure 2. Application agent searching and consuming web services transparently.

2.2 Agents Offering Web Services

In the case when agents are to expose their functionality to external entities (non-agent software) there has to be a mechanism for registering the offered services into the UDDI to assure that the service is locatable for the outside world. That involves the translation of DFAgentDescriptions to WSDLs representing the services.

In our architecture, the process of registering a service available via WS is not transparent to an agent. Instead, it has to explicitly request a registration in the WSPA that plays a different role than in the previous scenario. The approach where the DF automatically registers the services accessible via WS is avoided in order to maintain the standard FIPA elements as clean as possible and to leave the decision to offer a service as a WS to each individual agent. The WSPA handles the task of requesting the services from the providing agents located outside the platform. Unfortunately, it is not directly accessible to the external clients and can only be contacted by a special WS called Agent Dispatcher Web Service (ADWS) that receives the direct service invocations. The WSPA however is responsible for registering in the UDDI the actual tasks that the ADWS is able to provide, and does this based on the information provided by agents upon registration. The process of registration and invocation of services from the outside is depicted in Fig. 3.

3. Implementation

Integration of WS and an AP requires the implementation of a bridge that is able to listen for web requests and, at the same time, to communicate with agents residing at the AP. In this work such a bridge is built using several standard technologies in order to provide the functionality of the CAPNET Ontology Agent to the "outside world" and to consume resources external to the AP.

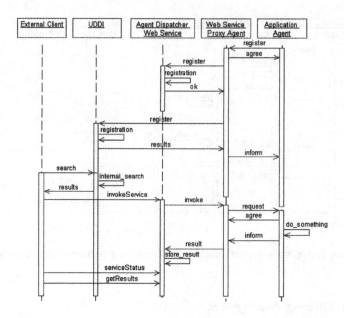

Figure 3. Application agent registering and providing web services.

The two components that allow offering the services of agents residing at the AP are the ADWS and the WSPA described in the following sections.

3.1 The Agent Dispatcher Web Service

This program itself is a simple WS that simplifies the work of contacting the functionality of agent provided services. It works in the following way: first, we register existing agent services with the WS dispatcher to make them available to other software. This registration is performed by the WSPA upon agent registration. In the case that a web enabled program needs to access services provided by agents, instead of having to implement agent communication mechanisms, it calls the ADWS providing only the name of the service and the input parameters. Then the dispatcher forwards the request to the WSPA and also returns the output to the calling program. In this scenario the client program needs only to know the name, the input format, and the output format of the service that wants to invoke. This assures that meanwhile these parameters do not change; the agent implementing this particular service can be changed or moved to a different physical location without affecting the client code.

In order to use the ADWS, existing agent services need to be registered on the dispatcher, and the client programs have to request the services through it. Since any WS registered with UDDI must be associated with a service type also known as a tModel in our case we have defined a tModel that allows service providers (APs in our case) to expose their functionality using a WS as an intermediary. Dispatcher's WSDL (and eventually the tModel) includes the following methods:

- *CallService(serviceName, parameters, timeout)*. This method allows to invoke the synchronous execution and will return the result to the corresponding agent or a failure message if the agent does not respond in a timely fashion (e.g. after a provided timeout period has expired)
- *invokeService(serviceName, parameters, timeout)*. This method sends a request for a service but terminates instantly returning a requestID that allows the client program to track the results of the asynchronous execution of the service.
- *serviceStatus(requestID)*. This method returns the status of a pending request and can return "done", "processing", "failed", "timedout" or "unknown" in case the dispatcher does not recognize the requestID as a valid ID one.
- *getResults(requestID)*. This method returns the results of the service with invokeService and if called on request with a serviceStatus other than "done", returns a message error.
- *getServiceDescription(serviceName)*. Returns the service description, parameters and results in a semantically meaningful format such as DAML-S.

3.2 The Web Service Proxy Agent

This agent living inside the AP plays two important roles. First, it provides functionality very similar to the DF but in this case, the registration process involves the creation of one or more entries in the ADWS and the registration in the UDDI of these services allowing external clients to request them. The entries in the dispatcher provide all the information that the WS requires to invoke the service on the WSPA that is responsible also for requesting the service to the provider agent and returning the results. It means that the WSPA will be the internal client (inside the AP) for the offered agent services. This makes the provider agents "unaware" (sure, they can already know what the WSPA function is) that they are providing the service to a non-agent entity. In our implementation, the ADWS is able to contact the WSPA via .NET Remoting and to invoke the required service from it. This will cause the WSPA to request the service from the registered service providing agent(s).

The WSPA also plays the role of provider or "wrapper" of WS for the internal agents that require access to WS. To do this, WSPA needs to be able to consume WS (and it is, since previously we stated that it is responsible for registering the services of the agents on the UDDI). Thus, WSPA receives a request from an agent, in which the WS, its parameters and all the required information are specified. This kind of information typically is given by the WSDF to agents when a direct or federated search is performed.

4. Case Study

As a case study, we discuss in this section the integration of the services offered by the Ontology Agent (OA) of CAPNET and its ontology library (OL) with the requirements of KSNet [12] for such a service. Ontologies containing taxonomies and/or rules constitute the centrepiece of the knowledge retrieval, sharing and reuse mechanisms either on the web or among agents. KSNet proposes a view integrating the concept of networked intelligent organization, Web Intelligence (WI) and WS into a collaboration environment and tries to solve the knowledge logistics problem. In this scenario, it is necessary to share ontologies for user request processing. The application includes different ontology types such as: top-level, application, knowledge source (KS), domain and tasks & methods ontology to mention just few of them. The ontologies need to be stored in a common OL that allows sharing and reusing them. So, the access to this library is an important issue to guarantee the overall systems efficiency. This is a clear case of an application that benefits from having a dedicated agent that manages, controls access and provides answers accessing a set of explicit ontologies, which is exactly what the CAPNET's OA is able to perform.

In KSNet, there are several Knowledge Fusion Agents (KFA), whose task is to generate a solution set (if it exists) to a user request using the application ontology. (AO). In the implementation of this application, the KFAs were external clients for the CAPNET's OA and they had to invoke its services via the WS interface provided by the proposed framework (fig. 1). In doing so, they had to contact the ADWS to invoke the required service (which was previously registered by the OA in the WSPA). Then the ADWS forwards the request to the WSPA responsible to request the service from the OA and then returns the results to the ADWS for delivery to the KFA that made the request. After the KFA receives the data from the OA, it generates a part of the program based on this data and user requirements and interests, then combines it with a template that has an algorithm and strategy definition for an automatic answer generation that is immediately compiled to generate the executable program that will further respond to queries like this (fig 4). By using this framework KSNet had access to an OA that fulfilled all its requirements of ontology processing and the communication with this agent was made in a natural for KSNet way.

In order to measure the efficiency of the framework a test case was defined and executed in order to get a list of all the requirements made by the KFA to the OA (167 in total) and the time it took to execute the whole exercise (240 minutes). Then the same set of queries was formulated to the OA by an agent living inside the CAPNET, and the time was measured. Requesting the information via WS was 42% slower than requesting them locally, which is easily understandable since in the latter scenario no WS invocation took place and two method invocations and three messages less were required by each query.

After that, in order to make these results as accurate as possible, the time it took the KFAs to perform their own tasks was calculated and subtracted from the difference of times. That led us to a 27% of delay (64.8 Min) due to communication issues involved in using the framework. The final test was to measure the time needed to invoke an isolated WS that implemented a simulation of the OA (had the same average response times) and the result was that it took 238.2 Min. which means that the delay induced for consuming the service of an agent via a WS was 0.75% of the overall time.

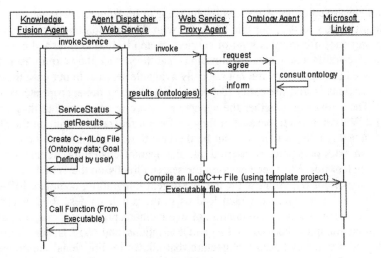

Figure 4. The UML sequence diagram shows the KF scenario

5. Discussion

DSE for e-Business require that users deploy their own services and use the services of other users and businesses, build and tailor new services from existing ones, and finally, access services in an intelligent and semi-autonomous way. Development of dynamic service is based on existing infrastructures, service coordination mechanisms and semantic interoperability. They include J2BB, complimentary Jini system, ONE, .NET, P2P architectures, UDDI, SOAP. On the other hand, service coordination and trading mechanisms include eCo, BizTalk, ebXML, eSPEAK, RosettaNet. Finally, ontology frameworks (DAML, OIL), industry standardization (XML, RDF), and WSDL are used to guarantee semantic operability of the WS. Nevertheless, despite of the existence of these technologies and implementations, it is not obvious how they can be combined to form a DSE required for open, large scale, heterogeneous e-Business environments. To approach this goal, WI plays an important role.

WI explores fundamental and practical impacts of AI and advanced information technologies on the next generation of Web-empowered systems, services, and environments [13]. Within this paradigm, the issue to create an innovative, technologically well-founded environment supporting high level, dynamic composition of heterogeneous on-line services is highlighted. To do this, three basic elements are required: (i) open network architecture supporting many heterogeneous, autonomous interacting entities for on-line open systems, (ii) dynamic value creation enabling effective service composition, and (iii) service level interoperability. This paper is an attempt to contribute to the solution of the first and the third problems.

As shown in the paper, the case of agents consuming WS is easy to model because agents could have the built-in functionality allowing them to search and consume these resources by themselves. Nevertheless, even when this is technically possible, it is not an elegant solution. A more suitable one is to implement a wrapper or proxy to provide the access to WS, but this leaves us with the question on who is responsible for locating and offering this kind of services to application agents, and even if it is necessary/desirable that agents are conscious that the service they require is actually a WS outside of the platform and not a locally available service. In our case the answer to this questions is that the entity responsible for locating the appropriate WS is the WSDF. The answer on whether the agents are aware or unaware that they are consuming a WS is left open, because if they perform a federated search on the DF they can get mixed results, which may not be the best thing to do, but can be easily corrected if an extra parameter is inserted into the SearchConstraints. Agents are free to specifically look for WS if they perform the search directly on the WSDF.

As an important requirement for the WS-Agent integration, complete FIPA compliance had to be maintained which lead us to the problems described in [14]. Our approach is in some way a combination of two methods proposed there, consisting in a referential mapping between DFAgentDescriptions and WSDL descriptions for services and a gateway-based architecture that allows bi-directional communication respectively. Extra elements, such as ADWS, WSDF and WSPA described above complete the architecture presented in this paper. The ADWS is one of the key elements of this framework providing the following advantages:

- The proposed approach to WS-MAS integration is based on standard technologies both on the WS and Agent sides.
- The programs that use various agent provided services need only to access the WS dispatcher program.
- The client systems can be of any type as long as they can invoke WS.
- Multiple agents running on one or more machines can provide the same service so that the client programs can still work if one of the provider agents crashes.
- Multiple instances of the WS dispatcher can be used and the same agent can make its services available through multiple dispatchers.

There are also some restrictions on using the ADWS. First, services registered with the dispatcher can only take string arguments and return strings, and typically XML will be used to represent complex data types, either for input or output data. Second, a service accessible through the dispatcher must be uniquely identified by name; so if several services are registered with the same name they are assumed to provide the same functionality. Presenting some ambiguity, this also allows the dispatcher to use any available agent to improve fault tolerance, and even in future implementations of the dispatcher to balance the load between the provider agents.

Even though the performance tests have been made mostly to prove of concept, they will certainly provide a good basis for comparison with other approaches.

6. Conclusions

Web-agent based architecture is a good basis for WI support of continuous business engineering. WS allow minimizing the effort needed to interconnect systems of disparate nature. Intelligent web-agents can act in a distributed environment, independently from the users and apply ontologies for knowledge representation and interchange.

Agents' properties and functions exposed in a way described in this paper enable to organize the agent community in a way to support autonomic Web. Developed framework allows an easy integration between WS and MAS that permits to join these two major players in the WI scenario.

Acknowledgements

Partial support for this research work has been provided by the Mexican Petroleum Institute within the project D.00006 "Distributed Intelligent Computing".

References

1. Plummer D., Smith D., Web Services and Software E-Services: What's in a Name? Application Integration and Middleware Strategies Research Note COM-12-0101, Gartner Group, October 30, (2000).
2. Brown, T.M. The Integration Report. eAI Journal 2 (2003) 23—25.
3. SOAP-Reference V1.1 . URL: http://www.w3.org/TR/SOAP/
4. Huhns, M., Stephens, L. Multiagent Systems and Societies of Agents. In: Weiss, G. (ed.): Multiagent systems: a Modern Approach to Distributed Artificial Intelligence. The MIT Press, Cambridge, Massachusetts, London (2000) 79—120.
5. Agentcities RTD Project, URL: http://www.agentcities.org/EURTD/
6. Lyell M., Rosen L., Casagni-Simkins M., Norris D. On Software Agents and Web Services: Usage and Design Concepts and Issues. AAMAS'2003, Workshop on Web Services and Agent-Based Engineering, Melbourne, Australia, July 14-15 (2003).
7. Montebello M., Abela C. DAML enabled Web Services and Agents in the Semantic Web. In Proc. of the 3rd Conference Object-Oriented Programming for the Net world, (2002).
8. Jennings, N. An Agent-based Approach for Building Complex. Software Systems. Comm. ACM, 44, No. 4 (2001) 35-41.
9. Sheremetov L., Contreras M., Valencia C., Intelligent Multi-Agent Support for the Contingency Management System. International Journal of Expert Systems with Applications (Special Issue), Pergamon Press, 26(1) (2004) 57-71.
10. Sheremetov L., Contreras M., Chi M., German E., Alvarado M. Towards the Enterprises Information Infrastructure Based on Components and Agent. In Proc. of the 5th International Conference on Enterprise Information Systems, Angers, France, 23-26 April, (2003) 340-347.
11. Foundation for Intelligent Physical Agents Documentation, (2002), http://www.fipa.org.
12. Smirnov, A., Pashkin, M., Chilov, N., Levashova, T., Haritatos, F. A KSNet-Approach to Knowledge Logistics in Distributed Environment. Proceedings of the Int. Conference on Human-Computer Interaction in Aeronautics (HCI-Aero 2002), USA, Menlo Park, AAAI Press (2002) 88—93.
13. Zhong N., Liu J., Yao Y. In Search of the Wisdom Web. Computer 35 (11) (2002) 27-31.
14. Dale J., Exposing Web Services. Agentcities.NET iD2, Lisbon, 9-10th September (2002).

An Agent Based System for the Contextual Retrieval of Medical Information

Marcela Rodríguez[1,2] and Alfredo Preciado[1]

[1]Departamento de Ciencias de la Computación, CICESE, Ensenada, México
{marcerod, alprecia}@cicese.mx
[2]Facultad de Ingeniería, UABC, Mexicali, México

Abstract. As in any other organization, hospital personnel absorb information from their environment, turn it into knowledge, and then make decisions based on it. Hospital Information Systems that provide access to electronic patient records and the proliferation of Medical Digital Libraries on the Web, are a step in the direction of providing accurate and timely information to hospital staff in support of adequate decision-making. A recent trend in the development of these systems is the support for ubiquitous computing technology that can be used by the hospital staff to access medical information anywhere and anytime. Physicians often use information from previous clinical cases in their decision-making. However, they seldom consult the records of previous patients, to a large extent because they are difficult to locate. In this paper, we present a ubiquitous computing medical system, which main components are context-aware agents that autonomously achieve information management tasks on behalf of the user, such as retrieving and recommending links to previous patient's records and to information of medical digital libraries which are accessible through the Web.

1. Introduction

Over the past decade, health care consumers have begun to benefit from new Web-based systems to guide decision making on treatments and tests [15]. Important efforts have been invested in the past few years in the development of medical digital libraries which are accessible through the Web. In order to validate the effectiveness of the Internet as a mechanism for the delivery of medical guidelines, a study in a real healthcare setting provided evidence of their high user acceptance [8].

Physicians, who are in a continuous learning process through their daily practice, are motivated to seek information to reduce the uncertainty of the route they ought to follow for the patient's treatment when faced with a complex clinical case [5][14]. However, given their current workloads, they don't usually have the time to search for information on the Web, which provides a convenient delivery mechanism to convey semi-structured medical information to healthcare workers. On the other hand, doctors often use information from previous clinical cases in their decision-making. For this, they might rely on their own experience or consult other colleagues who are more experienced on a given subject, or just to have a second opinion. Physicians,

J. Favela et al. (Eds.): AWIC 2004, LNAI 3034, pp. 64-73, 2004.

however, seldom consult the clinical records of previous patients, to a large extent because they are difficult to locate, or because the data that could be used to retrieve them, such as the patient's name or the date of a given case, are difficult to recall.

The development of hospital information systems that provide access to electronic patient records is a step in the direction of providing accurate and timely information to hospital staff in support for adequate decision-making. A recent trend in the development of these systems is the support for ubiquitous computing technology that can provide timely access to information according to the context of use.

We have implemented the agent-based Context-aware Hospital Information System (CHIS), which selects and adapts the information to be displayed on ubiquitous devices, such as PDAs and large displays, according to the hospital worker's identity, role, and location [10][11][7]. In this paper, we seamlessly integrate to CHIS autonomous agents: A Knowledge Management agent (KM-a) that opportunistically presents references to previous patient's clinical records to the physician while she analyzes a patient's clinical case. At the same time, the Medical Guide proxy-agent (MGp-a) automatically presents the hospital's medical guide relevant to the case being consulted. This agent continuously perceives the user's information needs to suggest links to medical guides from Web digital libraries. Physicians based on this information and their medical judgment can make more accurate clinical decisions.

2. Contextual Retrieval of Medical Information

Traditional Web information retrieval systems are isolated from the context in which a request occurs. Information requests occur for a reason (related to the current user's activity), and that reason grounds the query in contextual information necessary to interpret and process it. Without access to this context, requests become highly ambiguous, resulting in incoherent results, and unsatisfied users [4]. This is evident in the health-care domain, in which vast quantities of medical information are now available through the web and can easily lead to information overload [12]. One way to overcome such a problem is to provide an environment that proactively retrieves and presents information based on the hospital professionals' context, thus providing Context-Aware information Retrieval (CAR) [3]. Context-aware computing technology is a key element to construct this new generation of Web retrieval systems by sensing the changes on the users' activities, to predict users' interests and then, retrieve information based on them.

Ubiquitous and context-aware computing technology may provide support to healthcare professionals for opportunistically acquiring, managing, and sharing knowledge, which are issues faced everyday by hospital workers. We have generated scenarios to bridge the gap between the medical knowledge management practices and an idealized pervasive hospital environment. These scenarios address current sources of misshapes or look to simplify time consuming tasks, such as searching in digital libraries from the Web through the use of ubiquitous computing technology.

2.1 A Medical Knowledge Management Scenario

In the next scenario we illustrate how pervasive technology, such as handhelds computers and large public displays, provides timely access to medical knowledge by using a context-aware retrieval approach.

While Dr. Garcia is evaluating the patient in bed 234, her PDA alerts her that a new message has arrived. Her handheld displays a hospital floor map indicating her that the X-ray results of patient in bed 225 are available. Before Dr. Garcia visits this patient, she approaches the nearest public display that detects the physician's presence and provides her with a personalized view of the Hospital Information System. In particular, it shows a personalized floor map highlighting recent additions to clinical records of patients she is in charge of, messages addressed to her, and the services most relevant to her current work activities. Dr. Garcia selects the message on bed 225, which opens windows displaying the patient's medical record and the X-ray image recently taken. Aware of the context of the situation (patient's original diagnosis, the fact that X-rays where just taken from the patient's hand, etc.), the system automatically opens a window with the hospital's medical guide that relates to the patient's current diagnosis, and shows an icon which displays references to previous similar patient's cases. Dr. Garcia analyses the X-ray image and writes on it to emphasize the clinical problem. As she is interested in knowing about the efficiency of the treatment received by other patients with similar problems, she selects a reference to a previous patient's case. By the doctor's interaction with the information on the public display, the system infers she is still interested in learning more about this case, in particular, in alternative treatments for this medical condition. Then the application suggests links to medical digital libraries from the Web that are considered by the hospital's clinicians as reliable sources of medical information She selects the first recommended Web link which presents information about alternative treatments. Thus, Dr. Garcia uses this trusted medical information combined with their medical experience to make a more precise decision about the treatment to follow.

2.2 Design Issues Raised by the Scenario

The above scenario illustrates how current clinical practices can be improved with the use of interactive public displays and handhelds computers running context-aware applications. With this ubiquitous computing technology medical staff, which is highly mobile, can locate relevant documents, such as patient's records, laboratory results, and forms to be filled; locate patients and colleagues; and locate and track the availability of devices, such as medical equipment and beds, which are moved within the hospital [10]. From the scenario, we observe that the application takes into account contextual information such as, person's location, role, and identity to adapt and personalize the presentation of information to the user, which enhances the user's interaction with computational devices of the hospital [6].

Physicians often use information from preceding cases in their decision-making. For this, they might rely on experience, but they seldom examine the records of previous patients, to a large extent because they are difficult to locate or they can not recall the name of the patient or date of a given case. They also use information from the hospital's medical guide, but they not often consult information from medical guides of other digital libraries since searching information from the Internet is time consuming. The electronic patient record allows medical staff to access relevant medical information with little effort from the user. In order to provide this information, the pervasive environment takes into account contextual information, such as, type of clinical problem, and if the device is a large display on which the user can clearly appreciate and analyze documents and images. The environment may also opportunistically display medical guides relevant to the patient's diagnosis as supporting information for doctors.

3. Context-aware Hospital Information System (CHIS)

In order to create a pervasive hospital environment with the above features, we used autonomous agent which allowed us to implement a system that is adaptive to users and reactive to user's context to provide high quality services. Thus, we built the Context-aware Hospital Information System (CHIS) as an agent-based system by using the SALSA middleware [13]. SALSA is a class framework for implementing autonomous agents that act on behalf of users, represent services, or wrap a system's functionality. It allows for a seamless integration of new proactive components since no modifications are required to other components.

3.1 Architecture of CHIS

The architecture of CHIS, illustrated in Figure 1, includes the following components:

Location-aware Client: Physicians and nurses carry a handheld computer that estimates their location, provides them with information relevant to their location, and allows them to fill requests and communicate with other members of the staff. The interface of the location-aware client is based on the Instant Messaging (IM) paradigm, through which users are notified of the availability of other users and their location. This information is displayed in the form of a list (as in traditional IM systems) or in a map of the area surrounding the user. The location-aware client provides access to the Hospital Information System. In addition, the client has a *Location-estimation Agent* that estimates the user's position.

Hospital Information System (HIS): This system manages and stores the patient's clinical records and other data relevant to the hospital, such as what patients are in what beds.

Hospital IS agent (HIS-a): This agent acts as proxy of the HIS, it provides access to, and monitors the state of, the information contained in it. Rules are used to indicate what type of information should be delivered to a user given its current location and role. For instance, when the HIS agent becomes aware that the physician is near a patient and that this patient's lab results are available, it notifies this to the doctor's client. This agent runs as a daemon on a computing device with connectivity to an agent directory and the IM server.

Broker Agent: The broker is used for agent-to-agent and user-to-agent communication. For this, we use an open-source Instant Messaging (IM) Server to report the state of people and agents and to handle the interaction among people,

68   Marcela Rodríguez and Alfredo Preciado

agents, and devices through XML messages. For instance, all communication between the Location-aware Client and the Hospital IS Agent will go through this server.

Agent Directory: to which agents representing services and users will register. Agents Directories are located in one or more *HTTP servers*, which handle the XML/HTML communication required to register or locate an agent in a Directory

Context-aware agent (Ca-a): All messages that depend on contextual variables for their delivery are transferred to this agent. This agent monitors the environment to determine whether conditions are met for the delivery of a message.

Access points. Wireless connectivity between the system's components, such as servers and mobile clients, is achieved through the IEEE 80211b standard.

Public Display agent (PD-a): This component acts as a proxy for the large public display. It monitors the user's action on the display and tracks its state (availability, users accessing it and open applications). The agent incorporates an IM client that lets it be aware of the status and location of users and other devices. It is also through this client that it communicates with other agents or users to notify its availability. Applications running in the public display also communicate with other components of the architecture thru the public display agent. These applications include PublicCalendar and PublicMap which are discussed in Section 4.

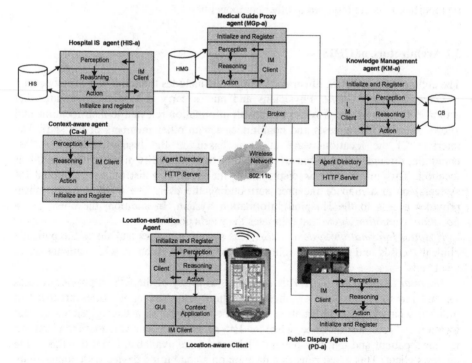

Fig. 1. Architecture of the Context-aware Hospital Information System.

3.2 Agents as Proxies to Medical Knowledge

As physicians often use information from previous cases and the hospital's medical guides available on the Web, the system opportunistically recommends links to information relevant to the clinical case being consulted. For this, the system infers the current physician's interests by taking into account contextual information, such as the document being displayed, and the user's manipulation of the document. The recommended clinical cases are ranked by similarity with the current case. For instance, it may be more relevant for the physician to consult first how she solved previous cases akin to this, and after that, find out the treatment or diagnostic given by other clinicians to similar problems. Besides, the most significant clinical cases are those that coincide with the personal patient's data such as gender, age or weight, which may be factors correlated with the causes of a medical problem or treatment. Depending with the type of diagnosis some of these data will be more relevant than other to retrieve previous cases. Based on the description of the patient's diagnosis, the system presents the hospital's medical guide related with this particular case.

To retrieve relevant medical information we integrated to the CHIS architecture several agents that handle the process of seeking and retrieving information as shown on Figure 1:

The *Knowledge Management agent (KM-a)* uses the Case-based Reasoning (CBR) paradigm aimed at solving new problems by retrieving and reusing similar experiences of past cases [1]. The model of the case memory consists in organizing specific medical cases with the same diagnosis under a generalized episode (GE) [1]. Each GE contains indices that are features that discriminate between GE's cases, for instance, medical treatment, or the name of the physician who treated that patient. Thus, the GE is an indexing structure for matching and retrieving similar cases. The KM-a first identifies the features that best describe the patient's medical condition given by the diagnosis, which are translated to a search query. Then the agent retrieves a set of plausible candidates by comparing the query to the descriptions of the generalized episodes in the index structure. The agent will use specific patient data (gender, age, etc.) as a criterion to rank the retrieved cases. References to these previous cases are presented to the user when requested. Finally, the KM-a updates the case memory by (a) adding a reference to the patient's case as a leaf of the GE tree, if one of the recommended treatments was applied, (b) as a leaf indicating that it is a case by the physician in particular, and (c) creating a new GE if it is a new clinical case.

The *Medical Guide proxy-agent (MGp-a)* is responsible for displaying the hospital's medical guide relevant to the case being consulted if one is found available. This agent also considers information of the diagnosis, symptoms and treatment to formulate a search query used to retrieve the hospital's medical guide related with this particular case.

Through a sample application, we next describe how these components and those of the CHIS architecture described earlier, interact to support the work of healthcare professionals.

4. Sample Application

We revisit the scenario presented in Section 2 to describe the functionality of the extended architecture. As illustrated in the sequence diagram of Figure 3, when a user is in front of the public display, the Public Display agent (PD-a) will acknowledge the presence of the user by displaying her photograph (Fig. 2(A)), indicating that she has been logged into the system. Then the PD-a personalizes the applications on the display for her. In our scenario, as Dr. Garcia is the first user to access the public display, she will be shown personalized applications, such as a PublicMap. This application indicates the location of hospital staff and services available (printer, public display, etc) and highlights the beds of patients assigned to the current user of the display. The PublicMap also displays messages addressed to Dr. Garcia that are dependent on location. This includes messages related to her patients, such as new additions to their electronic records (e.g. analysis results or a medical note). Dr. Garcia, who is interested in looking at the recently taken X-rays, selects bed 225. The PD-a requests the electronic patient's records to the HIS Agent and these are presented to the user in two windows, one with the main page of this patient's medical records (Fig. 2(B)), and a second one with its latest addition, in this case, the X-ray image (Fig. 2(C)) of interest to the doctor.

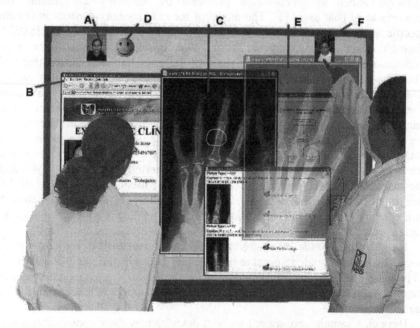

Fig. 2. Interacting with the Context-aware Hospital Information System

As represented in the sequence diagram of Figure 4, when the Public Display agent retrieves the information most recently added to the patient's record, it notifies to the KM-a and MD-a that this document has been presented to the user. The KM-a formulates the search query based on the diagnosis and personal information of the patient, and the MD-a formulates its query based on information that describes the patient's medical condition, such as, symptoms and diagnosis. Based on these queries, the agents retrieve medical information from the Case Base (CB) repository and from the Hospital's Medical Library (HML) respectively. The retrieved information will be sent to the PD-a that will adapt it on the display. For instance, while the medical guide is automatically displayed, the links to previous clinical cases will be represented with the KM-a icon. In our scenario, while Dr Garcia analyzes the X-ray image and the medical guide retrieved by the MGp-a, she selects the KM-a agent's icon for additional recommendations, then the links to previous relevant cases are displayed.

Finally, the Doctor selects the link to the first recommended case, which is ranked as the most relevant since it is one of her patients and the medical condition is the most similar to the new patient's case. When the physician prescribed the treatment to her patient, the KM-a perceives that it is highly similar to the case consulted earlier. Then the agent updates its case-base by adding this case to the same generalized episode.

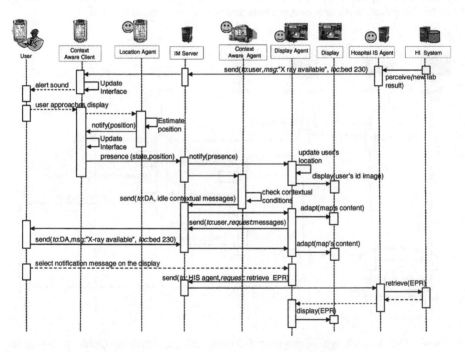

Fig. 3. Context-aware Access to Medical Information

5. Conclusions

The ubiquitous nature of Internet enables health-care professionals to easily access medical information at any time. Physicians, who constantly are learning from their practices in their workplace, are potential consumers of medical information available on the Web, such as medical digital libraries. They seek for information to ask their clinical questions, which enables them to make a better informed decision. With adequate support to estimate the context of work, such as location, identity, and/or role, context-aware systems can opportunistically deliver information that is relevant to the user's activities. In this paper, we have presented how a context-aware retrieval approach allows hospital's professionals to timely access medical information to support the decision making process. For this, we extend the Context-aware Hospital Information System to support context-aware retrieval of medical knowledge information. The ubiquitous system components were identified as agents that autonomously retrieve and present information according to the user's context. This had synergistic effects. For instance, a Public Display agent, representing the artifact, can be aware of the presence and location of users within the hospital; the Knowledge Management agent can interact with the Public Display agent through the instant messaging server and extensions to the XML-based protocol to present timely clinical information. Even tough using instant messaging and agents as a basis for our architecture imposes some performance overhead, these are more than compensated for the simplicity with new components and services can be integrated.

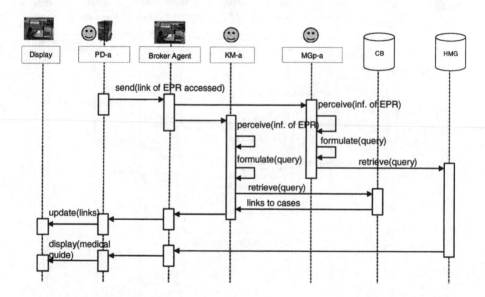

Fig. 4. The Knowledge Management Agent and the Medical Guide proxy-agent Retrieving Medical Information

References

1. Aamodt, A., Plaza, E. Case-Based Reasoning: Foundational Issues, Methodological Variations, and System Approaches. AI Communications. IOS Press, Vol. 7 No.1, (1994) 39-59.

2. Baeza, Y.R., and Ribeiro, N.B.: Modern Information Retrieval. Ed.Addison-Wesley (1999).
3. Brown P.J., Jones, G.J.F.: Context-aware Retrieval: Exploring a New Environment for Information Retrieval and Information Filtering. Personal and Ubiquitous Computing, Vol.5 (2001) 253-263.
4. Budzik, J., Hammond, K.: User Interactions with Every Applications as Context for Just-in-time Information Access: Proc.of Intelligent User Interfaces 2000. ACM Press (2000) 44-51.
5. Casebeer, L. L., Strasser, S. M., Spettell, C., Wall, M. T., Weissman, N., Ray, M. N., Allison, J. J.: Designing Tailored Web-Based Instruction to Improve Practicing Physicians' Preventive Practices. Journal of Medical Internet Research, Vol 5. No. 3, (2003)
6. Dey, A.K.: Understanding and Using Context. Personal and Ubiquitous Computing, Springer-Verlag, London, UK; Vol. 5, No.1, (2001) 4-7.
7. Favela, J., Rodríguez, M., Preciado, A., and González, V.M.: Integrating Context-aware Public Displays into a Mobile Hospital Information System. To be published in IEEE Transactions on Information Technology in Biomedicine (2004).
8. Jeannot, J.G., Scherer, F., Pittet, V., Burnand, B., Vader J.P.: Use of the World Wide Web to Implement Clinical Practice Guidelines: A Feasibility Study. Journal of Medical Internet Research, Vol. 5, No. 2, (2003)
9. Ji, W., Naguib, R.N.G., and Ghoneim, M.A.: Neural Network-Based Assessment of Prognostic Markers and Outcome Prediction in Bilharziasis-Associated Bladder Cancer. IEEE Trans. on Information Technology in Biomedicine, Vol. 7 No.3, (2003) 218-224.
10. Muñoz, M., Gonzalez, V.M., Rodriguez, M., and Favela, J.: Supporting Context-aware Collaboration in a Hospital: An ethnographic informed design, 9th International Workshop on Groupware, CRIWG'03. Springer LNCS 2806, (2003) 330-344.
11. Muñoz, M., Rodriguez, M., Favela, J., Gonzalez, V.M., and Martinez-Garcia A.I.: Context-aware mobile communication in hospitals. IEEE Computer Vol. 36, No. 8, (2003) 60-67.
12. Pratt, W., Fagan, L.: The Usefulness of Dynamically Categorizing Search Results. Journal of the American Medical Informatics Association. Vol. 7 No. 6 (2000) 605-617.
13. Rodríguez, M. and Favela, J.: Autonomous Agents to Support Interoperability and Physical Integration in Pervasive Environments. In Proceedings of the Atlantic Web Intelligence Conference, AWIC 2003, Springer-Verlag, (2003) 278-287.
14. Schoen DA.: The reflective practitioner: how professionals think in action. New York: Basic Books, (1983)
15. Schwitzer, G.: A Review of Features in Internet Consumer Health Decision-support Tools. Journal of Medical Internet Research, Vol. 4, No. 2 (2002)

Attribute Reduction for Effective Intrusion Detection*

Fernando Godínez[1], Dieter Hutter[2], and Raúl Monroy[3]

[1] Centre for Intelligent Systems, ITESM–Monterrey
Eugenio Garza Sada 2501, Monterrey, 64849, Mexico
fgodinez@itesm.mx
[2] DFKI, Saarbrücken University
Stuhlsatzenhausweg 3, D-66123 Saarbrücken, Germany
hutter@dfki.de
[3] Department of Computer Science, ITESM–Estado de México
Carr. Lago de Guadalupe, Km. 3.5, Estado de México, 52926, Mexico
raulm@itesm.mx

Abstract. Computer intrusion detection is to do with identifying computer activities that may compromise the integrity, confidentiality or the availability of an IT system. Anomaly Intrusion Detection Systems (IDSs) aim at distinguishing an abnormal activity from an ordinary one. However, even in a moderate site, computer activity very quickly yields Giga-bytes of information, overwhelming current IDSs. To make anomaly intrusion detection feasible, this paper advocates the use of Rough Sets previous to the intrusion detector, in order to filter out redundant, spurious information. Using rough sets, we have been able to successfully identify pieces of information that succinctly characterise computer activity without missing chief details. The results are very promising since we were able to reduce the number of attributes by a factor of 3 resulting in a 66% of data reduction. We have tested our approach using BSM log files borrowed from the DARPA repository.

1 Introduction

Computer intrusion detection is concerned with studying how to detect computer attacks. A *computer attack*, or *attack* for short, is any activity that jeopardises the integrity, confidentiality or the availability of an IT system. An attack may be either physical or logical. There exists a number of Intrusion Detection Systems (IDSs); based on the detection scheme they belong to either of two main categories: *misuse-detection* and *anomaly-detection* IDSs.

Misuse-Detection IDSs aim to detect the appearance of the signature of a known attack in a network traffic. While simple, *misuse-detection IDSs* do not scale up, both because they are useless to unknown attacks and because they are easily cheated upon an attack originating from several sessions.

---

* This research is supported by three research grants CONACyT 33337-A, CONACyT-DLR J200.324/2003 and ITESM CCEM-0302-05.

J. Favela et al. (Eds.): AWIC 2004, LNAI 3034, pp. 74–83, 2004.
© Springer-Verlag Berlin Heidelberg 2004

To get around this situation, *anomaly-detection IDSs* count on a characterisation of ordinary activity and use it to distinguish it from an abnormal one [1]. However, normal and abnormal behaviour differ quite subtly and hence are difficult to put apart. To compound the problem, there is an infinite number of instances of both normal and abnormal activity. Even in a moderate site, computer activity very quickly yields Giga-bytes of information, overwhelming current IDSs.

This paper aims to make anomaly-based intrusion detection feasible. It addresses the problem of dimensionality reduction using an attribute relevance analyser. We aim to filter out redundant, spurious information, and significantly reduce the number of computer resources, both memory and CPU time, required to detect an attack. We work under the consideration that intrusion detection is approached at the level of execution of operating system calls, rather than network traffic. So our input data is noiseless and less subject to encrypted attacks. In our reduction experiments, we use *BSM log files* [2], borrowed from the DARPA repository [3].

A BSM log file consists of a sequence of system calls. Roughly, Sun Solaris involves about 240 different system calls, each of which takes a different number of attributes. The same system call can even take distinct attributes in separate entries. This diversity in the structure of a BSM log file gets in the way for a successful application of data mining techniques. Entries cannot be easily standardized to hold the same number of attributes, unless extra attributes are given no value. This lack of information rules out the possibility of using classical data mining techniques, such as ID3 [4] or GINI [5]. Fortunately, rough sets [6] work well under diverse, incomplete information.

Using rough sets, we have been able to successfully identify pieces of information that succinctly characterise computer activity without missing chief details. We have tested our approach using various BSM log files of the DARPA repository. More precisely we used 8 days out of 25 available from 1998 as our training data. The results we obtained show that we need less than a third part of the 51 identified attributes to represent the log files with minimum loss of information.

This paper is organized as follows: in section 2 we briefly overview the importance of Intrusion Detection Systems and the problem of information managing. Section 3 is a brief introduction to the Rough Set Theory especially the parts used on the problem of dimensionality reduction. In section 4 we describe the methodology of our experiments. Section 5 describes our experimental results. Finally some conclusions are discussed in section 6.

2   Information Managing in Intrusion Detection Systems

An anomaly-based IDS relies on some kind of statistical profile abstracting out normal user behaviour. User actions may be observed at different levels, ranging from system commands to system calls. Any deviation from a behaviour profile is taken as an anomaly and therefore an intrusion. Building a reliable user profile requires a number of observations that can easily overwhelm any

IDS [7], making it necessary to narrow the input data without loosing important information. Narrowing input data yields the additional benefit of alleviating intrusion detection. Current reduction methods, as shown below, eliminate important information getting in the way for effective intrusion detection.

2.1 Attribute Reduction Methods

Log files are naturally represented as a table, a two dimensional array, where rows stand for objects (in our case system calls) and columns for their attributes. These tables may be unnecessarily redundant. The problem of reducing the rows and columns of a table, we respectively call *object reduction* and *attribute reduction*. To the best of the authors' knowledge, the attempts to reduce the number of attributes prior to clustering have been few while this is still a big concern as there might be unnecessary attributes in any given source of information.

Lane *et al* have suggested an IBL technique for modeling user behavior [8, 9], that works at the level of Unix user commands. Their technique relies upon an arbitrary reduction mechanism, which replaces all the attributes of a command with an integer representing the number of that command's attributes (e.g. `cat /etc/password /etc/shadow > /home/mypasswords` is replaced by `cat <3>`). According to [8, 9], this reduction mechanism narrows the alphabet by a factor of 14, but certainly at the cost of loosing chief information. This is because the arguments cannot be put away if a proper distinction between normal and abnormal behavior is to be done. For example, copying the password files may in general denote abnormal activity. By contrast our method keeps all these attributes as they are main discriminants between objects and thus an important source of information.

Knop *et al* have suggested the use of correlation elimination to achieve attribute reduction [10]. Their mechanism uses a correlation coefficient matrix to compute statistical relations between system calls. [4]. These relations are then used to identify chief attributes. Knop *et al*'s mechanism relies upon an numerical representation of system call attributes to capture object correlation. Since a log file consists of mainly a sequence of strings, this representation is unnatural and a source of noise. It may incorrectly relate two syntactically similar system calls with different meaning. By comparison, our method does not relies on correlation measures but in data frequency which is less susceptible to representation problems.

2.2 Object Reduction Methods

Most object reduction methods rely on grouping similar objects according to their attributes. Examples of such methods are the Expectation-Maximization procedure used by Lane *et al* [8, 9] and an expert system based grouping method developed by Marin *et al* [12]. The more information we have about the objects

---

[4] Knop *et al*'s method resembles Principal Component Analysis [11]

the more accurate the grouping will be. This comes with a computational over-head, the more attributes we use to make the grouping the more computationally intense the process becomes. All these methods can benefit from our work since a reduction previous to clustering can reduce the number of attributes needed to represent an object, therefore reducing the time needed to group similar ones.

In general attribute reduction method are not directly capable of dealing with incomplete data. These methods rely on the objects having some value assigned for every attribute and a fixed number of attributes. In order to overcome these problems the use of another method is proposed, Rough Set Theory. Even though the Rough Sets Theory has not been widely used in dimensionality reduction for security logs, its ability to deal with incomplete information (one of the key features of Rough Sets) makes it very suitable for our needs since entries in a log do not have the same attributes all the time. This completes our revision of related work. Attention is now given to describing Rough Sets.

3   Dealing with Data Imperfection

In production environments, output data are often vague, incomplete, inconsistent and of a great variety, getting in the way of its sound analysis. Data imperfections rule out the possibility of using conventional data mining techniques, such as ID3, C5 or GINI. Fortunately, the theory of rough sets [6] has been specially designed to handle these kinds of scenarios. Same as in fuzzy logic, in rough sets every object of interest is associated with a piece of knowledge indicating relative membership. This knowledge is used to drive data classification and is the key issue of any reasoning, learning, and decision making.

Knowledge, acquired from human or machine experience, is represented as a set of examples describing attributes of either of two types, condition and decision. *Condition attributes* and *decision attributes* respectively represent a priori and a posteriori knowledge. Thus, learning in rough sets is supervised.

Rough sets removes superfluous information by examining attribute dependencies. It deals with inconsistencies, uncertainty and incompleteness by imposing an upper and an lower approximation to set membership. Rough sets estimates the relevance of an attribute by using attribute dependencies regarding a given decision class. It achieves attribute set covering by imposing a discernibility relation. Rough set's output, purged and consistent data, can be used to define decision rules. A brief introduction to rough set theory, mostly based on [6], follows.

3.1   Rough Sets

Knowledge is represented by means of a table, so-called an *information system*, where rows and columns respectively denote objects and attributes. An information system, $\mathcal{A}$, is given as a pair $\mathcal{A} = (U, A)$, where U is a non-empty finite set of objects, the *universe*, and A is a non-empty finite set of *attributes*.

A *decision system* is an information system that involves at least (and usually) one decision attribute. It is given by $\mathcal{A} = (U, A \cup \{d\})$, where $d \notin A$ is the decision attribute. Decision attributes are often two-valued. Then the input set of examples is split into two disjoint subsets: positive and negative. An element is in positive if it belongs to the associated decision class and is in negative otherwise. Multi-valued decision attributes give rise to pairwise, multiple decision classes. A decision system expresses our knowledge about a model. It may be unnecessarily redundant. To remove redundancies, rough sets define an equivalence relation up to indiscernibility. Let $\mathcal{A} = (U, A)$ be an information system. Then, every $B \subseteq A$ yields an equivalence relation up to indiscernibility, $IND_{\mathcal{A}}(B) \subseteq (U \times U)$, given by:

$$IND_{\mathcal{A}}(B) = \{(x, x') : \forall a \in B. \, a(x) = a(x')\}$$

A *reduct* of $\mathcal{A}$ is the least $B \subseteq A$ that is equivalent to A up to indiscernibility. In symbols, $IND_{\mathcal{A}}(B) = IND_{\mathcal{A}}(A)$. Then the attributes in $A - B$ are considered expendable. An information system typically has many subsets B. The set of all reducts in $\mathcal{A}$ is denoted $RED(\mathcal{A})$.

An equivalence splits the universe, allowing us to create new classes, also called *concepts*. A concept that cannot be completely characterised gives rise to a rough set. A rough set is used to hold elements for which it cannot be definitely said whether or not they belong to a given concept. For the purpose of this paper reducts is the only concept that we need to understand thoroughly. We will now explore two of the most used reduct algorithms.

3.2   Reduct Algorithms

First we need to note that currently the algorithms supplied by the Rosetta library (which is described in 3.3) support two types of discernibility: i)*Full*: In this case the reducts are extracted relative to the system as a whole. With the resulting reduct set we are able to discern between all relevant objects. ii)*Object*: This kind of discernibility extract reducts relative to a single object. The result is a set of reducts for each object in $\mathcal{A}$. We are mainly interested in two reduct extraction algorithms supplied by the Rosetta library, Johnson's Algorithm and Genetic Algorithm.

Johnson's algorithm implements a variation of a simple greedy search algorithm as described in [13]. This algorithm extracts a single reduct and not a set like other algorithms. The reduct B can be found by executing the following algorithm where $\mathcal{S}$ is a superset of the sets corresponding to the discernibility function $g_A(U)$ and $w(S)$ is a weight function assigned to $S \in \mathcal{S}$ (Unless stated otherwise the function $w(S)$ denotes cardinality): i)$B = \emptyset$, ii)Select an attribute a that maximizes $\sum w(S) | \forall S, a \in S$, iii)Add a to B, iv)Remove $S | a \in S$ from $\mathcal{S}$, v)When $\mathcal{S} = \emptyset$ return B otherwise repeat from step ii.

Approximate solutions can be provided by leaving the execution when an arbitrary number of sets have been removed from $\mathcal{S}$. The support count associated with the extracted reduct is the percentage of $S \in \mathcal{S} : B \cap S \neq \emptyset$, when computing the reducts a minimum support value can be provided. This algorithm has the advantage of returning a single reduct but depending on the desired value for the minimal support count some attributes might be eliminated. If we use a support of 0% then all attributes are included in the reduct, if we use a value of 100% then the algorithm executes until $S = \emptyset$.

The **Genetic Algorithm** described by Øhrn and Viterbo in [14] is used to find minimal hitting sets. The algorithm's fitness function is presented below. In the function S is the multi-set given by the discernibility function, α is a weighting between subset cost and the hitting fraction, and ε is used for approximate solutions.

$$ f(B) = (1 - \alpha) \times \frac{cost(A) - cost(B)}{cost(A)} + \alpha \times min\left\{ \varepsilon, \frac{|[S \in S]|S \cap B \neq \emptyset|}{|S|} \right\} $$

The subsets B of A are found by an evolutionary search measured by $f(B)$, when a subset B has a hitting fraction of at least ε then it is saved in a list. The size of the list is arbitrary. The function $cost$ specifies a penalty for an attribute (some attributes may be harder to collect) but it defaults to $cost(B) = |B|$. If $\varepsilon = 1$ then the minimal hitting set is returned. In this algorithm the support count is the same as in Johnson's algorithm.

3.3   Rosetta Software

The Rosetta system is a toolkit developed by Alexander Øhrn [15] used for data analysis using Rough Sets Theory. The Rosetta toolkit is conformed by a computational kernel and a GUI. The main interest for us is the kernel which is a general C++ class library implementing various methods of the Rough Set framework. The library is open source thus being modifiable by the user. Anyone interested in the library should refer to [15].

In the next section we will see the application of Rough Sets to the problem of dimensionality reduction in particular attribute reduction and our results in applying this technique.

4   Rough Set Application to Attribute Reduction

This section aims to show how rough sets can be used to find the chief attributes which ought to be considered for session analysis. By the equivalence up to discernibility (see section 3.1), this attribute reduction will be minimal with respect to content of information.

Ideally, to find the reduct, we would just need to collect together as many as possible session logs and make Rosetta to process them. However this is computationally prohibitive since one would require to have an unlimited amount of resources, both memory and CPU time. To get around this situation, we ran a number of separate analysis, each of which considers a session segment, and then collected the associated reducts. Then, to find the *minimum common reduct*, we performed an statistical analysis which removes those attributes that appeared least frequently. In what follows, we elaborate on our methodology to reduct extraction, which closely follows that outlined by Komorowski [6].

4.1   Reduct Extraction

To approach reduct extraction, considering the information provided by the DARPA repository, we randomly chose 8 logs (out of 25), for the year 1998, and put them together. Then the enhanced log was evenly divided in segments of 25,000 objects, yielding 365 partial log files. For each partial log file, we made Rosetta extract the associated reduct using Johnson's algorithm and selecting a 100% support count (see Section 3.2).

After this extraction process, we sampled the resulting reducts and using an frequency-based discriminant, we constructed a minimum common reduct (MCR). This MCR is so that it keeps most information of the original data minimizing the number of attributes. The largest reduct in the original set has 15 attributes and our minimum common reduct has 18 attributes. This is still a 66.66% reduction in the number of attributes. The 18 chief attributes are shown below:

Access-Mode	device-ID	exec-arg-1	Effective-Group-ID
Owner	arg-value-1	Socket-Type	Process-ID
Owner-Group	arg-string-1	Remote-IP	System-Call
File-System-ID	arg-value-2	Audit-ID	
inode-ID	arg-value-3	Effective-User-ID	

Before concluding this section, we report on our observations of the performance of the algorithms found in Rosetta, namely Johnson's algorithm and the genetic algorithm based reduction mechanism.

4.2   Algorithm Selection

Previous to reduct extraction, we tested on the performance of the two Rosetta reduction algorithms, in order to find which is the most suitable to our work. Both reduction algorithms (see section 3.2) were made find a reduction with 25 log files. Log files were selected considering different sizes and types of sessions. A minimum common reduct set containing 14 attributes was obtained after the 25 extraction processes. This amounts to a reduction of 72.5% in the number of attributes. In general, both algorithms yielded similar total elapsed times. Sometimes, however, Johnson's algorithm was faster. As expected, the total elapsed time involved in reduct extraction grows exponentially with the number of objects to be processed. For a 1,000 object log file the time needed to extract the reduct is 3 seconds and for a 570,000 is 22 hours. Also the size of the reduct increases according to the diversity of the log. For a 1,000 object log long, we found a reduct of 8 attributes, while for a 570,000 one, we found a reduct of 14 attributes.

However, for longer log files, the instability of the genetic algorithm based mechanism become apparent. Our experiments show that this algorithm is unable to handle log files containing more than 22,000 objects, each with 51 attributes. This explains why our experiments only consider Johnson's algorithm.

Even though the algorithms accept indiscernibility decision graphs (that is relations between objects) we did not use them, both because we wanted to keep the process as unsupervised as possible and because in order to build the graphs we needed to know in advance the relation between the objects which is quite difficult even with the smaller logs with 60,000 objects. In the next section we will review our experimental results to validate the resulting reducts.

5   Reduct Validation — Experimental Results

This section describes the methodology used to validate our output reduct, the main contribution of this paper. The validation methodology basically appeals to so-called association patterns.

An *association pattern* is basically a pattern that, with the help of wild-cards, matches part of an example log file. Given both a reduct and a log file, the corresponding association patterns are extracted by overlaying the reduct over that log file, and reading off the values [15]. Then the association patterns are compared against another log to compute how well they cover that log file information. Thus, our validation test consists of checking the quality of the association patterns generated by our output reduct, considering two log files. The rationale behind it is that the more information about the system the reduct comprehends the higher the matching ratio the association patterns of that reduct will have.

To validate our reduct, we conducted the following three step approach. For each one of the 8 log files considered through our experiments, i) use the output reduct to compute the association patterns, ii) cross validate the association patterns against all of the log files, including the one used to generate them and iii) collect the results. Our validation results are summarized in Table 1. The patterns contain only relations between attributes contained in the final reduct set. A set of patterns was generated from each log file.

Training Log	Testing log							
	A	B	C	D	E	F	G	H
A	93.7	89.7	90.8	90.3	90.9	91.1	89.9	90.9
B	90.9	93.1	91.2	91.3	90.9	92.4	91.4	90.1
C	90.2	90.8	92.8	90.7	92.1	90.1	90.6	91.0
D	90.3	89.3	91.3	93.1	91.5	90.5	92.9	91.1
E	89.8	89.1	92.2	92.3	93.4	89.9	92.1	90.1
F	89.7	89.3	91.4	92.8	90.7	92.9	92.3	90.8
G	89.2	90.3	91.5	92.6	91.2	90.7	93.1	90.6
H	90.1	89.5	91.2	91.3	90.8	90.2	90.9	92.5
Size	744,085	2,114,283	1,093,140	1,121,967	1,095,935	815,236	1,210,358	927,456

Table 1. Covering % of the Association Patterns

These association patterns are able to describe the information system to some extent. That extent is the covering percentage of the patterns over the information system. The first column indicates the corresponding log file used to generate the association patterns. The first row indicates the log file used to test the covering of the pattern. In contrast if we were to generate a set of patterns using all attributes, then those patterns will cover 100% of the objects in the table that generated them. The result is the percentage of objects we were able to identify using the attributes in our reduct.

These experiments were conducted on a Ultra Sparc 60 with two processors running Solaris 7. Even though it is a fast workstation the Reduct algorithms are the most computational demanding in all the Rough Set Theory. The order of the reduction algorithms is $O(n^2)$ with n being the number of objects. With 700,000 an overhead in time was to be expected.

Calculating the quality of the rules generated with the extracted reducts is also time consuming. The generation of the rules took 27 hours (we used the larger tables to generate the rules) and another 60 hours to calculate the quality of the generated rules. In order to test the rules with another table we needed to extend the Rosetta library, that is because of the internal representation of data depends on the order an object is imported and saved on the internal dictionary of the table (every value is translated to a numerical form). The library has no method for importing a table using the dictionary from an already loaded table. To overcome the above deficiencies we extended the Rosetta library with an algorithm capable of importing a table using a dictionary from an already loaded table. This way we were able to test the rules generated in a training set over a different testing set. We also tested the rules upon the training set.

In the end the quality of the reduction set is measured in terms of the discernibility between objects. If we can still discern between two different objects with the reduced set of attributes then the loss of information is said to be minimal. Our goal was to reduce the number of attributes without loosing the discernibility between objects, so more precise IDSs can be designed. The goal was achieved.

Even though the entire reduct extraction process is time consuming, it only needs to be done once and it can be done off-line. There is no need for live data, the analysis can be done with stock data. Once the reduct is calculated and its quality verified we can use only the attributes we need thus reducing the space required to hold the logs and the time used processing them to make a proper intrusion detection. The last section of this paper present our conclusions and projected future work.

6   Conclusions and Future Work

Based on our results we identified the chief attributes of a BSM log file without sacrificing discernibility relevant information. With growing amount of information flowing in an IT system there was a need for an effective method capable of identify key elements in the data in order to reduce the amount of memory and time used in the detection process. The method is expected to produce similar results if applied to different multi-variable log files. Our results prove that Rough Sets provide such a method. As future work we will experiment on object reduction to facilitate even more the detection task. So far the reduction obtained should be sufficient to explore intrusion detection methods that are computational intensive and were prohibitive.

References

[1] Kim, J., Bentley, P.: The Human Immune System and Network Intrusion Detection. In: Proceedings of the 7th European Conference on Intelligent Techniques and Soft Computing (EUFIT'99), Aachen, Germany, ELITE Foundation (1999)

[2] Sun MicroSystems: SunSHIELD Basic Security Module Guide. Part number 806-1789-10 edn. (2000)

[3] Haines, J.W., Lippmann, R.P., Fried, D.J., Tran, E., Boswell, S., Zissman, M.A.: 1999 DARPA intrusion detection system evaluation: Design and procedures. Technical Report 1062, Lincoln Laboratory, MIT (2001)

[4] Quinlan, J.R.: Learning efficient classification procedures and their application to chess and games. Machine Learning: An artificial intelligence approach. Springer, Palo Alto, CA (1983)

[5] Breiman, L., Stone, C.J., Olshen, R.A., Friedman, J.H.: Classification and Regression Trees. Statistics-Probability Series. Brooks/Cole (1984)

[6] Komorowski, J., Polkowski, L., Skowron, A.: Rough sets: A tutorial. In: Rough-Fuzzy Hybridization: A New Method for Decision Making. Springer-Verlag (1998)

[7] Axelsson, S.: Aspects of the modelling and performance of intrusion detection. Department of Computer Engineering, Chalmers University of Technology (2000) Thesis for the degree of Licentiate of Engineering.

[8] Lane, T., Brodley, C.E.: Temporal Sequence Learning and Data Reduction for Anomaly Detection. ACM Transactions on Information and System Security **2** (1999) 295–331

[9] Lane, T., Brodley, C.E.: Data Reduction Techniques for Instance-Based Learning from Human/Computer Interface Data. In: Proceedings of the 17th International Conference on Machine Learning, Morgan Kaufmann (2000) 519–526

[10] Knop, M.W., Schopf, J.M., Dinda, P.A.: Windows performance monitoring and data reduction using watchtower and argus. Technical Report Technical Report NWU-CS-01-6, Department of Computer Science, Northwestern University (2001)

[11] Rencher, A.: Methods in Multivariate Analysis. Wiley & Sons, New York (1995)

[12] Marin, J.A., Ragsdale, D., Surdu, J.: A hybrid approach to profile creation and intrusion detection. In: Proc. of DARPA Information Survivability Conference and Exposition, IEEE Computer Society (2001)

[13] Johnson, D.S.: Approximation algorithms for combinatorial problems. Journal of Computer and System Sciences **9** (1974) 256–278

[14] Viterbo, S., Øhrn, A.: Minimal approximate hitting sets and rule templates. International Journal of Approximate Reasoning **25** (2000) 123–143

[15] Øhrn, A., Komorowski, J.: ROSETTA: A Rough Set Toolkit for Analysis of Data. In Wong, P., ed.: Proceedings of the Third International Joint Conference on Information Sciences. Volume 3., Durham, NC, USA, Department of Electrical and Computer Engineering, Duke University (1997) 403–407

Computing Minimal Probabilistic Rules from Probabilistic Decision Tables: Decision Matrix Approach

Wojciech Ziarko and Xiang Xiao

Computer Science Department
University of Regina
Regina, Saskatchewan, S4S 0A2, Canada

Abstract. The article presents a method for computing maximally general minimal length probabilistic decision rules from probabilistic decision tables using the idea of decision matrices. The method reduces the problem of rule computation to the problem of identification of prime implicants of a suitably defined Boolean function. The presentation is developed in the context of the variable precision rough set model, which underlies the methodology of probabilistic decision table acquisition from data. A computational example is included to illustrate the application of the method to a real-life problem.

1 Introduction

One of the fundamental tasks of data mining systems is identification of potentially interesting or useful patterns in data referred to as *probabilistic rules* [17] (the term "association rules" [18] has also been used in recent years). In general, the probabilistic rules are statements of the form **if** *(input_conditions)* **then** *(result_condition)* with the associated probabilistic confidence factor P. The rule of this kind specifies the likelihood of the occurrence of the *result_condition* on an object e from the universe of interest U, given that it satisfies all input conditions. The likelihood is given by the conditional probability estimate $P(result\_condition|input\_conditions)$, which is typically computed from available data. For example, a probabilistic rule might state, in reference to a car engine condition, that **if** *(oil_pressure = low **and** engine_vibrations = high **and** operating_temperature = high)* **then** *(engine_failure = yes)* with probability 0.85.

The probabilistic rules are important in many applications involving decision making or predictions, including data mining, machine learning, expert systems etc. The first methods for computing probabilistic rules from data were developed and implemented in the context of rough set theory in 1980's [17], followed by algorithms specifically oriented to deal with some classes of data mining tasks, such as, for example, the "a priori" algorithm [18]. Some of these algorithms perform constrained search for rules, while others are concerned with finding a "locally minimal cover" subset of all minimal length probabilistic rules [3][12][14][6][15][16]. Although the latter approach was proven efficient and satisfactory for many applications, particularly in the context of machine learning, many potentially useful or interesting rules were missed. Consequently, for data mining applications, there is a need to compute all potentially interesting rules rather than focusing on a specific subset of them.

In the framework of rough set theory[6], special interest has been devoted to maximally general, or minimal length rules (minimal rules), which minimize number of input conditions subject to satisfaction of a confidence requirement. In particular, deterministic minimal rules have the implied confidence requirement equal to 1. Algorithms for computing all minimal deterministic decision rules involve applying the ideas of *decision matrices* or *discernibility matrices* [2][4]. However, in data mining problems deterministic rules occur rather infrequently, restricting the practical applicability of the algorithms to very specific problems. To deal with this issue, we present extended methodology for computation of all minimal length probabilistic rules via decision matrices [4]. In the extended methodology, derived in the framework of Variable Precision Model (VPRSM) of rough sets [8][5] [9][7], all minimal length probabilistic rules are computed, subject to the satisfaction of the minimum confidence requirement.

The paper is organized as follows. In the next section, we introduce the basic concepts of the VPRSM and of probabilistic decision tables [10]. This is followed by the introduction of decision matrices, decision functions and of the primary rule computation algorithm referred to as MINRUL-PROB. Finally, we present a comprehensive example of the application of the presented method to insurance company data [1] [11].

2   Basics of the Variable Precision Rough Set Model

The VPRSM, as well as the basic rough set model introduced by Pawlak, is developed within the context of a universe of objects of interest U, for example, the universe might be the collection of patients, sounds, web pages etc. It is assumed that objects are represented in terms of some observable properties belonging to finite domains. Such properties are referred to as attributes. Formally, the attributes are finite-valued functions assigning unique attribute values to objects, i.e. each attribute is a mapping $a : U \to Dom(a)$, where $Dom(a)$ is attribute a domain.

We will divide the attributes into two categories:

- The set of *condition attributes* $a \in C$, representing the "input" information about objects, that is information that we are able to obtain with available means, for example from sensors. This information is typically used in developing model for predicting the values of *decision attributes* $d \in D$.
- The *decision attributes* $d \in D$, representing the classification target, for example, a medical diagnosis in a clinical application. It can be assumed, without loss of generality, that there is only one binary-valued decision attribute d with two values v_{d_1} and v_{d_0}, which are dividing the universe into two sets: set X representing our prediction target (v_{d_1}) and its complement $U - X$ (v_{d_0}).

The VPRSM assumes the knowledge of an equivalence relation, called the *indiscernibility relation, $IND(C) \subseteq U \otimes U$* with finite number of equivalence classes, that is defined according to identity of values of the condition attributes C. Objects in each equivalence class of $IND(C)$ have identical values of the condition attributes. Based on size and frequency distribution information within each equivalence class (also called a C-elementary set) E of the relation $IND(C)$, we can estimate the following two probabilistic measures:

- The probability $P(E)$ of the elementary set, which is typically estimated based on data by $P(E) = \frac{card(E')}{card(U')}$, where *card* denotes set cardinality and $U' \subseteq U$, $E' \subseteq E$ are respective finite subsets of the universe corresponding to the available collection of sample data.
- The conditional probability $P(X|E)$, which represents the likelihood of an event that an object belonging to the C-elementary set E would also belong to the set X. The conditional probability $P(X|E)$ is typically estimated by calculating the relative degree of overlap between sets X and E, that is $P(X|E) = \frac{card(X' \cap E')}{card(E')}$, where $X' \subseteq X$, $E' \subseteq E$ are finite subsets of the universe.

Each C-elementary set E is represented by a set of attribute-value pairs with attributes belonging to C, values of which are common on all objects in the set E. We will refer to such a set of attribute-value pairs as a *description* of the elementary set E. It is formally defined as

$$des(E) = \{(a, a(e)) : a \in C, e \in E\} \tag{1}$$

where $a(e)$ is a value of the attribute a on object $e \in U$.

For example, Table 2 illustrates the classification of a domain U of driver records, as provided by an insurance company [1], in terms of the condition attributes $C = \{C1, C2, C3, C4, C5\}$. Among other things, the table specifies descriptions of all elementary sets as combinations of values of the attributes, the probability of each elementary set $P(E)$ and conditional probabilities $P(X|E)$ with respect to the target subset X.

The frequency distribution information represented by the probability estimates can be used to construct generalized rough approximations of the target subset $X \subseteq U$. The defining criteria are expressed here in terms of conditional probabilities and of the *prior* probability $P(X)$ of the set X in the universe U. Two *precision control* or *probabilistic significance* criteria parameters are used [13].

The first parameter, referred to as the *lower limit l*, satisfying the constraint $0 \leq l < P(X) < 1$, represents the highest acceptable degree of the conditional probability $P(X|E)$ to include the elementary set E in the negative region of the set X. In other words, the *l-negative region* of the set X, $NEG_l(X)$ is defined as

$$NEG_l(X) = \cup\{E : P(X|E) \leq l\} \tag{2}$$

The *l*-negative region of the set X is a collection of objects for which the probability of membership in the set X is *significantly lower* than the prior probability

$P(X)$, that is, the membership probability in the absence of any information about objects of the universe U.

The second parameter, referred to as the *upper limit u*, satisfying the constraint $0 < P(X) < u \leq 1$, defines the *u-positive region* of the set X. The upper limit reflects the least acceptable degree of the conditional probability $P(X|E)$ to include the elementary set E in the positive region, or u-lower approximation of the set X. The u-positive region of the set X, $POS_u(X)$ is defined as

$$POS_u(X) = \cup\{E : P(X|E) \geq u\}. \tag{3}$$

The u-positive region of the set X is a collection of objects for which the probability of membership in the set X is *significantly higher* than the prior probability $P(X)$.

The objects which are not classified as being in the u-positive region nor in the l-negative region belong to the (l, u)-boundary region of the set X, denoted as

$$BNR_{l,u}(X) = \cup\{E : l < P(X|E) < u\}. \tag{4}$$

The boundary is a specification of objects about which it is known that their associated probability of belonging, or not belonging to the target set X, is not significantly different from the prior probability $P(X)$.

A table summarizing the probabilistic distribution information along with the specification of the assignment of each elementary set E to exactly one of the VPRSM approximation regions is referred to as *probabilistic decision table*. In the table, each elementary set E is assigned a unique designation of its VPRSM approximation region based on the preset values of the probabilistic significance parameters l and u. An example probabilistic decision table is shown in Table 2. In this table, the abbreviations *POS, NEG, BND* in the column *REGION* denote positive, negative and boundary regions of the target set X respectively.

3   Decision Matrices and Rules

The decision matrix is a systematic summary of all differences between positive region rows versus all other rows of a decision table. In the process of decision matrix computation, the positive region rows are compared to all rows belonging to boundary or negative regions and results of the comparison are summarized in the matrix form. In the following subsections, we provide a precise definition of the decision matrix and discuss a decision matrix-based method for computation of probabilistic decision rules. All the definitions and rule computing methods presented here are general and can be used to deal with multiple-valued attributes. If there are more than two values of the decision attribute then the original problem of n decisions can be decomposed into n binary decision problems.

3.1   Decision Matrix

To define decision matrix precisely, let i $(i = 1, 2, ...n)$ be an index numbering all positive region rows, or equivalently, elementary sets of positive region of the probabilistic decision table. Similarly, let j $(j = 1, 2, ...m)$ be an index numbering all remaining rows of the table, corresponding to all remaining elementary sets.

With each pair (i, j) we associate the set of attribute-value pairs

$$M_{ij} = \{(a, a(i)) : a(i) \neq a(j) \text{ and } a \in C\} \tag{5}$$

where $a(i)$ is the common value of the attribute a as assigned to all objects belonging to the corresponding elementary set E_i. The matrix element M_{ij} contains all attribute-value pairs appearing in the description of the elementary set E_i and which do not appear in the description of the elementary set E_j. That is, M_{ij} represents the complete information distinguishing elementary sets E_i and E_j. The distinguishing attribute-value pairs, for different combinations of i and j, can be summarized in the form of a matrix, referred to as a decision matrix

$$M = [M_{ij}]_{n \times m} \tag{6}$$

where n is the number of elementary sets of the positive region of the target set X and m is the number of elementary sets in the union of boundary and negative regions of X.

3.2   Decision Functions and Minimal Rules

Each row i, $(i = 1, 2, ...n)$ of the decision matrix can be associated with a Boolean function called a *decision function* [4], which is inspired by the idea of a *discernibility function* introduced in [2]. The decision function B_i is constructed out of the row i: $(M_{i1}, M_{i2}, ...M_m)$ of the decision matrix by formally treating each attribute-value pair occurring in component M_{ij} as a Boolean variable and then forming the Boolean conjunction of disjunctions of components belonging to each set M_{ij} $(j = 1, 2..., m)$. That is,

$$B_i = \bigwedge_j \bigvee M_{ij} \tag{7}$$

where $\bigwedge$ and $\bigvee$ are respectively the generalized conjunction and disjunction operators.

In the context of probabilistic decision tables, a rule r with respect to a value v_{d1} of the decision attribute d can be represented as a set of attribute-value pairs:

$$cond(r) = \{(a_{i_1}, v_{i_1}), (a_{i_2}, v_{i_2}), ..., (a_{i_k}, v_{i_k})\} \tag{8}$$

such that

$$a_{i_j} \in C, \quad v_{i_j} \in Dom(a_{i_j}), \quad \{a_{i_1}, a_{i_2}, ..., a_{i_k}\} \subseteq C \tag{9}$$

and

$$supp(r) = \bigcup \{E : des(E) \supseteq cond(r)\} \subseteq POS_u(X) \qquad (10)$$

The *rule support set*, $supp(r)$ is a union of all elementary sets whose description match rule conditions. Traditionally, the rule r can be denoted as an implication

$$cond(r) \rightarrow (d, v_{d_1}) \quad or \quad (a_{i_1} = v_{i_1}) \wedge (a_{i_2} = v_{i_2}), \wedge ... \wedge (a_{i_k} = v_{i_k}) \rightarrow (d, v_{d_1}) \quad (11)$$

According to this notation, the collection of attribute-value pairs occurring on the left hand side of the rule r is referred to as the rule condition part, denoted as $cond(r)$. Two rules r1 and r2 are comparable if either $cond(r1) \subseteq cond(r2)$ or $cond(r2) \subseteq cond(r1)$. The set of rules for $d = v_{d_1}$ is partially ordered with respect to the relation of inclusion. ¿From the practical perspective, the most important problem is finding the minimal elements of the partially ordered rule set. The minimal rules minimize the number of rule conditions subject to constraint (10). It can be proven [4], that for each positive region elementary set E, all minimal length rules matching the description of this set correspond to prime implicants of the decision function, where prime implicant is a minimal conjunction of a Boolean function variables or their negations, which is logically equivalent to the function (i.e. its logical value is true only if the function's value is true). Consequently, the computation of the rules in the deterministic case can be reduced to the computation of the prime implicants. This can be accomplished via symbol manipulation algorithms based on laws of Boolean algebra, such as distributivity and absorption laws. In addition, the resulting rule sets computed for each row of the decision matrix have to be combined by set theoretic union operation to produce complete collection and to eliminate potential duplicates. In the case of probabilistic rules computed with probabilistic decision tables, the rules need to be associated with two additional parameters: *the rule probability or strength* and the *rule confidence factor*, as defined below.

Rule r strength, denoted as $P(r)$, is defined as the probability of the rule support set $P(supp(r))$, which can be computed directly from the probabilistic decision table by:

$$P(r) = P(supp(r)) = \sum_{E \subseteq supp(r)} P(E) \qquad (12)$$

Rule r confidence factor, denoted here as $P(d|r)$, is defined as the conditional probability of the occurrence of the decision attribute value $d(e) = v_{d_1}$ on an object $e \in U$, given that the object satisfies rule conditions, that is that $des(e) \supseteq cond(r)$. This probability can also be computed directly from the probabilistic decision table by:

$$P(d|r) = \frac{\sum_{E \subseteq supp(r)} P(E)P(X|E)}{\sum_{E \subseteq supp(r)} P(E)} \qquad (13)$$

Based on the above, we can derive the general procedure for computing all minimal probabilistic rules for the positive region $POS_u(X)$ of the target set X. The procedure can also be used, after minor adaptation, to compute rules for other approximation regions of X, or combinations of them. The procedure requires the construction of the decision matrix for the positive region prior to the computation of rules. Once the decision matrix was constructed, the core steps to compute the rules are summarized in the following algorithm.

Algorithm $MINRUL - PROB$

Step 1. *Compute the decision matrix for the positive region $POS_u(X)$ of current decision category X.*

Step 2. *Compute decision function $B_i = \bigwedge_j \bigvee M_{ij}$ for each elementary set E_i, $(i = 1, 2, ..., n)$ such that $E_i \subseteq POS_u(X)$.*

Step 3. *For each $E_i \subseteq POS_u(X)$, $(i = 1, 2, ..., n)$, compute the set of all minimal rules MIN_i matching this class description by evaluating and simplifying the associated decision function B_i to find all its prime implicants.*

Step 4. *Compute the union $\bigcup MIN_i$ of minimal rule sets obtained in* **Step 3** *to find all minimal rules for the current decision category.*

Step 5. *For each rule r, obtained in Step 4:*

1. *Identify the collection of all elementary sets E whose descriptions match $cond(r)$, i.e. such that $des(E) \supseteq cond(r)$.*
2. *Compute rule strength and support coefficients from the probabilistic decision table according to formulas (13) and (14).*

The computational complexity of the algorithm is determined by the method required for finding prime implicants of the decision functions. The prime implicants can be calculated by using the distributive law of Boolean algebra to obtain disjunctive form of the Boolean expression and the absorption law to simplify it. This is of the order $O(p^q)$ in the worst case, where p is the number of attributes and q is the number of elementary sets in boundary and negative regions. Although this result seems to be discouraging in practical applications, the actual attribute values are usually obtained via discretization process, which makes the decision table relatively small. The discretization results in fewer, typically several, values per attribute. What really matters here is not the size of the original data, but the size of the decision table representing classes of objects rather than individual objects.

4   Computational Example

In this section we provide a computational example of the application of the presented method to real life data provided by an insurance company [1] [11]. The data consists of 98042 drivers' records reflecting such information about drivers as their gender, age, size of the population center they are living in, number of past driving convictions and accidents and occurrence of an accident in the most recent year. The data was a subject of a comprehensive study [1] during

Attribute Code	Attribute	0	1	2	3	4	5
				Domain codes			
C1	SEX		M	F			
C2	AGE		≥ 60	$\geq 20, \leq 59$	≤ 19		
C3	CITY_SIZE		$\geq 180K$	$\geq 30K$	$\geq 10K$	$\geq 5K$	$< 5K$
C4	CONVICTIONS		< 2	$\geq 2, \leq 5$	> 5		
C5	ACCIDENTS		< 2	$\geq 2, \leq 5$	> 5		
D	HAS_ACCIDENT	No	Yes				

Table 1. Driver-Attribute Discretization Criteria

which it was grouped into categories defining the study's condition attributes, as summarized in Table 1. The decision attribute is the occurrence of an accident in the most recent year, represented by *HAS_ACCIDENT*.

For the purpose of this example, the selected target value of the decision category X was *HAS_ACCIDENT=No*. The prior probability for this decision category, as estimated from the data, is $P(X) = 0.9308$. The decision matrix approach was used to identify all minimal probabilistic rules for this decision category. Such rules characterize the segment of the population that has significantly lower than average incidence of being in accidents. Any increase, or decrease, of non-accident probability exceeding 5% was considered significant. Consequently, the significance parameters l and u were selected to be within +,- 5% of the average non-accident probability (the prior probability) of 0.9308, i.e. $l = 0.8819$ and $u = 0.9319$. With these assumptions, the probabilistic decision table was computed, as shown in Table 2. Each elementary set of the table is supported by relatively many cases ranging, depending on the set, from 242 to 16745 cases. The positive region rows of the table were numbered with the index i, while remaining rows were numbered with the index j in preparation for decision matrix computation.

Following the probabilistic decision table derivation, the decision matrix for positive region $POS_u(X)$ of the target set X was computed. The resulting partial decision matrix is shown in Table 3. Based on the matrix, the Boolean decision functions were computed from each row of the matrix. For example, partial decision function for row 1 is:

$$((C1,2) \vee (C2,1)) \wedge (C1,2) \wedge ((C1,2) \vee (C2,1)) \wedge ((C1,2) \vee (C2,1) \vee (C3,1)) \wedge \dots$$

The prime implicants for the decision functions were then computed using the laws of Boolean logic, which yielded the two implicants:

$$(C1,2) \quad and \quad (C2,1) \wedge (C3,4)$$

These implicants correspond to the following two minimal rules:

1. $C1 = 2 \rightarrow HAS\_ACCIDENT = No$, with strength 0.426 and confidence 0.9537;
2. $C2 = 1 \wedge C3 = 4 \rightarrow HAS\_ACCIDENT = No$, with strength 0.0233 and confidence 0.9540;

i	j	C1	C2	C3	C4	C5	$P(E)$	$P(X \mid E)$	REGION
-	1	1	2	1	1	1	0.0734	0.9031	BND
-	2	1	1	1	1	1	0.0934	0.9022	BND
-	3	1	2	5	1	1	0.0169	0.9177	BND
-	4	1	2	3	1	1	0.0134	0.9214	BND
-	5	1	1	2	1	1	0.0240	0.9228	BND
-	6	1	1	5	1	1	0.1708	0.9294	BND
-	7	1	1	1	2	1	0.0024	0.7934	NEG
-	8	1	2	1	2	1	0.0065	0.8141	NEG
-	9	1	2	5	2	1	0.0082	0.8422	NEG
-	10	1	2	2	1	1	0.0151	0.9100	BND
-	11	1	2	1	1	2	0.0026	0.8157	NEG
-	12	1	1	5	2	1	0.0031	0.8155	NEG
-	13	1	1	3	1	1	0.0235	0.9245	BND
1	-	2	1	1	1	1	0.0760	0.9410	POS
2	-	1	1	4	1	1	0.0125	0.9438	POS
-	14	1	2	4	1	1	0.0073	0.9244	BND
-	15	1	2	5	1	2	0.0030	0.8418	NEG
-	16	1	1	1	1	2	0.0030	0.8362	NEG
-	17	1	1	5	1	2	0.0045	0.8682	NEG
3	-	2	2	1	1	1	0.0649	0.9356	POS
4	-	2	2	5	1	1	0.0809	0.9583	POS
5	-	2	2	3	1	1	0.0113	0.9567	POS
6	-	2	1	5	1	1	0.1243	0.9664	POS
7	-	2	1	4	1	1	0.0108	0.9659	POS
8	-	2	1	2	1	1	0.0189	0.9512	POS
9	-	2	2	2	1	1	0.0128	0.9555	POS
10	-	2	1	3	1	1	0.0201	0.9554	POS
11	-	2	2	4	1	1	0.0060	0.9581	POS

Table 2. Example Probabilistic Decision Table with $PX) = 0.9308$ and $l = 0.8819$, $u = 0.9319$

Each rule has significantly higher confidence than the average probability of X occurrence. The first rule indicates that females are significantly safer drivers than males, as it is confirmed in over 40% of sample cases. The second rule indicates that drivers from smaller population centers and of older age are also significantly safer than average.

5   Conclusions

The article introduces a new method for computing probabilistic decision rules. The method is based on the idea of decision matrix derived from probabilistic decision table. It proves that the rule acquisition from data is not always a search process, as opposed to what was suggested by some researchers before. In our approach, the rules are computed by simplifying a Boolean expression and no

i/j	1	2	3	4	5	...
1	(C1,2)(C2,1)	(C1,2)	(C1,2)(C2,1)	(C1,2)(C2,1)(C3,1)	(C1,2)(C3,1)	...
2	(C2,1)(C3,4)	(C3,4)	(C2,1)(C3,4)	(C2,1)(C3,4)	(C3,4)	...
3	(C1,2)	(C1,2)(C2,2)	(C1,2)(C3,1)	(C1,2)(3,1)	(C1,2)(C2,2)(C3,1)	...
4	(C1,2)(C3,5)	(C1,2)(2,2)(C3,5)	(C1,2)	(C1,2)(C3,5)	(C1,2)(C2,2)(C3,5)	...
5	(C1,2)(C3,3)	(C1,2)(C2,2)(C3,3)	(C1,2)(C3,3)	(C1,2)	(C1,2)(C2,2)(C3,3)	...
6	(C1,2)(C2,1)(C3,5)	(C1,2)(C3,5)	(C1,2)(C2,1)	(C1,2)(C2,1)(C3,5)	(C1,2)(C3,5)	...
7	(C1,2)(C2,1)(C3,4)	(C1,2)(C3,4)	(C1,2)(C2,1)(C3,4)	(C1,2)(C2,1)(C3,4)	(C1,2)(C3,4)	...
8	(C1,2)(C2,1)(C3,2)	(C1,2)	(C1,2)(C2,1)(C3,2)	(C1,2)(C2,1)(C3,2)	(C1,2)	...
9	(C1,2)(C3,2)	(C1,2)(C2,2)(C3,2)	(C1,2)(C3,2)	(C1,2)(C3,2)	(C1,2)(C2,2)	...
10	(C1,2)(C2,1)(C3,3)	(C1,2)(C3,3)	(C1,2)(C2,1)(C3,3)	(C1,2)(C2,1)	(C1,2)(C3,3)	...
11	(C1,2)(C3,4)	(C1,2)(C2,2)(C3,4)	(C1,2)(C3,4)	(C1,2)(C3,4)	(C1,2)(C2,2)(C3,4)	...

Table 3. Partial Decision Matrix

search is involved. The computed rules are optimal in a sense, as they minimize the number of conditions and maximize the support. In the continuation of the research, the method will be applied to data mining problems.

Acknowledgments: The research reported in this article was supported in part by a research grant awarded to the first author by Natural Sciences and Engineering Council of Canada. Many thanks to Mr. Kwei Aryeetey for preparing the decision table used to illustrate the method and to Dr. Kwei Quaye for providing the insurance data.

References

1. Aryeetey, K. Ziarko, W. Quaye, K. Application of Variable Precision Rough Set Approach to Car Driver Assessment. In Kantardzic, M. Zurada, J. (eds.) New Generation of Data Mining Applications, (in print).
2. Skowron, A. Rauszer C. The Discernibility Matrices and Functions in Information Systems. ICS Report 1/91, Warsaw University of Technology.
3. Grzymala-Busse, J. LERS-A System for Learning from Examples Based on Rough Sets. In Slowinski, R. (ed.) Intelligent Decision Support: Handbook of Applications and Advances of Rough Sets Theory. Kluwer Academic Publishers, (1991) pp. 3-18.
4. Ziarko, W. Shan, N. A Method For Computing All Maximally General Rules in Attribute-Value Systems. Computational Intelligence: an International Journal, vol. 12, no. 2, (1996) pp. 223-234.

5. Katzberg, J. Ziarko, W. Variable Precision Rough Sets with Asymmetric Bounds. Proc. of the International Workshop on Rough Sets and Knowledge Discovery (RSKD'93) (1993) pp. 163-191.
6. Pawlak, Z. Rough sets - Theoretical aspects of reasoning about data. Kluwer Academic Publishers (1991).
7. Ślęzak, D., Ziarko, W. Bayesian Rough Set Model. In Proc. of FDM'2002. December 9, Maebashi, Japan, (2002) pp. 131-135.
8. Ziarko, W. Variable Precision Rough Sets Model. Journal of Computer and Systems Sciences, vol. 46. no. 1, (1993) pp. 39-59.
9. Yao, Y.Y., Wong, S.K.M. A Decision Theoretic Framework for Approximating Concepts. International Journal of Man-Machine Studies, 37, (1992) pp. 793-809.
10. Ziarko, W. Probabilistic Decision Tables in the Variable Precision Rough Set Model. Computational Intelligence: an International Journal, vol. 17, no 3, (2001) pp. 593-603.
11. Quaye, K. Using Prior Convictions and Accidents To Identify Unsafe Drivers - An examination of Saskatchewan's Delinquent Driver Program. Saskatchewan Government Insurance, Regina, Saskatchewan, Canada, (1997).
12. Grzymala-Busse, J. Ziarko, W. Data Mining Based on Rough Sets. Data Mining: Opportunities and Challenges. IDEA Group Publishing, (2003) 142-173.
13. Ziarko, W. Decision Making with Probabilistic Decision Tables. In Zhong, N. Skowron, A. Ohsuga, S. (eds.) New Directions in Rough Sets, Data Mining, and Granular-Soft Computing, Lecture Notes in AI 1711, Springer Verlag, 463-471.
14. Tsumoto, S. Modelling medical diagnostic rules based on rough sets. In Polkowski, L. Skowron, A. (eds.) Rough Sets and Current Trends in Computing, Lecture Notes in AI 1424, Springer Verlag (2001) pp. 475-482.
15. Wong, S.K.M. Ziarko, W. Algorithm for Inductive Learning. Bulletin of the Polish Academy of Sciences, vol. 34, 5-6, (1986) pp. 271-276.
16. Quinlan,R. C4.5: Programs for Machine Learning. Margan Kaufmann (1993).
17. Wong, S.K.M. Ziarko, W. INFER - An Adaptive Decision Support System Based on the Probabilistic Approximate Classification. Proc.of the 6th International Workshop on Expert Systems and Their Applications, Avignon, (1986) pp. 713-725.
18. Agrawal, R. Imielinski, T. Swami A. Mining Associations between Sets of Items in Massive Databases. In MD93, Washington, D.C., (1993) pp. 207-216.

A Framework for Extending Fuzzy Description Logic to Ontology Based Document Processing

Shailendra Singh, Lipika Dey, and Muhammad Abulaish

Department of Mathematics
Indian Institute of Technology, Delhi,
Hauz Khas, New Delhi, India
(lipika, shailen)@maths.iitd.ernet.in

Abstract. Ontologies have proved to be very useful in sharing concepts across applications in an unambiguous way. However, since web documents are not fully structured sources of information, it is not possible to utilize the benefits of a domain ontology straight away to extract information from such a document. In this paper we have proposed an uncertainty handling mechanism based on rough-fuzzy reasoning principles which can handle query-processing from unstructured web documents in an elegant way.

1 Introduction

In order to maximize the utility of web resources, it is essential to extract information from heterogeneous, unstructured web documents and reason with them. Several question-answering systems try to do this, though most of them still just list the relevant URLs. AnswerBus [8] is an open-domain question answering system based on sentence level Web information retrieval.

Though these systems work quite well, certain problems related to the nuances of Natural Language remain unsolved. For example we posted two queries to AnswerBus: (i) *What is a wine with fruity flavour, light hop, strong taste?* The answer was *"Sorry, I found no answer for your question"*. However when we asked (ii) *"What is a red wine with fruity flavour, light hop, strong taste?"* there were 3 answers. One of this was *"The nose on this beer is ripe and fruity with slightly vinous esters, married to interesting hop notes - the colour of a glorious red ruby wine"*. Clearly, this could be one of the answers for the earlier question also, since "red wine is a special class of wine". We feel that such systems can be greatly benefitted by integrating uncertainty handling mechanisms and underlying ontological structures with them.

Ontology based knowledge representation scheme provides a platform for sharing concepts across various applications in an unambiguous way [1], [2], [3], [4], [5]. Though a lot of focus is currently given on standardizing ontology representation languages for general domain representations, most of these assume that the concept world is exactly defined in terms of properties and values. The problem with this approach is that such a structure cannot be used straight away for retrieving information from an unstructured text document. Description logics have

J. Favela et al. (Eds.): AWIC 2004, LNAI 3034, pp. 95-104, 2004.

proved to be a useful tool in ontological engineering. However, in order to reason with contents of web resources, it is essential to extend Description Logic to query answering services [9], [10]. Since natural language resources contain imprecise, often vague or uncertain descriptions of concepts, for practical applications to question answering it is essential to extend Description Logic to handle imprecision. It has been shown in [9] how by placing certain restrictions on the use of variables in a query, Description Logic can be extended to DAML+OIL. They have focussed on Boolean queries to determine whether a query without free variables is true with respect to a Knowledge Base. Holldobler et al. [11] proposes a fuzzy Description Logic with Hedges as concept modifiers.

As another example, we consider another question *"What is a red wine with fruity flavour, light hop, not light taste"?* One of the answers generated by AnswerBus was *"The mystical magic of this well is reflected in the rich golden colour, fruity flavour and full hop aroma of this light and refreshing ale."* Clearly this is not a desirable answer. The problem lies in the wrong interpretation of terms "not light". The answers are based on string matching and it is not considered that "not light" is closer to "strong" than "light".

Looking at these problems of dealing with natural language texts, we were motivated to design a document analysis system which can do the following
- Identify implicit concepts in a document using underlying Ontological structures and treat words as concepts rather than patterns.
- Handle imprecision of natural language texts arising due to linguistic qualifiers through the use of fuzzy Description Logic [11], [12].

In this paper, we have proposed a framework for reasoning with imprecise and unstructured knowledge sources with an underlying ontological structure. The system reasons about relevance of documents using a rough-fuzzy reasoning mechanism. The salient features of this work are:
- We have provided a complete framework for incorporating fuzzy concept modifiers into an ontological structure.
- We propose a reasoning mechanism which can be used to match document concepts with user given concepts more satisfactorily by increasing the scope of the question to include related concepts.
- Finally a relevance computation function can be used to compute the overall relevance of a document using the extended query. The relevance computation mechanism uses hedge algebra to handle linguistic qualifiers.

2   Enriching Ontological Description with Linguistic Qualifiers

Ontology provides a shared conceptualization of domains to heterogeneous applications. Usually a concept is defined in terms of its mandatory and optional properties along with the value restrictions on those properties.

In general there is no ontological framework for qualifying a property. Even if linguistic variables like low, high etc. are used, they are most often used as value restrictions. For example, the wine ontology [3] defined by W3C group, uses the *properties hasflavour, hascolor, hasbody* etc. for describing any class of wine. The value restrictions on *hasflavour* is the set {Delicate, Moderate, Strong} and that of *hascolor* is {Red, White, Rose}. This ontology also describes a set of instances of wines of various types and describes them in terms of the above mentioned properties. Using Description Logic it is possible to retrieve information from this knowledge base.

However, some web documents describing wine are produced below:

- "BARBERA is a full bodied, fairly acidic red wine grown originally in California's coastal areas is now the major component of the red jug wines produced in California's Central Valley";
- "CABERNET FRANC is a light, fruity red wine from France's Loire Valley, often blended with Merlot. Basically used as a blending grape in California, especially with Cabernet Sauvignon."

If the user is looking for a wine that is "medium bodied, not acidic, light flavoured", then definitely CABERNET FRANC is a better choice than BARBERA.

We propose a framework in which a general set of concept modifiers can be associated to ontology. The role of these modifiers will be to change the degree of a property value. This set is a collection of hedges as described in [11] and is a partially ordered set. For example, the hedges "pale, slight, light, moderate, very, deep, dark, rich" can be associated to the wine ontology. We change the wine description ontology to include in addition to its original definition, the description of linguistic qualifiers and their associations to the property values. We accomplish this through multiple inheritance of each "Winedescriptor" property. "FuzzyQualifier" is a new subclass which can take values from the set of hedges only. The hedges are ordered by increasing instance number of nodes. Each property like "WineTaste", "WineFlavour" etc. are subclasses of "WineDescriptor". Now we introduce fuzzy property classes like "FuzzyTaste", "FuzzyBody" etc. as subclasses which multiply inherit from "FuzzyQualifier" and the respective class descriptor. These property classes inherit the possible values from a property descriptor class and the concept modifiers from the fuzzy qualifier class. Thus a description of a wine can be generated in terms of a list of concept modifiers followed by a property value. Parts of the OWL code that is generated by our scheme for the wine ontology is shown below:

```
<owl:Class rdf:ID="FuzzyQualifier">
 <rdfs:subClassOf>
  <owl:Restriction>
   <owl:onProperty>
    <owl:DatatypeProperty rdf:about="#has-qualifier"/>
   </owl:onProperty>
   <owl:cardinality rdf:datatype="http://www.w3.org/2001/XMLSchema#int"
   >1</owl:cardinality>
  </owl:Restriction>
 </rdfs:subClassOf>
 </owl:Class>
<owl:Class rdf:ID="FuzzyBody">
  <rdfs:subClassOf rdf:resource="#WineBody"/>
  <rdfs:subClassOf rdf:resource="#FuzzyQualifier"/>
  <rdfs:subClassOf>
```

```
    <owl:Restriction>
     <owl:onProperty>
      <owl:DatatypeProperty rdf:about="#has-qualifier"/>
     </owl:onProperty>
     <owl:maxCardinality
rdf:datatype="http://www.w3.org/2001/XMLSchema#int"
     >8</owl:maxCardinality>
    </owl:Restriction>
   </rdfs:subClassOf>
   <rdfs:subClassOf>
    <owl:Restriction>
     <owl:onProperty>
      <owl:DatatypeProperty rdf:about="#has-value"/>
     </owl:onProperty>
     <owl:allValuesFrom rdf:resource="#WineBody"/>
    </owl:Restriction>
   </rdfs:subClassOf>
   <rdfs:subClassOf>
    <owl:Restriction>
     <owl:onProperty>
      <owl:DatatypeProperty rdf:about="#has-qualifier"/>
     </owl:onProperty>
     <owl:allValuesFrom rdf:resource="#FuzzyQualifier"/>
...............
<j.0:FuzzyQualifier rdf:ID="Instance_56"
   j.0:has-qualifier="not"/>
<j.0:FuzzyQualifier rdf:ID="Instance_57"
   j.0:has-qualifier="mild"/>
<j.0:FuzzyQualifier rdf:ID="Instance_58"
   j.0:has-qualifier="moderate"/>
<j.0:FuzzyQualifier rdf:ID="Instance_59"
   j.0:has-qualifier="very"/>
```

With this definition an entity can have property value ∂A, where ∂ is a list of concept modifiers. This can be interpreted as having the value A to a certain degree. For example the wine BARBERA which has taste "fairly Acidic", has certain degree of membership to the "Acidic Taste" category which is definitely not 1. With a predefined set of concept modifiers, given an entity description in terms of these, the relevance of the entity to a user query can be computed as a function of its membership to the user given description. Thus if a user asks for a "very strong" wine, the relevance of two wine descriptions which are "light" and "very, very, strong" respectively, can be computed.

2.1 Computing Relevance of Property Values with Concept Modifiers

Let $H = \{h_1, h_2, ..., h_p\}$ be a set of hedges, among which each element of H is either positive or negative with respect to all other hedges including itself. The function sign: $H \times (HU\oslash) \rightarrow \{-1,+1\}$ is defined in [11] as

$$\text{sign}(h_i, h^*) = \begin{cases} -1 & \text{if } h_i \text{ is negative wrt } h^*, \\ 1 & \text{if } h_i \text{ is positive wrt } h^* \end{cases} \qquad (1)$$

$\oslash$ is the set of all property values in the domain. The set of fuzzy qualifiers operates with hedge algebra as defined by [11]. An entity can have property value ∂A, where ∂ is a list of concept modifiers. $\partial = h^*$, where $h \in H$ and $A \in \oslash$. This membership value of ∂A can be calculated using the algorithm presented in [11]. Using this algorithm one can compute the membership of any arbitrary combination of the concept modifiers by raising the membership to the appropriate power β.

Table 1. Membership calculation for concept modifiers

	Sig	β
Strong	1	2.0
Light	-1	0.5
Very	1	2.0
Moderate	-1	0.5
Very Strong	+1	4.0
Very light	-1	0.2
		5.0
Moderate Light	+1	0.7
		5.0

In our adaptation of this approach, we have made the following modifications. The set H is defined as follows:
$H = \{h_0, h_1, ..., h_p\}$ where $h_0 = $ not. While the remaining set of modifiers behave in the same way as before. The sign of h_0 is defined as follows:

$$\text{sign}(h_0, h^*) = \begin{cases} -1 & \text{if sign } (h^*, A) = +1 \text{ for any } A \\ 1 & \text{if sign } (h^*, A) = -1 \text{ for any } A \end{cases} \qquad (2)$$

Table 1 below shows the computation of a four member set containing {strong, light, very, moderate} with partial relationships defined between strong and light and between very and moderate, where mol stands for "more or less". Thus if it is given that "a wine is red has value 0.7", then the membership of "the wine is very red" = 0.49, "the wine is not red = -0.7", "the wine is not very red =-.49". This rightly interprets than it is more correct to say that the wine is not very red than to say the wine is not red.

3 Accepting User Query

A query is assumed to have a mandatory component – entity name, followed by an optional list of property specification. The property specification is a variable length list of property qualifiers and values. Thus a query assumes the following structure: Query: [Entity name: [{Property}: <List of Qualifiers>* <Property value>]]*]. Thus a sample query in the wine domain can be
[wine:[{Flavour}:<Light>(Fruity)]
        [{Colour}:<very deep>(red)]
        [{Taste}:<Very strong>(acidic)]].

For queries pertaining to an arbitrary entity that does not belong to any defined ontology, currently the system accepts any string given as property name and value. However, the concept modifiers can function correctly only if they are part of the defined modifier resource. For example looking for a bright celestial body resembling a comet, without any underlying ontology one can construct the query as:
[celestial body: [{appearance}<bright>]
            {like}<very much><comet>].

Since our emphasis is on ontology based query processing, the system expects concepts to be from a particular domain. If so, then it is logical to expect that the entities are described in terms of a pre-defined set of concepts.

4 Query Extension Using Related Concepts

Question answering systems usually extend a given user question by extending the user query to include relevant words [13]. In our work however, we extend the query with ontologically related concepts. Since ontologies are generated by domain experts, this leads to a better approximation of query. The ontologically related concepts to be included into a query is determined from the type of the question.

Along the lines of rough approximation, we define two approximations of the question – the lower approximation and the upper approximation. Let Q be the user query consisting of a set of concepts C.

Definition 1. Lower approximation of Q includes all those concepts which are semantically equivalent to the concepts. Mathematically,

$$\underline{Q(C)} = \left\{ c' \mid c' \equiv c \text{ where } c \in C \right\} \qquad (3)$$

If the underlying ontology is the English language, then all words synonymous to the original set of words will be included in $\underline{Q(C)}$.

Upper approximation of Q includes all concepts which are related to the concepts in the original query through the class-subclass relations. We define two types of upper approximations that can be obtained depending on the type of the query.

Definition 2. The generalized upper approximation of a query Q, denoted by $\overline{Q_G}(C)$, extends the set of query concepts C by including all concepts which are super classes of the original concepts. Thus

$$\overline{Q_G(C)} = \left\{ c' \mid c \subseteq c', \text{ where } c \in C \right\} \tag{4}$$

Definition 3. The specialized upper approximation of a query Q, denoted by $\overline{Q_S}(C)$, extends the set of query concepts C by including all concepts which are super classes of the original concepts. Thus

$$\overline{Q_S(C)} = \left\{ c' \mid c' \subseteq c, \text{ where } c, c' \in C \right\} \tag{5}$$

The query type will determine which type of approximation is to be taken. For example, let us look at the following queries:
1. Get a wine with a fruity flavor: If fruity is replaced by anything that is a specialization of fruit like orange, strawberry, grapes etc. the quality of answer remains same.
2. What is a fruit? : If fruit is replaced by a subclass like citrus fruit or berry, the answers retrieved with the specialized concepts may not give the exact answer.

We are yet to find a satisfactory way of determining which approximation is better under given circumstances. We work with the union of both the approximations. Since concepts in the original query and those included in the approximated extension cannot have the same weight while calculating document relevance, we associate weights to the concepts in the approximated query.

Let the original query be denoted by Q and let A denote the approximated query. The weight of any concept $c \in A$ is computed in terms of its closeness to concepts in Q.

Thus ...$c \in A$, $w(c) = \sup_{d \in Q} \{1/(dist(c,d) +1)\}$, where $dist(c,d)$ is the number of classes lying between c and d in the ontology tree, along a class-subclass hierarchy.

The above measure ensures that if c is a concept from the original query it is retained with weight 1.0. New concepts are inducted with a weight that is determined by the minimum distance of the concept from one of the query concepts.

5 Query Processing Framework

To find the relevant documents, we compute the similarity between the extended query and the unstructured texts. The query is assumed to be in the structured format presented in section 3.

To extend a query with its approximation, we consider all entities and values in the original query, and extend it to include other terms from the ontology. Thus we include all classes which are either generalizations or specializations of the original value concepts, in conjunction to the appropriate property.

Locating Relevant Concepts in Document. Each document is considered in its text form as a collection of words. HTML tags are deleted in case it is an HTML document.

Since a document as a whole may not be relevant to the query, we first try to locate appropriate portions in the document which are likely to be relevant to the query. We call the relevant portion the *"property window"*. For each property specified in the query, the property window for that property is the portion of the document which contains information about it. In our implementation we have used a sentence containing property names as a property window. A single property window may be verified by multiple property queries since a single sentence can have more than one property definition in it. Once we find the property windows, we look for qualifier-value matches within the window. Those properties for which a window could not be located, we consider the values in the approximations of the query and try to locate them in the document. These values are considered to be relevant only in conjunction with the properties that have not been already located. The sentences which contain the values serve as "value windows" for these properties. Once again, the same value window may be chosen for multiple properties since in absence of a specific property name, it is not possible to decide the value is pertaining to which property.

Computing relevance in terms of value matches between query and document.
In this phase we initiate an activation mechanism to locate the query values within property windows. A value may be a concept in the original query or in the extended query. When a value concept A is located in the document, a search for the modifiers preceding it is initiated. This may yield a list of modifier concepts. The final match is expressed as a similarity measure between the original query concepts and the concepts found in the document.

Let δ be the concept modifier for c in original query. Let β be the power determined for δ using algorithm of [11]. We find the concept modifier in the document for the related concept by initializing η to blank and then while earlier token in the sentence is a hedge h $\in$H, we concatenate h to η so that η becomes hη. We then determine β', the required power for η. The relevance of the value is then computed as

$$Rel(A) = 1, \text{ if } w(A)=1 \text{ and } \beta=\beta'$$
$$\text{/* denotes an exact match for value as well as qualifier*/}$$
$$\text{else } Rel(A) = w(A).e^{-|\beta-\beta'|}$$

This value is always less than or equal to 1.0, for each property value **A**. The final relevance of a document is computed as a normalized value of all matches with concepts in approximate query. We now present a few results with respect to the following queries:

- Query 1-[<colour><dark><red>][<Flavour><slight><Fruity>
        [<taste><mild><acidic>]
- Query 2-[<finish><slight><bitter>][<Flavour><strong><malty>
  We compute the relevance of each of the following documents. with respect to the above queries.
- Document 1 - Great *dark amber colour* with *red* highlights and a very dense tan head. The smell is very nice, hints of *malty* caramel and some *fruit*. Medium bodied, *malty flavour* with some other *fruit* highlights. The *taste* isn't too great, especially considering the style. The after *taste* is *very dry* and *bitter*, but not horrible at all. **Relevance wrt Query 1 = 0.743, Relevance wrt Query 2 = 0.94**.
- Document 2 – Acrodizer: *Deep copper_brown*. Nose of *red* wine, cedar, and strawberries, but loses a point for too strong of an alcohol *aroma*. A little thin initially on the tongue, with not too much carbonation but also not much alcohol present on the tongue, so the experience is all kind of mellow and soft. *Mild* cedar allspice oak and cranberry *flavour*. Fairly week on the tongue, and *flavour* wise there is not anything which stands out to make a *strong* case. **Relevance wrt Query 1 = 0.076, Relevance wrt Query 2 = 0.0**.
- Document 3 – SYRAH A deep red colour Rhone wine with an almost blackberry taste, slightly drier and less fruity than Zinfandel. The wine can be quite complex. Syrah is the base of most red Rhone blends (often with Grenache and Mourvedre). California produces some excellent Syrahs. **Relevance wrt Query 1 = 0.37, Relevance wrt Query 2 = 0.079**.
- Document 4 – Changxao: Small head that fades fast, good lacing though. Nice color with a *malty flavour*. Taste is malty and *slight bitter*, mouthfeel is a little thin, the *finish* is nice. Overall a good drinking beer that's not too expensive. **Relevance wrt Query 1 = 0.163, Relevance wrt Query 2 = 0.628**.

The results show that the concept modifiers can give better match for queries in the wine domain. For both the queries the maximum match is for document 1, which is a red wine with malty and fruity flavour. It also has a bitter finish. For the second query the last document also has a high degree of match, since it is also malty and bitter. Document 2 has little match with query 1 since it is red but no match with query2.

6 Conclusion

In this paper, we have presented a basic framework for integrating concept modifiers into an ontological framework. The ontological structures are enhanced with concept modifiers to model linguistic qualifiers since we found that documents rarely contained isolated values. We have also shown how query approximations can be done by extending the original query to include additional concepts from the ontology. This can enable extraction of more relevant documents through the search engines by using relevant concepts also. Finally, we have shown how relevance of documents can be computed using concept modifiers. However, the key problem that remains is the virtually endless number of concept modifiers and property-value pairs that can crop up in a domain, which cannot be taken care of in an ontology. We are therefore working on a system which can learn the possible values and qualifiers from a training set.

References

1. Zhong, N., Liu, J., Yao, Y. Y.: In search of the wisdom web. IEEE Computer, Vol. 35(11). (2002) 27-31
2. World wide web consortium. http://www.w3.org/
3. WineOntology.
   http://kaon.semanticweb.org/Members/rvo/WebOnt_Guide/wines.owl/view
4. Gal, A., Modica, G., Jamil, H.: Improving web search with automatic ontology matching. http://citeseer.nj.nec.com/558376.html
5. Ramsdell, J. D.: A foundation for a semantic web.
   http://www.ccs.neu.edu/home/ramsdell/papers/swfol/swfol.pdf. (2001)
6. Srinivasan, P., Ruiz, M.E., Kraft, D.H., Chen, J.: Vocabulary Mining for Information Retrieval: Rough Sets and Fuzzy Sets. Information Processing and Management, Vol. 37. (2001) 15-38
7. Ross, T.: Fuzzy Logic for Engineering Applications. McGraw-Hill Book Company, New York, NY, ISBN: 0-07-053917-0. (1995)
8. Zheng, Z.: AnswerBus Question Answering System. Human Language Technology Conference (HLT 2002). San Diego, CA (2002)
9. Horrocks, I., Tessaris, S.: Querying the semantic web: a formal approach. In Proceedings of the 13th International Semantic Web Conference (ISWC 2002). Lecture Notes in Computer Science, Vol.2342. Springer-Verlag (2002) 177-191
10. Horrocks, I., Tessaris, S.: A conjunctive query language for description logic aboxes. In Proceedings of the 17th National Conference on Artificial Intelligence (AAAI 2000). (2000) 399-404
11. Hölldobler, S., Khang, T., D., Störr, H., P.: A fuzzy description logic with hedges as concept modifiers. In Proceedings InTech/VJFuzzy'2002. Science and Technics Publishing House, Hanoi, Vietnam (2002) 25-34
12. Zadeh, L., A.: A fuzzy-set-theoretic interpretation of linguistic hedges. Journal of Cybernetic, Vol. 2. (1972)
13. Li, X., Roth, D.: Learning Question Classifiers. In Proceedings of the 19th International Conference on Computational Linguistics. (2002)

On Correction of Semantic Errors
in Natural Language Texts
with a Dictionary of Literal Paronyms*

Alexander Gelbukh,[1,2] Igor A. Bolshakov [1]

[1] Center for Computing Research
National Polytechnic Institute, Mexico City, Mexico
{gelbukh,igor}@cic.ipn.mx; www.Gelbukh.com

[2] Department of Computer Science and Engineering, Chung-Ang University,
221 Huksuk-Dong, DongJak-Ku, Seoul, 156-756, Korea

Abstract. Due to the open nature of the Web, search engines must include means of meaningful processing of incorrect texts, including automatic error detection and correction. One of wide-spread types of errors in Internet texts are malapropisms, i.e., semantic errors replacing a word by another existing word similar in letter composition and/or sound but semantically incompatible with the context. Methods for detection and correction of malapropisms have been proposed recently. Any such method relies on a generator of correction candidates—paronyms, i.e., real words similar to the suspicious one encountered in the text and having the same grammatical properties. Literal paronyms are words at the distant of few editing operations from a given word. We argue that a dictionary of literal paronyms should be compiled beforehand and that its units should be grammeme names. For Spanish, such grammemes are (1) singulars and plurals of nouns; (2) adjectives plus participles; (3) verbs in infinitive; (4) gerunds plus adverbs; (5) personal verb forms. Basing on existing Spanish electronic dictionaries, we have compiled a dictionary of one-letter-distant literal paronyms. The size of the dictionary is few tens thousand entries, an entry averaging approximately three paronyms. We calculate the gain in number of candidate search operations achievable through the proposed dictionary and give illustrative examples of correcting one-letter malapropisms using our dictionary.

1   Introduction

Linguistic studies based on various Internet search engines repeatedly show that completely correct texts in any language are rather rare exceptions among lots of texts containing errors of various kinds. For any task of creation of specialized corpora or databases extracted from Internet search engines or robots, a module that tries to automatically correct the extracted texts seems absolutely necessary.

---

* Work done under partial support of Mexican Government (CONACyT, SNI, COFAA-IPN) and Korean Government (KIPA Professorship for Visiting Faculty Positions in Korea). The first author is currently on Sabbatical leave at Chung-Ang University.

J. Favela et al. (Eds.): AWIC 2004, LNAI 3034, pp. 105-114, 2004.

106   Alexander Gelbukh and Igor A. Bolshakov

There are different types of errors introduced into texts by their authors. Modern widespread authoring tools, such as Microsoft Word or Microsoft FrontPage, easily detect *orthographical* errors—misspellings leading to a letter string that does not exist in the given language as a correct word, e.g., **wors* for *word*. However, such tools usually fail to detect so-called real-word errors: mutilations of a word that lead to another existing word, e.g., *?work, ?wore,* or *?worn* for *word*. What is more, such tools sometimes introduce such errors by automatically "correcting" misspelled words by substituting them with existing words without asking the user whether this was the intended word.

The presence of some of such real-word errors—namely, *syntactic* errors—is relatively easy to detect using syntactic analysis. For example, the phrase **every wore* (or *worn*) *in this text is spelled correctly* is ungrammatical and thus probably contains a misspelled word. However, when the grammatical characteristics of the new word coincide with those of the intended one, even a grammar checker fails to detect a problem, as, for example, in the phrase *?every work in this text is spelled correctly* (for *every word...*), which is perfectly grammatical, while does not make sense, or at least is suspicious, semantically.

Such *semantic* errors cannot be automatically detected or corrected so far. They usually replace a real word by another one existing in the language but semantically incompatible with context, which results in violation of human knowledge and/or common sense and impedes comprehension of the text. Indeed, if the replacing word has the same syntactic function in the sentence, neither orthography nor syntax is violated, so that spelling and grammar checkers fail to detect the problem. Semantic errors replacing a word by another one similar to the intended word in letter composition and/or sound are named *malapropisms*. A Spanish example is *visitar el centro histérico* 'to visit hysterical center' for the intended word *histórico* 'historical'.

Two methods of malapropism correction have been proposed recently [4, 3]. Both of them rely on a generator of correction candidates for malapropisms, i.e., a set of real words similar to the suspicious one encountered in the text, with the same grammatical properties. Such similar words are usually called *paronyms*. Two words that are literal paronyms are at the distant of few editing operations from one another, where by operations insertion, omission, replacement of a letter, or permutation of two adjacent letters is meant. If only one such operation is applied to a string, the resulting letter string is said to be at the distance 1 from the source string. In this paper we study only such 1-distance literal paronyms.

We argue for that a dictionary of literal paronyms should be compiled beforehand for each language. The preferable unit for an entry of such a dictionary is a grammeme. For Spanish, such grammemes are (1) singulars and plurals of nouns;

- adjectives plus participles;
- verbs in infinitive;
- gerunds plus adverbs;
- personal verb forms.

Based on available lexicographic material on Spanish, we have elaborated a dictionary of one-letter-distant literal paronyms. The size of the dictionary proved to be ca. 38,000 words, with an entry (set of literal paronyms of a headword) averaging approximately three. The gain in the number of search operations necessary to find all correction candidates using the proposed dictionary is about 248 times; see calculations below.

More specifically, the objectives of this paper are:

- To discuss distances between words as letter strings;
- To choose the most suitable unit for paronym dictionaries;
- To present the compiled paronym dictionary and to theoretically evaluate the gain achievable using this dictionary as compared with the blind search of correction candidates;
- To outline shortly two possible resources as a basis of practical use of the compiled dictionary;
- To trace three demonstrative examples of correcting one-letter malapropisms.

We illustrate our considerations mostly on English examples, in all cases when it does not contradict our main motivation of applying our method to processing Spanish texts.

2   Distance between Words as Letter Strings

For any known method of malapropism detection, a generator of correction candidates is necessary. The candidates should be in some sense "similar" to the given word. Such generation is analogous to generation of the candidates for orthographical errors but differs in the way the similarity is measured and in the restrictions that apply.

Indeed, word forms of a natural language are rare interspersions in the space of all letter strings. For approximate evaluation of this rarefaction, consider that in such highly inflexional language as Spanish there exist ca. 800,000 different word forms, whereas in low inflexional English, say, three times less. The number of all possible strings over a given alphabet consisting of A letters with the lengths equal to the mean length L of a real word in a corresponding dictionary is A^L, i.e. $33^9 \approx 4.6 \times 10^{13}$ in Spanish and $26^8 \approx 2.1 \times 10^{11}$ in English. This means that a real word form occurs on average once among 58 million senseless strings in Spanish and 788 thousand in English. The change of the mean length of word form in a dictionary to the mean textual value decreases this contrast, still leaving it huge.

If word forms as letter strings were absolutely stochastic in structure, the probability to meet two forms at a short distance would be inconsiderable. In fact, however, words are built of few thousands of radices and even fewer prefix and suffix morphs (these are few hundreds in languages like Spanish). Some semantic and morphonological restrictions are imposed on compatibility of radixes, prefixes, and suffixes, since not all combinations are reasonable and not all reasonable ones are utterable.

Just this circumstance facilitates the candidate search for replacement of one real word by another. For *orthographical* errors, a wrong string can be arbitrary and the task to gather beforehand, for each such string, all similar real words seems impractical. However, the environments of a real word form, as our considerations show, contain few real words, which can be found beforehand. Being collected in a special dictionary, they could be used for malapropism correction, cutting down the search space of candidates.

Indeed, for correction of one-letter error in a string with the length L, it is necessary $A(2L+1)+L-1$ checks, which for a word of nine letters equals to 616. For two-letter errors, already ca. 360,000 checks are necessary. In the same time, beforehand gathered one-letter-apart candidates are only few units and for two-letter-apart ones, few tens. For words that are not in the dictionary of substitutes, the candidate search is not needed, which also cuts down the search.

Let us consider the distance between literal strings in more detail. One literal string of the length L can be formed from any other one by a series of editing operations [5, 6, 9]. Consider strings over an alphabet of A letters. The elementary editing operations are: replacement of a letter with another letter in any place within the source string (here there are $(A-1)L$ options); omission of a letter (L options); insertion of a letter (here, $A(L+1)$ options); permutation of two adjacent letters ($L-1$ options).

The string obtained with any of these $A(2L+1)+L-1$ operations is at the distance 1 from the source string, i.e., within the sphere of radius 1 in the string space. Making another elementary step off, we form a string on the sphere with radius two with regard to the source one, etc. Points obtained with minimum R steps are on R-sphere, whereas the points of r-spheres with $r < R$ and the source point itself are not included in the R-sphere. Here are English examples:

- *word* Vs. *world*, *ethology* Vs. *etiology*, *ethology* Vs. *ethnology* are at the distance 1,
- *hysterical* Vs. *historical*, *dielectric* Vs. *dialectic*, *excess* Vs. *access*, *garniture* Vs. *furniture* are at the distance 2,
- *company* Vs. *campaign*, *massy* Vs. *massive*, *sensible* Vs. *sensitive*, *hypotenuse* Vs. *hypothesis* are at the distance 3 or more.

Though the mean distance between word forms is large in any language, they prove to gather together in clusters. Firstly, such clusters contain elements of morphological paradigms of various lexemes, word forms within them being usually at a distance of 0 to 3 from each other. Just such a cluster is a lexeme, and one of the composing forms is used as its dictionary name. Secondly, paradigms of various lexemes with similar morphs can be close to each other, sometimes even with intersection (such intersections give rise to morphological ambiguities).

3   Preferable Unit of Paronym Dictionary

For our purposes, of interest are the paradigm pairs with the same number of elements and correlative elements at the same distance. E.g., all four elements of paradigms of Eng. verbs *bake* and *cake* differ in the first letter only. Let us call such paradigms parallel. If the distance equals to 1, let us call them close parallel.

Thus, any element $\lambda(\chi)$ of the paradigm of λ, where χ is a set of intra-lexeme coordinates (i.e., morphological characteristics selecting a specific word form), can be obtained from the correlated element of the parallel paradigm using the same editing operator $R_i(\ )$, where i is the cardinal number of the operator in an effective enumeration of such operators. Then the relation between dictionary names (they correspond to $\chi = \chi_0$) and specific word forms of parallel lexemes can be represented by the proportion

$$\frac{\lambda(\chi)}{\lambda(\chi_0)} = \frac{R_i(\lambda(\chi))}{R_i(\lambda(\chi_0))} \tag{1}$$

This formula means that for any suspicious form $\lambda(\chi)$ in text, it is necessary to find its dictionary form $\lambda(\chi_0)$, and, if a close parallel $R_i(\lambda(\chi_0))$ for it exists, $R_i(\lambda(\chi))$ should be tried as a correction candidate. For such tries, the syntactic correctness usually pertains, and some try can correct the error.

This parallelism permits to unite sets of word forms, storing in the dictionary only one their representative, i.e., the dictionary name of each lexeme. However, strictly parallel paradigms are not so frequent in highly inflectional languages. More usually the parallelism between subparadigms can be found. As such subparadigms, it is reasonable to take grammemes corresponding to fixed combinations of the characteristics χ.

For example, noun lexemes of European languages have grammemes of singular and plural. They play the same role in a sentence but differ in the sets of collocations they can be in.[1] This division of wordforms by grammatical number serves our purposes as well.

Spanish verbs have grammemes of personal forms, infinitive, participles, and gerund. These grammemes differ in their role in a sentence, so that their separate use keeps syntactic correctness of text after restoration of the error.

A dictionary name is assigned to each grammeme, e.g., adjectives and participles are represented in Spanish by their singular forms of masculine. For such dictionary entry and specific word forms, the formula (1) pertains.

In the cases when the parallelism is not valid for some forms of two grammemes under comparison, the correction attempt will fail. If such cases are rare, it is not very problematic.

4 Compiled Dictionary and Gain Achieved

No general-purpose electronic dictionary proved to be useful for our goal to compile the dictionary of literal paronyms. So we used the lexicographic materials put at our disposal by our colleagues from the Polytechnic University of Barcelona, Spain.

The following grammemes were taken for the target Spanish dictionary:

- Nouns of masculine gender in singular number, together with the verbal infinitives,
- Nouns of masculine gender in plural number,
- Nouns of feminine gender in singular number,

---

[1] By collocations we mean semantically meaningful and syntactically connected (in the sense of dependency grammars; possibly through a chain of functional words) pairs of words. Some authors mean by collocations co-occurrences within a text unit [10]. We believe that even in this case collocation properties of plurals and singulars differ.

- Nouns of feminine gender in plural number,
- Adjectives together with verbal participles (singular masculine form representing all forms),
- Adverbs together with verbal gerunds,
- Verbs in infinitive,
- Verbs in 3rd person present indicative (representing all personal forms of non-compound tenses)

Here are some examples of the entries of the dictionary:

...	fajas *nfp*	coartando *v*
aliño *nms*	lajas *nfp*	**cubando** *v*
alijo *nms*	majas *nfp*	cebando *v*
aliso *nms*	pajas *nfp*	cucando *v*
ali *nms*	rajas *nfp*	cunando *v*
ami *nms*	**bajezas** *nfp*	curando *v*
aliado *nms*	majezas *nfp*	cuñando *v*
alzado *nms*	**bajistas** *ncp*	...
aliar *v*	bañistas *ncp*	**alude** *v*
alias *nmn*	cajistas *ncp*	acude *v*
altar *nms*	...	elude *v*
alzar *v*	**apical** *adj*	ilude *v*
alear *v*	amical *adj*	**aluja** *v*
alfar *v*	**apilonado** *v*	aleja *v*
aviar *v*	apisonado *v*	alija *v*
adiar *v*	apitonado *v*	aloja *v*
alias *nmn*	apiñonado *adj*	aluna *v*
aliar *v*	**apiojado** *v*	aluza *v*
alicorear *v*	apiolado *v*	amuja *v*
alicortar *v*	...	atuja *v*
...	**cuando** *adv*	aduja *v*
bajas *nfp*	ciando *v*	aguja *v*
balas *nfp*	cuanto *adv*	**alumbra** *v*
batas *nfp*	puando *v*	adumbra *v*
bayas *nfp*	ruando *v*	alambra *v*
bazas *nfp*	**cuanto** *adv*	...
babas *nfp*	cuando *adv*	
cajas *nfp*	**cuartando** *v*	

The meaning of the marks next to the words is as follows: *nms* stands for noun, masculine, singular; *nmn* for noun, masculine, neutral number, *nfp* for noun, feminine, plural; *ncp* for noun, common gender, plural; *adj* for adjective, *v* for verb, *adv* for adverb. In the examples one can observe mixed groups, in which substitutes for a word of a certain morphological part of speech is a word of another morphological part of speech, though the same syntactic function: for example, (*el*) *aliar* / (*el*) *alias*.

The statistics for each type of grammemes and totaling parameters are in Table 1.

Table 1. Statistics of the dictionary on grammeme basis

Syntactic part of speech	Source entries	Entries with paronyms	Average group
Nouns masculine singular, with infinitives	24,805	8,598	2.73
Nouns masculine plural	9,568	2,034	2.38
Nouns feminine singular	11,656	2,862	2.89
Nouns feminine plural	7,901	1,864	2.66
Adjectives with participles	23,255	6,349	2.14
Adverbs with gerunds	13,592	5,775	3.03
Verbs in infinitive	11,831	5,385	2.99
Verbs in 3rd person present indicative	11,785	5,512	2.96
Total	**114,393**	**38,379**	**2.74**

One can see that the entries with paronyms cover ca. 33.6% of the source dictionary and amount ca. 38 thousand of the entries of the compiled dictionary. On average, the groups of paronyms contain 2.74 elements, this figure weakly depending on a specific grammeme.

The main gain in candidate search is reached due to looking up only the candidates given in the paronymy dictionary. Using the total number of tries for a 9-letter Spanish word, we get the gain coefficient $G_1 = 616 / 2.74 = 225$.

The source dictionary contains ca. 114,000 grammemes and the revealed paronymous grammemes are supposedly the most frequent among them. With the reasonable assumption that the rank distribution of all words in the dictionary conforms to Zipf law, we have the additional gain coefficient $G_2 = \ln 114,300 / \ln 38,400 = 1.103$ due to that all other 75,900 grammemes are ignored in the candidate search. The total gain is $G_1 \times G_2 \approx 248$.

5   Resources for Testing Collocations

The developed dictionary of paronyms can be used only in conjunction with a resource for testing whether or not a given pair of content words can constitute a collocation. In [3] two such resources have been proposed, with different strategy of the decision.

The resource of the first type is a machine-readable collocation base. For English, the market can only propose Oxford collocations dictionary [8] in printed form. However, the availability of the large collocation base for Russian [2] shows that such bases will be at hand for other languages in the foreseeable future.

Two words V and W are admitted to form a collocation recorded in this collocation base if both words are in its dictionary and potential syntactical link between them corresponds to the features also recorded in the base.[2]

---

[2] Hence a simplistic syntactic analysis of the text under revision is necessary.

The resource of the second type can be a search engine for Internet, e.g., Google [3]. For using it, a simpler criterion of statistical nature is applied. The words V and W are considered combinable into a collocation, if the mutual information inequality is satisfied [7; cf. 10]:

$$\ln \frac{N(V,W)}{N_{max}} > \ln \frac{N(V)}{N_{max}} + \ln \frac{N(W)}{N_{max}}, \qquad (2)$$

where $N(V,W)$ is the number of web pages where V and W co-occur, $N(V)$ and $N(W)$ are the numbers of the web pages where each words occurs evaluated separately, and N_{max} is the total number of pages collected by Google for the given language. The latter value can be approximately calculated through the numbers of pages where the most used (functional) words of a given language occur [1]. It was shown [1] that the number of Spanish-language pages in Google was ca. 12.4 million at the end of 2002.

The inequality (2) rejects those potential collocations whose components co-occur in a statistically insignificant number.

6 Illustrative Examples

Let us track the occurrences of malapropisms in the following three intended Spanish sentences:

* *Seguimos la cadena causal entera* 'we follow the whole causal chain'.
* *La gente espera una tormenta de granizo* 'people expect a tempest of hail'.
* *Visitaremos el centro histórico* 'we will visit the historical center'.

The intended words are now changed to malapropos: *causal* to *casual*, *granizo* to *granito*, and *histórico* to *histérico*, given the following erroneous variants:

* *Seguimos la cadena <u>casual</u> entera* 'we follow the whole <u>casual</u> chain'.
* *La gente espera una tormenta de <u>granito</u>* 'people expect a tempest of <u>granite</u>'.
* *Visitaremos el centro <u>histérico</u>* 'we will visit the <u>hysterical</u> center'.

Let is trace the two different recourses for collocation testing.

Collocation base. In the base, the following collocations are supposed: *seguir la cadena, cadena causal, cadena entera, gente espera, esperar una tormenta, tormenta de granizo, visitar el centro, centro histórico*. At the same time, the malapropos combinations *cadena casual* 'casual chain', *tormenta de granito* 'tempest of granite', *tormenta de grafito* 'tempest of graphite', and *centro histérico 'hysterical center'* are not present in the base. Thus the malapropos words *casual, granito,* and *histérico* will be detected immediately. Accessing to dictionary of literal paronyms, we will find the following candidates: *causal* for *casual*; *grafito* and *granizo* for *granito*; *histórico* for *histérico*. The unique candidates among them correspond to collocations recorded in the base, thus indicating the true way for correction. Among the two options to correct the second sentence, only *granizo* restores the collocation, so only this word will be proposed to the user for correction.

Google. If only access to Google (but not to a collocation database) is available, malapropism detection and correction is possible on the statistical threshold rule (1). We gathered the necessary statistics of occurrences and co-occurrences in Google (see Table 2).

Table 2. Statistics for detection and correction

Intended combination	Statistics				
	Intend. combin.	Malaprop. combin.	1st word (invariable)	2nd word (intended)	2nd word (malapropos)
cadena causal	1,080	21	786,000	80,800	140,000
tormenta de granizo	802	0/0	191,000	30,900	98,100
centro histórico	110,000	75	403,000	883,000	10,600

One can see that malapropos word combinations occurred in insignificant numbers rejected by the statistical criterion after taking into account that all words under consideration are rather frequent in Internet. For the second sentence, both malapropos combination and the alternative candidate for correction (*grafito*) give zero number of co-occurrences among millions of Spanish web-pages.

Hence, the results are incentive to continue the research.

7   Conclusion and Future Work

To drastically speed up the search of candidates for malapropism correction, we have proposed a dictionary of literal paronyms. Such paronyms are real words at the distance 1 between them in the letter string space.

Significant limitations on further experimentations with our dictionary are laid by that

- We possess currently only a small collocation base for Spanish (less that 10,000) and its broadening will take some time.
- In statistical threshold formula, we use the number of strict co-occurrences of the collocation-forming words, while Google does not permit us to estimate more realistically the situations when these words are separated by several other words.

It is worthwhile to gather also literal paronyms distanced by 2. For example, the malapropos words in *materialismo dieléctrico* 'dielectric materialism' and in *orugas en la piel* 'tracks on the skin' are at the distance 2 from intended words *dialéctico* 'dialectic' and *arrugas* 'wrinkles'.

As another tool accelerating the candidate search, a dictionary of sound paronyms can be introduced. In Spanish, the sound distance between *k*, *qu* and *c* (before *a, e, u*) is equal to zero (all of them are pronounced as [k]), whereas in letter space this distance is 1 or 2; an example of English strings with zero distance in the sound is *right*, *Wright*, *write*. Thus, the transition to the phonological space can sometimes simplify the search.

References

1. Bolshakov, I. A., S. N. Galicia-Haro. *Can We Correctly Estimate the Total Number of Pages in Google for a Specific Language?* In: A. Gelbukh (Ed.) *CICLing-2003, Computational Linguistics and Intelligent Text Processing.* Lecture Notes in Computer Science, No. 2588, Springer-Verlag, 2003, p. 415-419.
2. Bolshakov, I. A., A. Gelbukh. *A Very Large Database of Collocations and Semantic Links.* In: M. Bouzeghoub *et al.* (Eds.) *NLDB-2000, Natural Language Processing and Information Systems.* Lecture Notes in Computer Science, No. 1959, Springer-Verag, 2001, p. 103-114.
3. Bolshakov, I. A., A. Gelbukh. *On Detection of Malapropisms by Multistage Collocation Testing.* In: A. Dusterhoft, B. Talheim (Eds.) 8th *Intern. Conference on Applications of Natural Language to Information Systems NLDB-2003,* GI-Edition, Lecture Notes in Informatics, v. P-29, Bonn, 2003, p. 28-41.
4. Hirst, G., D. St-Onge. *Lexical Chains as Representation of Context for Detection and Corrections of Malapropisms.* In: C. Fellbaum (ed.) *WordNet: An Electronic Lexical Database.* The MIT Press, 1998, p. 305-332.
5. Kashyap, R. L., B. I. Oomen. *An effective algorithm for string correction using generalized edit distances. I. Description of the algorithm and its optimality. Information Science,* 1981, Vol. 23, No. 2, p. 123-142.
6. Mays, E., F. J. Damerau, R. L. Mercer. *Context-based spelling correction. Information Processing and Management.* 1992, Vol. 27, No. 5, p. 517-522.
7. Manning, Ch. D., H. Schütze. *Foundations of Statistical Natural Language Processing.* The MIT Press, 1999.
8. *Oxford Collocations Dictionary for Students of English.* Oxford University Press. 2003.
9. Wagner, R.A., M. J. Fisher. *The string-to-string correction problem. J. ACM,* Vol. 21, No. 1, 1974, p. 168-173.
10. Biemann, C., S. Bordag, G. Heyer, U. Quasthoff, C. Wolff. *Language-independent Methods for Compiling Monolingual Lexical Data.* In A. Gelbukh (Ed.), *CICLing-2004, Computational Linguistics and Intelligent Text Processing.* Lecture Notes in Computer Science, N 2945, Springer, 2004, pp. 214-225.

Web-Based Sources for an Annotated Corpus Building and Composite Proper Name Identification

Sofía N. Galicia-Haro[1], Alexander Gelbukh[2,3], and Igor A. Bolshakov[2]

[1] Faculty of Sciences
UNAM Ciudad Universitaria Mexico City, Mexico
sngh@fciencias.unam.mx

[2] Center for Computing Research
National Polytechnic Institute, Mexico City, Mexico
{gelbukh,igor}@cic.ipn.mx; www.Gelbukh.com

[3] Department of Computer Science and Engineering, Chung-Ang University,
221 Huksuk-Dong, DongJak-Ku, Seoul, 156-756, Korea

Abstract. Nowadays, collections of texts with annotations on several levels are useful resources. Huge efforts are required to develop this resource for languages like Spanish. In this work, we present the initial step, lexical level annotation, for the compilation of an annotated Mexican corpus using Web-based sources. We also describe a method based on heterogeneous knowledge and simple Web-based sources for the proper name identification required in such annotation. We focused our work on composite entities (names with coordinated constituents, names with several prepositional phrases, and names of songs, books, movies, etc.). The preliminary obtained results are presented.

1. Introduction

Obtaining usage information of language from collections of texts, i.e. corpus, has been a common practice in lexicography. In natural language processing, the use of very large corpora is also a common practice for linguistic phenomena research that mainly appears in unrestricted materials. Researches recognize the potential of very large corpus usage for problem solving in the lexical, syntactic and semantic levels of analysis. However, the useful corpora required in natural language processing need annotations, i.e., lexical, syntactic and semantic marks.

Training methods to resolve distinct natural language processing tasks have been the main usage of annotated corpus. Manual work is the most employed method and the more accurate for corpus compilation and annotation. To reduce economic and manual efforts we intend to make by automatic processes most of the work to compile and annotate such type of corpus.

There is a wide range of possible usages of the WEB for corpus construction, from a specific retrieval of contexts [7] to a whole use, since it has been even proposed to use the WEB itself as a very huge corpus [8]. We use the Web as the main source of appropriate Mexican texts for our purposes. We selected four Mexican newspapers daily published in the Web with a high proportion of their paper publication.

J. Favela et al. (Eds.): AWIC 2004, LNAI 3034, pp. 115–124, 2004.
© Springer-Verlag Berlin Heidelberg 2004

After text processing of Web-based sources for adequate format assignment we found that almost 50% of the total unknown words were proper names. Proper names have been mainly studied in the field of Information Extraction that requires the robust handle of proper names for successful performance in diverse tasks as pattern filling with correct entities that perform semantic roles [11]. The research fulfilled in the Message Understanding Conference (MUC) structure entity name task and it distinguishes three types: ENAMEX, TIMEX and NUMEX [5]. In this paper, we are concerned with ENAMEX entity (organizations, persons and localities) identification but we focused our work on names with coordinated constituents, names with several prepositional phrases, and titles.

Name entity recognition (NER) works in MUC have been dedicated to English. NER works in Language-Independent NER, the shared task of Computational Natural Language Learning (CoNLL) covered Spanish in 2002 [14]. A wide variety of machine learning techniques was used with good results for name entity (NE) classification. However composite names were limited: NE are non-recursive and non-overlapping, in case a NE is embedded in another one only the top level entity was marked, and test files do not include proper names with coordinated constituents.

In this work, we present some observations and results about text collection compilation, then we describe the development of the lexical annotation for our corpus. Then we present the heterogeneous method for proper name identification, it is based on local context, rules, statistics, heuristics and the use of Web-based lists. We present the definition of composite proper names, the method to identify them and finally the obtained results.

2. Characteristics of Annotated Corpus

Corpus compilation implies different problem solutions of the self texts. Ideally, it is desirable to obtain a large and representative sample of general language, it could be expected a larger quantity of words as longer is the corpus. A big quantity of words should imply bigger dictionary language coverage and it mainly should imply greater evidence of the diverse linguistic phenomena required. To be representative supposes several cultural language levels, several themes and genres. However these qualities do not imply each other, in some cases instead they are contrary. One contraposition that must be considered is that between quality and quantity. A big corpus does not guarantee to posses the expected quality.

The corpus should be balanced among those qualities. However, it seems to be not possible to balance appropriately a corpus, not without huge effort. In addition the sampling methods are quite expensive, for example those for quality selection. To reduce time and costs we must assume the obvious problems related to work with unbalanced data.

Because of the huge efforts to compile a corpus with all desired qualities, we limited the corpus qualities to those that are relevant for our goals: required information and size. The main goal for the Mexican corpus compilation is the syntactic analysis of unrestricted texts, similar to those of newspaper texts. One of the main problems in the syntactic analysis is the correct attachment of noun and prepositional phrases.

Therefore, it is important that the corpus contains extensive use of prepositional phrases and predicates.

About information required in a corpus, for example, [2] notes different use of prepositional phrases according to the text genre. [13] found significant differences of subcategorization frequencies in different corpus. Discourse and semantic influence were identified as the sources for those differences. The former is caused by the changes of language form used in different types of discourse. The semantic influence is based on semantic context of discourse. Therefore a corpus with different genres should be quite adequate for our goal.

About the big size of the corpus, the current corpora have a range from millions of words to hundred of millions of words depending on its type, i.e. plain text or diverse type of annotations. [1] argue that a corpus must be big enough to avoid sparse data and reflect natural use of language in order to obtain a good probability approximation. They use the one million of words Wall Street Journal corpus. Other authors, on the contrary, do not use the whole corpus for their research but a subcorpus with specific characteristics [12] which requires huge manual efforts. Therefore, we consider the size of tenths of millions of words and Web-based sources.

2.1. Corpus Annotation

There are several levels for corpus annotation: lexical, syntactic, semantic, etc. and even more levels of annotation could exist inside each level. Lemma and part of speech assignments are considered in lexical annotation. There is a wide variety of annotation schemes. For example, the Penn Tree-bank [9] uses 36 marks for part of speech and 12 for punctuation and other symbols. The Brown Corpus [6] uses 87 simple annotations but it permits composed annotations.

The sentence structure in the syntactic level is generally showed grouping words by parenthesis, and labeling those groups additionally. Since a complete structure requires more learning time of the scheme by annotators and more time for sentence annotation, there are different grades of sentence hierarchic structure realization. For example, in the Penn Tree-bank development the distinction of sentence arguments and adjuncts was ignored in a first stage. Nevertheless, the argument annotation is crucial for the semantic interpretation of verbs. In the semantic level, it has been considered the signification annotation and a type of concept.

The first step in the compilation of a Mexican Spanish corpus is the lexical level; other stages will consider the syntactic and semantic annotation.

3. Corpus Compilation

3.1. Plain Text and Word Compound

The WEB organization of the four Mexican newspapers daily published permitted us an automatic extraction for monthly and yearly periods in a quite short time. The texts correspond to diverse sections: economy, politics, culture, sport, etc. from 1998 to 2002.

The size of the original texts was 2540 MB from which we obtain 1592 MB in plain text with some marks. These texts were obtained by the following steps:
1. HTML labels deleting. Since there is no consistent use of HTML formats even inside each newspaper, several programs were developed to obtain plain texts.
2. Article structure assignment. The texts were automatically labeled with marks of title, subtitle, text body and paragraph. The paragraph assignment was respected as it was defined in the Internet publication (not exactly as its paper publication). The paragraphs were automatically split in sentences by means of punctuation-based heuristics.
3. "Wrong" and "correct" word assignment. We obtained all different words from the texts. The "correct" words were automatically annotated using the orthographic tool of a word processor and two Spanish dictionaries. Therefore, "correct" words were those recognized by such resources. Initially, from 747,970 total different words, 60% were marked as wrong words, among them we encountered the following three cases:

a) Some specific Mexican words. A manual non exhaustive work let us identify words used in Mexico that does not appear in DRAE[1], neither in María Moliner dictionary, like *ámpula*, but it appears in DEUM[2]. Other "wrong" words were words of Indian origin (náhuatl, maya, otomí, etc.). For example: *zotehuela, xochimilca, xoconostle*, etc.

To override this problem we obtained lists of this type of words from the WEB and from specialized manuals in order to compare text words against that of Web-based sources. We obtained a new group of "correct" words of Indian origin.

b) Word forms not contained in dictionaries. Some heuristics based on suffixes were used to detect diminutives, plurals and other regular word forms.

c) Composed words by hyphens. Groups of words connected by hyphens are quite common in English. On the contrary, stylistic Spanish manuals suggest a minimal use of hyphens. However, newspaper texts show the use of hyphens for diverse purposes:
- Emphasize a group of words. Ex: *única-y-mejor-ruta* (the only and best route)
- Evocate slogans. Ex: *sí-se-puede* (it is possible)
- Indicate slow pronunciation of one word. Ex: *é-x-i-t-o* (successful).
- Give different attributes. Ex: *étnico-nacionalista* (ethnical, nationalist)
- Show links among corporations or real names. Ex: *ABB-Alsthom, ADM-Dreyfus-Novartis-Maseca*
- Give a route. Ex: *Durango-Zacatecas*
- For some English words. Ex: *e-mail, e-business, zig-zag*, etc.
- Indicate football matches or other kind of sport games. Ex. *Pachuca-Santos*.

There were found some mistakes introduced by copying texts of the newspaper edition containing the natural use of hyphens for syllable separation. Ex: *De-rechos* (ri-ghts)

All the previous cases were treated first as a compound of words if the words individually could be considered as "correct" words. If such heuristic was wrong a second one treats them as a one word, joining the elements divided by hyphens, if the whole element could be found as a "correct" word. In general, a tag of noun or adjective can

---

[1] Spanish language dictionary of the Real Spanish Academy. Espasa, Calpe, 21 ed. 1995
[2] Usual Spanish in Mexico Dictionary. Ed. Colegio de México. México, 1996.

be assigned. Future work should consider some semantic mark-up for all detected uses of hyphens.

Since the orthography of words of Indian origin is not quite well known by Mexican speakers, there are many spelling mistakes of this type. A future work will consider some kind of error correction, since typographic error, spelling check errors and words in capital letters without accents were considered as wrong words.

4. Linking of composed prepositions. There are many composed prepositions in Spanish besides simple prepositions. Words groups as *al cabo de, con respecto a*, require a manipulation as a set (*con_respecto_a, a_fin_de, al_cabo_de*).

5. Foreign words. The Web-based sources contain foreign words. We use the orthographic tool of a word processor to detect some English and French "correct" words.

6. Proper names annotation. There were found 168,333 different words with capital letters either initializing each word or totally filling them. They are repeated in the texts counting 1804,959 occurrences. Initially, manual work was considered for 160 words having more than 1000 occurrences but they count only 420964 of total words (23% of total occurrences). Therefore, some kind of proper name identification is necessary.

- Acronyms. Ex: PRD, PT, ONU
- Proper names including prepositions and coordination. Ex: *Convergencia por la Democracia, Ley del Impuesto sobre la Renta, Luz y Fuerza del Centro.*
- Names. Ex: *San Lázaro, Benito Juárez, El séptimo sello.*

The corpus building involves tasks of different nature as we already described in the above subsections. Among them the detection of correct words and the proper name identification are required. The former needs complex tools to detect and correct wrong spelling. The second is being developed and it is described in sections 4 and 5.

3.2. Lexical Level Annotation

There are Spanish corpora with lexical level annotations, for example the LEXESP[3] corpus. As LEXESP corpus has been used for research purposes at our laboratory, we decided to use the same 275 different lexical labels for our corpus. The main reason for such quantity of labels in Spanish is agreement (gender, person and number).

The LEXESP corpus has the PAROLE[4] categories that considers the following POS classification:

- Adjective (A). Example: *frágiles* <AQ0CP00>
- Adverb (R). Example: *no* <RG000>
- Article (T). Example: *la* <TDFS0>
- Determinant (D), see figure 1. Example: *tal* <DD0CS00>
- Noun (N). Example: *señora* <NCFS000>
- Verb (V). Example: *acabó* <VMIS3S0>

---

[3] The LEXESP corpus was kindly provided by H. Rodríguez from Universidad Politécnica de Cataluña, Barcelona, Spain.

[4] http://www.ub.es/gilcub/castellano/proyectos/europeos/parole.html

Table 1. Characteristics of determinants

Type		Person	Gender		Number		Case	Posses
Value	Key		Value	Key	Value	Key		
Demonstrative	D	1	Feminine	F	Singular	S	0	0
Possessive	P	2	Masculine	M	Plural	P		
Interrogative	T	3	Common	C	Invariable	N		
Exclamatory	E							
Undefined	I							

- Pronoun (P). Example: *ella* <PP3FS000>
- Conjunctions (C). Example: *y* <CC00>
- Numerals (M). Example: *cinco* <MCCP00>
- Prepositions (SPS00). Example: *ante* <SPS00>
- Numbers (Z). Example: *5000* <Z>
- Interjections (I). Example: *oh* <I>
- Abbreviations (Y). Example: *etc.* <Y>
- Punctuation (F). All punctuation signs (.,:;-¡!'¿?"%). Example: "." <Fp>
- Residuals (X). The words that do not fit in previous categories. Ex.: *sine* <X>
  (Latin)

Example of the POS for the ambiguous word *bajo*:

```
bajo   bajar(verb)     <VMIP1S0>   bajo(preposition) <SPS00>
       bajo(adverb)    <RG000>     bajo(noun) <NCMS000>
       bajo(adjective) <AQ0MS00>
```

We only detail the complete key in PAROLE for determinants (see Table 1), showing the considered features. The "common" value in gender is employed for both feminine and masculine, for example *alegre* (cheerful). The "invariable" value in number is used for both singular and plural, for example: *se* (personal pronoun).

The POS annotation was realized with the MACO [4] program developed by the Natural Language Processing group of the Artificial Intelligence section of Software Department in Polytechnic University of Catalonia in collaboration with the Computational Linguistic Laboratory of the Barcelona University. In addition, some modifications have been included in the labels to consider marks for clitics inside verbal forms.

4. Composite Proper Names in Newspaper Texts

We selected one Mexican newspaper (MNP#2) in order to analyze how composite proper names could be identified and delimited. A Perl program extracted groups of words that we called "compounds" containing capitalized words joined with no more than three functional words. They were left and right limited by a punctuation mark and a non-capitalized word if they exist. We manually analyzed the compounds of approximately 2000 sentences randomly selected.

We classified the proper names in two categories: non-ambiguous and ambiguous identification.

Non-ambiguous identification. Most of compounds without functional words are proper names with non-ambiguous identification, mainly those with high frequency scores. Other characteristics defining non-ambiguous identification are: 1) Redundancy: information obtained from juxtaposition of proper names and acronyms, for example: *Asociación Rural de Interés Colectivo (ARIC)*, and 2) Flexibility: long proper names do not appear as fixed forms. For example: *Instituto para la Protección al Ahorro, Instituto para la Protección al Ahorro Bancario, Instituto para la Protección del Ahorro Bancario*, all of them correspond to the same entity. More variety exists for names translated from foreign languages but the differences are functional words.

Ambiguous identification. Three main syntactic causes of ambiguous identification are: coordination, prepositional phrase attachment, and embedded sentences. The last one corresponds to names composed of several words where only the first one is capitalized, titles of songs, books, etc. As far as we observed, the titles found in MNP#2 are no delimited by punctuation marks. This use is rather different to that considered in CoNLL-2002 files, where the titles are delimited by quotation marks.

- *Coordination.* In the simpler and more usual case, two names with the conjunction cover the last embedded substructure. For example: *Ley de Armas de Fuego y Explosivos, Instituto Nacional de Antropología e Historia*. However, there are other cases where the coordinated pair is an internal substructure of the entire name, for example: *Mesa de [Cultura y Derechos] Indígenas*. Other compounds are ambiguous since one coordinated name could be also coordinated, for example: *Comisión Federal de Electricidad y Luz y Fuerza del Centro, Margarita Diéguez y Armas y Carlos Virgilio*.
- *Prepositional phrases.* We consider a diverse criterion than that considered in CoNLL: in case a NE is embedded in another one or in case a NE is composed of several entities all should be identified since syntactic analysis should find their relations for deep understanding. For example: *Teatro y Danza de la UNAM* (UNAM's Theater and Dance), *Comandancia General del Ejército Zapatista de Liberación Nacional* (General command of..) A specific grammar for composite proper name identification should cope with the already known prepositional phrase attachment problem. Therefore, diverse knowledge was considered to decide on splitting or joining prepositional phrases.

5. Method

Identification of composite proper names in our texts collection was mainly based on their syntactic-semantic context, on discourse factors and on their specific construction. The heterogeneous knowledge contributions required are:
- *Local context.* It has been considered in different tasks. We use it for title identification. Two words preceding the capitalized word were defined as left limit; one of them could be a cue of the manually compiled list of 26 items plus synonyms and variants (gender, number). For example, in the following sentences the cue is underlined: *En su libro La razón de mi vida (Editorial Pax)*... (In his book The reason of my life (Pax publisher), ...*comencé a releer La edad de la discreción de Simone de Beauvoir*,... (I began to reread Simone de Beauvoir's The age of discretion),

...en su programa Una ciudad para todos que... (in his program A city for all that ...)

The right limit consider all posterior words until a specific word or punctuation sign is found, they could be: 1) proper name, 2) sign of punctuation (period [10], comma, semicolon, etc.) and/or 3) conjunction. In the above examples: "(", "*Simone de Beauvoir*" and the conjunction "que" delimit the names.

- *Linguistic knowledge.* It is settled by linguistic restrictions, they mainly correspond to preposition use, discourse structure and punctuation rules. For example: 1) lists of groups of capitalized words are similar entities, and then the last one should be a different coordinated entity. For example: *Corea del Sur, Taiwan, Checoslovaquia y Sudáfrica.* 2) preposition use, considering the localization meaning, direction meaning, etc. For example: two proper names joined by destination preposition ("a", "hasta") should be separated if they are preceded by a preposition denoting an origin position ("de", "desde"). For example: *de Salina Cruz a Juchitán.*
- *Lists.* Many NER systems use lists of names. We included two Web-based sources (list of personal names: 697 items, list of main Mexican cities: 910 items) and one manually compiled list of similes [3] to disambiguate identification of coordinated proper names.
- *Heuristics.* One example is: a personal name should not be coordinated in a single proper name. For example: *Margarita Diéguez y Armas y Carlos Virgilio*, where Carlos is an item of personal names list.
- *Statistics.* Statistics of groups of capitalized words were obtained from MNP#2 (from one word to three contiguous words, capitalized words related to acronyms). The top statistics for such groups were used to split composite names, for example: *Comandancia General del Ejército Zapatista de Liberación Nacional* could be separated in: *Comandancia General* and *Ejército Zapatista de Liberación Nacional.*

Knowledge application

A Perl program process sentences in two steps to disambiguate identification of composite proper names: 1) compounds extraction using a dictionary with part of speech, 2) decision on splitting, delimiting or leaving as is each compound. The order of decisions in the second step is: 1) look up the compound in the acronym list, 2) decide on coordinated groups ambiguity using the list of similes, rules, and statistics, 3) decide on prepositional phrase ambiguity using rules, lists, heuristics and statistics, 4) delimit possible titles using context cues, rules, and statistics, and 5) decide on the rest of groups of capitalized words using heuristics and statistics.

Results

We test the method on 200 sentences of MNP#4. They were manually annotated and compared against the results of the method. The results are presented in **Table 2** where:

Precision: # of correct entities detected / # of entities detected
Recall: # of correct entities detected / # of entities manually labelled

Table 2. Results in a testing set of sentences

	NUMBER OF:			
	COORD. GROUPS	PREP. PHRASE GROUPS	TITLES	ALL
Precision	61	70	55	88
Recall	51	68	55	85

Table 2 indicates the performance for coordinated names (53 items), prepositional groups (84 items), and titles (11 items). The last column shows the performance for total proper names (753 items) including the previous ones. The main causes of errors were: 1) over splitting of prepositional phrases, 2) foreign words (names, cities, prepositions), 3) names missing in the available lists, and 4) missing signs for delimitation of titles and punctuation marks inside titles.

Conclusions

We presented the development of a resource for the linguistic processing of Mexican Spanish texts: a collection of Web-based sources to build an annotated corpus. We detailed the things found and results on text collection, processed automatically. We explained the process used for part of speech annotation. The main advantage of our method is that most of the work was realized in an automatic form to reduce time and costs.

One of the main problems in lexical level annotation was proper name identification. We present a method for identification of composite proper names (names with coordinated constituents, names with several prepositional phrases, and names of songs, books, movies, etc.). We are interested in minimum use of complex tools. Therefore, our method use extremely small lists and a dictionary with part of speech. Since limited resources use cause robust and velocity of execution.

The strategy of our method is the use of heterogeneous knowledge to decide on splitting or joining groups of capitalized words. Results were obtained on 200 sentences corresponding to different topics. The preliminary results show the possibilities of the method.

References

1. Berthouzoz, C. and Merlo, P. Statistical ambiguity resolution for principle-based parsing. In Proceedings of the Recent Advances in Natural Language Processing (1997) 179–186
2. Biber, D. Using Register. Diversified Corpora for general Language Studies. Computational Linguistics Vol. 19–2 (1993) 219—241
3. Bolshakov, I. A., A. F. Gelbukh, and S. N. Galicia-Haro: Stable Coordinated Pairs in Text Processing. In Václav Matoušek and Pavel Mautner (Eds.). Text, Speech and Dialogue. Lecture Notes in Artificial Intelligence, N 2807, Springer-Verlag (2003) 27–35

4. Carmona, J., S. Cervell, L. Màrquez, M.A. Martí, L. Padró, R. Placer, H. Rodríguez, M. Taulé & J. Turmo. An Environment for Morphosyntactic Processing of Unrestricted Spanish Text. First International Conference on Language Resources and Evaluation. Granada, Spain (1998)
5. Chinchor N.: MUC-7 Named Entity Task Definition http://www.itl.nist.gov/iaui/894.02/ relatedprojects/muc/proceedings/muc7toc.html#appendices (1997)
6. Francis, W. N. and Henry Kučera. Frequency Análisis of English Usage: Lexicon and Grammar. Houghton Mifflin (1982)
7. Gelbukh, A., G. Sidorov, and L. Chanona-Hernández. Compilation of a Spanish representative corpus. Proc. CICLing-2002, 3rd International Conference on Intelligent Text Processing and Computational Linguistics, Mexico City. Lecture Notes in Computer Science N 2276, Springer-Verlag (2002) 285–288
8. Kilgariff, A. *Web as corpus*. In: Proc. of Corpus Linguistics Conference, Lancaster University (2001) 342–344
9. Marcus, M., Santorini, B. and Marcinkiewicz, M. Building a large annotated corpus of English The Penn Treebank. Computational Linguistics Vol.19–2 (1993)
10. Mikheev A.: Periods, Capitalized Words, etc. http://www.ltg.ed.ac.uk/~mikheev/ papers.html
11. MUC: Proceedings of the Sixth Message Understanding Conference. (MUC-6). Morgan Kaufmann (1995) http://www.itl.nist.gov/iaui/894.02/related_projects/tipster/muc.htm
12. Ratnaparkhi, A. Statistical Models for Unsupervised Prepositional Phrase Attachment. In Proceedings of the 36th Annual Meeting of the Association for Computational Linguistics. Montreal, Quebec, Canada (1998) http://xxx.lanl.gov/ps/cmp-lg/9807011
13. Roland. D. and D. Jurafsky. How Verb Subcategorization Frequencies are Effected by Corpus Choice. In Proc. International Conference COLING-ACL'98. Quebec, Canada (1998) 1122–1128
14. Tjong Kim Sang, Erik F. Introduction to the CoNLL-2002 Shared Task: Language-Independent Named Entity Recognition. http://lcg-www.uia.ac.be/~erikt/papers/

Intelligent Automated Navigation through the Deep Web

Vicente Luque Centeno, Carlos Delgado Kloos, Luis Sánchez Fernández, and
Norberto Fernández García

Departamento de Ingeniería Telemática
Universidad Carlos III de Madrid,
Avda. Universidad, 30, E-28911 Leganés, Madrid, Spain

Abstract. The Deep Web, considered as the amount of built-on-demand
(non pre-built) Web pages has become a very important part of the Web,
not only because of its enormous size (it might considered that it is significantly bigger that the Superficial pre-built Web [12]), but because
these Web pages usually contain customized information extracted from
databases according to specific user's requests. These pages are commonly robot-unreachable, usually requiring a login identification process
or filling in some forms. Since pages within the Deep Web must be obtained within a navigation process, it is common that a single URL may
not be enough for reaching them, so full **navigation paths** need to be
stablished, usually by starting at a well-known URL and following some
links and filling in some forms.
On the other hand, Web Intelligence in a Web client might be considered as the property of properly combining several distributed data for
solving a specific problem. Automated navigation through the Deep Web
needs intelligence in order to reach relevant data which can be further
computed. Web automated navigation involves both **inter-document**
and **intra-document** navigations. Without intelligence at any of these
two, Web clients can not stablish proper Web Navigation paths to those
relevant data.
This article presents an approach to formalize specifications of automated
navigation on the Deep Web. These formalization has been expressed
both graphically and textually in a combination of two languages for
defining intelligent Web navigation behaviours at Web clients. Running
examples of programs developed with these languages have been successfully developed and tested on legacy well known Web sites with low cost
and a relatively high robustness.
Keywords: agents, target-oriented Web navigation, deep Web, legacy
Web, Web navigation paths

1 Introduction

The World Wide Web has rapidly expanded as the largest human knowledge
repository. Database managers have found on the Web an easy way to publish
enormous amounts of information anytime anywhere. Personalized Web sites

J. Favela et al. (Eds.): AWIC 2004, LNAI 3034, pp. 125–134, 2004.
© Springer-Verlag Berlin Heidelberg 2004

have become commonly used so that users can manage fruitful & dynamic information within them by just providing a login and a password and navigating within a customized Web site. Banking accounts, enterprises' intranets, auction Web sites, Web mail servers and a huge increasing amount of sites provide customized, dynamic and relevant information to their users once they get identified. However, users usually spend a lot of effort by interacting with these Web sites with browsers, because relevant information can usually be found disseminated. Intelligence could be used to properly combine all those Web-disseminated data and compute final results according to user's needs.

The W3C Semantic Web initiative [3] tries to solve this by explicitly declaring semantic descriptions in (typically RDF [16] and OWL [20]) metadata associated to Web pages and ontologies combined with semantic rules. This way, inference-enabled agents may deduce which actions (links to be followed, forms to be filled, ...) should be executed in order to retrieve the results for a user's query.

However, legacy Web sites don't provide support for Semantic Web techniques. Data not only should be properly extracted. It should also be properly homogeneized and combined with other heterogeneous relevant data in order to compute some results. These *intelligent* combinations might be difficult-to-be-expressed only with declarative metadata and semantic rules. However, expressing intelligence with data combinations within an imperative algorithm might be powerful enough to perform complex tasks, even though specific imperative algorithms can be difficultly be reused for other purposes.

2   Navigation Paths

Fortunately, it is possible to build task-oriented Web clients that automate these tasks for the user [6]. These programs need to automatically select and follow links and fill in forms emulating a human user behind a browser, but presenting only the final results for her, requiring less user's interactivity. These Web clients, referred as **wrapper agents** [5], can be used to automate tasks performed over well known Web sites, specially those involving a large amount of data or navigation paths which need some steps to be followed. Wrapper agents are also suitable for data integration across heterogeneous information sources.

Wrapper agents are quite different from search engine robots. Generic robots have no navigation path to be followed and they navigate through the superficial Web site (prebuilt pages), performing very simple generic tasks, having rather simple textual data extraction and performing simple computation with extracted data (mainly database indexation). Wrapper agents, instead, only follow links belonging to a well known **navigation path**. They might navigate through Deep Web sites, extracting only relevant data found within that path with powerful extraction rules and performing *ad-hoc* computation with those extracted data. Wrapper agents are useful for developing mediators that combine heterogeneous information from several information sources and automating complex tasks for the user.

Navigation paths should intelligently be specified in order to navigation agents can successfully arrive to relevant data. Navigation paths, in order to be fully specified should consist on both a **inter-document** and a **intra-document** navigation.

2.1 Inter-document Navigation

Inter-document navigation consists on obtaining from the (Deep) Web all those relevant documents which are needed to perform a specific task. Inter-document navigation should be aware to maintain session behaviours (cookies, referrer header, hidden form fields, dynamic urls, ...) to achieve that server applications can assimilate HTTP transactions belonging to the same HTTP session. Inter-document navigation involves both GET and POST HTTP requests as if they were requested by any human-driven browser.

Not only GET requests are needed to navigate to a well-known URL. Navigation paths might rarely be modelled as a URL list. Since URLs need to be properly found during the navigation path, being extracted from previously visited pages, only the initial URL should be *a-priori* known. Any other URL for GET or POST requests must be obtained during navigation, properly maintaining cookies, referrers and any other low level HTTP feature as a browser would do. Most packages, applications or libraries [2, 23, 1, 15, 13] for developing automated Web clients have little support for properly managing HTTP session support. However, we have extended the WebL [9] platform to provide further *inter-document* navigation support, specially for forms (hidden form fields, higher level of form filling) and SSL support.

2.2 Intra-document Navigation

Intra-document navigation consists of deeply analyzing documents retrieved by inter-document navigation in order to extract any relevant data to be further computed and intelligently combined with other different data (maybe from the same document, maybe from others). Intra-document navigation should be aware to the inherent semi-structured nature of HTML pages, firstly extracting any relevant data from the page and secondly computing some results. These results might be a result for the user, a partial/temporal result or just a URL or query-string that next inter-document navigation step should be aware of.

Data extraction from HTML pages becomes difficult, not only because HTML pages from different Web sites are rather heterogeneous and have little structuration, but because HTML tags are not very *semantically* expressive. Metadata and ontologies are usually desirable to automatically detect the nature of different parts of data. However, legacy HTML pages have no such metadata. Even more, since legacy HTML pages rarely conform to a well defined grammar like XHTML [14], RDF metadata can difficultly be applied.

Relevant data extraction techniques as regular expressions, SAX [10], DOM [18], JDOM [8], XSLT [17], XPath [21], XPointer [19] or XQuery [22] have been successfully applied to XML-ized HTML pages with different effort measures.

From all of them, XPath has been considered as a data extraction language suitable for our platform. Every page obtained from the inter-document navigation is internally processed by Tidy [11] in order to obtain a equivalent XHTML representation. XPath expressions can then safely be evaluated to address relevant parts of the documents considered as relevant. These parts of the document can be processed in order to be stored at local repositories, combined with some other data or simply considered for further inter-document navigation steps. XPath expressions result much simpler than SAX or DOM-like rules because XPath expressions provide a single-line, neutral, standard expression suitable for maintenance when structural changes occur in HTML visited pages. Maintenance cost is very important to be minimized in order to navigation paths can be properly be followed.

Though most usual data extractions can be safely be computed with XPath expressions, several data extraction rules might depend on other several addressing mechanisms, like XPointer's positions, or XQuery contextualization variables. For this reason, a new language, based on an extension of a subset of XPath 2.0 plus several new operators, has been defined. This language, called XTendedPath, can be safely used for intra-document navigation on mostly any HTML part of a Web page. Other language, called **XPlore**, has been defined for inter-document navigation. XPlore is both a graphical and textual formalism based on the **Message Sequence Charts** (MSC) [7], a formal method defined by the ITU (International Telecommunication Union) for specifying behaviours in distributed middle-ware systems. Combination of both XPlore (for inter-document navigation) and XTendedPath (for intra-document navigation) languages, as described in [4], can be used to express navigation paths to be surfed in the *deep Web*. A platform providing execution support for these two languages has also been implemented and successfully tested.

Once all relevant data are available at structured local repositories, further computing is often required to be performed over them, like comparisons, accumulations, re-orderings, or any kind of semantic reasoning which may decide things like which link should be followed next or whether an information retrieval process is near from being concluded. Though this computations can be easily programmed with any imperative programming language, Web site navigation skills need to be considered as well. XTendedPath is also well suited for defining user defined behaviours to be performed over data obtained from extraction rules.

3   Platform Support

XPlore programs are not directly compiled or interpreted as other programming languages. Though this could be possible, a more effective solution has been found by translating XPlore programs into well known programming languages which will indeed implement the required functionality in programmed libraries. Traducing XPlore programs to almost any programming language, like C or Java, is not difficult if good support is provided at system libraries. Our current prototype is able to translate XPlore programs to the WebL programming language [9]. WebL has been chosen because its good support for HTTP management. However, translation to other languages could also be possible.

One major lack of our platform nowadays consists in its lack of support of JavaScript execution. This has been solved by letting assistants to emulate JavaScript defined behaviour within their own code. This results in a major development effort, since JavaScript inverse engineering needs to be performed, though this is not always needed. However, XPlore and XTendedPath expressions can be easily used to emulate these actions.

4   Commented Example: Yahoo! Mail

A commented example showing XPlore usability is found in this section, where a graphically designed and implemented program lists messages from Yahoo! mail spool and deletes messages selected by some simple pattern matching. The navigation path, as shown at figure 1 starts by a well known URL at Yahoo! for having access to a mail account. This main page is retrieved from Yahoo! server through an HTTP GET request and stored as the first step on the navigation path. P1 variable can be considered as a repository for that page. After P1's retrieval, some intra-document navigation needs to be performed in order to manipulate P1's form. Two simple XPath expressions can be used to address form textual fields for login and password input fields and fill them with user defined data (her user identification). P1's form is then filled in and a boolean variable for looping control is initialized with a **true** value.

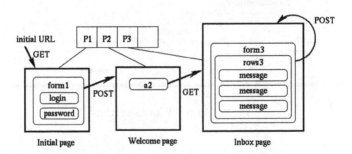

Fig. 1. Navigation path at Yahoo!

Next inter-document step involves posting P1's form. The query-string to be posted is extracted from P1's form's internal representation (the same where values were filled in by the user). Action's URL is extracted from P1's **action** attribute, as a browser would do. This URL is not hardcoded within the program, but dynamically extracted from a visited document with intra-document navigation, imitating a browser's behaviour. Yahoo! Web server receives the POST request, and, if identification was OK at Yahoo!, a page containing a *Welcome* message is returned and stored at P2 variable at the client side (if a wrong login and password pair is provided, P2 would be assigned a *Retry* message). P2 does not have yet included complete information on our mail inbox, but it contains a link where this can be obtained. In order to arrive to that page, a link containing the words *Bandeja entrada* (*mail inbox* in English) should be followed. a2 variable addresses such link with a XPath expression. Figure 2 shows the main XPlore navigation diagram for this task.

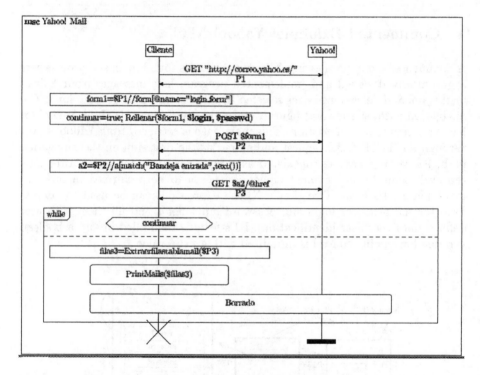

Fig. 2. Main XPlore diagram

Next page should be obtained with the URL specified in a2's `href` attribute. By following such link, P3 page is obtained from Yahoo! P3 contains the most important information about the most recent 25 messages in our incoming mail box. Relevant data of this page consists of a table containing major information of messages in our inbox. Figure 3 is a typical visualization window of this page, when viewed with a browser. The structure of this page is repeatedly used on any paginated message listing found within Yahoo! mail pages.

Next step in our task consists on printing header information for all incoming messages within that page. `rows3` variable is used to address the list of all messages declared within that page (as HTML table rows within the central table).

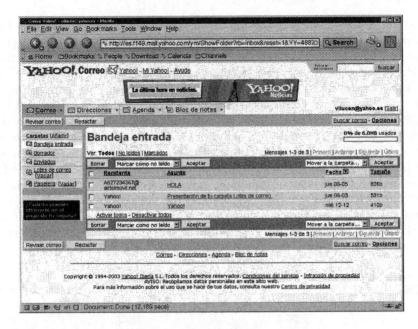

Fig. 3. Yahoo! Inbox

A simple XPath expression can be safely used to address such rows within the page. However intra-document navigation does not stop at this level. Every item in the `rows3` message list has a well known and viewable table cell structure composed of the subject, sender, date, size and other attributes of the message, being preceded by a checkbox form field which can be used to select the message in order to apply some action on it later. Access to the full mail message might be obtained by following the subject's link, but for the approach of this navigation task, P3 contains all needed & relevant information, and this might easily be printed as the XPlore routine at figure 4 shows.

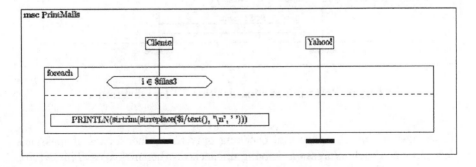

Fig. 4. Printing mails XPlore diagram

Once that all mail messages declared at this page have successfully been addressed by `rows3` variable and relevant information of this part of the page has been printed to the user, we can then call our *Deletion* routine for removing those messages selected by some user defined pattern matching. All messages within the table are contained in a single form, which can easily be addressed by its `name` attribute (namely `messageList`). In order to select messages, several rules might be defined by different users (depending on which kind of messages they might be receiving). Anyhow, it is quite common that some kind of user-definable pattern might be applied. If selectable messages come from the same source and the have same common words within the subject, they might be selected as those messages that contain some user defined variables *sender* and *subject* as substrings within the message's sender and the message's subject. In order to delete these messages, they should be properly selected by checking in their own checkbox and pushing on the *Delete* button when all selected checkboxes are properly left checked or unchecked. Figure 5 shows a *for-each* loop iterating

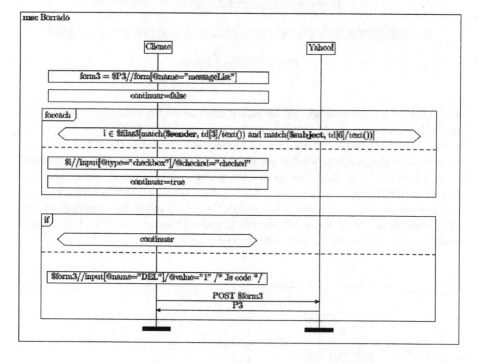

Fig. 5. Pattern matching deletion XPlore diagram

all messages within the page and checking only those checkboxes of messages selected by a XPath expression, leaving unchecked other messages. This XPath expression combines some user defined variables with information parts of the message and is a clear and simple example of user's and page's data integration.

A boolean flag detecting that at least one message has been selected is set to a *true* value to indicate that the main loop should iterate again. This boolean flag is also finally used to decide whether the *Delete* button should be pressed (to delete all selected messages) or not (if no message was selected). Since some JavaScript code changing this button's value attribute is invoked at deletion (in a button's *onclick* event), a XPath-based equivalent sentence involving this behaviour should be executed to update a form field's value, before posting the form. When the form is finally posted, a new updated, cleaned, version of P3 is obtained, with previously selected messages deleted. If no message is selected next, then no action should be performed and navigation should stop.

5 Conclusions

This article has presented some specification and graphical formalisms (MSC and XPath based) to express inter-document and intra-document navigation paths which can easily be defined by users that have some experience navigating a repeatedly used and well-known Web site.

Both inter-document and intra-document navigations are needed to fully exploit intelligent integration of data within the Deep Web. Wrapper agents can be easily built according to well defined navigation paths and a well known task to be performed. Some maintenance effort is needed in order to maintain these programs operative when changes occur within a Web site affecting a navigation path. This maintenance requires some *a-priori* knowledge of the Web site. Wrapper agents can nearly perform any task on behalf of the user, perhaps involving data combination from several heterogeneous Web sources.

Intelligent agents navigating a Web site according to metadata might also perform tasks for the user. However, our experience has found that, if well defined tasks need to be performed over well known Web sites, specific-purpose wrapper agents result more powerful than any metadata-driven generic technology. Metadata expressiveness imply that navigation paths should be built during navigation according to declarative knowledge within some metadata. In order to perform very specific tasks over well known Web sites, specific user's knowledge results cheaper and easy to be modelled if navigation paths are expressed using our formalisms. Even though an intelligent agent might be clever enough for properly filling in a specific form like Yahoo's!, users that already know how to do that in an efficient and simple manner, would prefer to formally express navigation paths in a formalism like ours, instead of letting a program try to guess the procedure.

Acknowledgements

The work reported in this paper has been partially funded by the project Infoflex *TIC2003-07208* of the Spanish Ministry of Science and Research.

134   Vicente Luque Centeno et al.

References

[1] Curl tool. curl.haxx.se/docs/httpscripting.shtml.
[2] Wget tool. sunsite.auc.dk/pub/infosystems/wget/.
[3] T. Berners-Lee, J. Hendler, and O. Lassila. The semantic web. In *Scientific American*, May 2001.
[4] V. L. Centeno, P. T. Breuer, L. S. Fernandez, C. D. Kloos, and J. A. H. Perez. Msc-based language for specifying automated web clients. In *The Eighth IEEE Symposium on Computers and Communications*, pages 407–412, Kemer, Antalya, Turkey, June 30 - July 3 2003.
[5] V. L. Centeno, L. S. Fernandez, C. D. Kloos, P. T. Breuer, and F. P. Martin. Building wrapper agents for the deep web. In *Third International Conference on Web Engineering ICWE 2003, Lecture Notes in Computer Science LNCS 2722*, Ed. Springer, pages 58–67, Oviedo, Spain, July 2003.
[6] V. L. Centeno, C. D. Kloos, P. T. Breuer, L. S. Fernandez, M. E. G. Cabellos, and J. A. H. Perez. Automation of the deep web with user defined behaviours. In *First International Atlantic Web Intelligence Conference, AWIC 2003, Lecture Notes in Artificial Intelligence LNAI 2663 (Subseries of Lecture Notes in Computer Science)*, Ed. Springer, pages 339–348, Madrid, Spain, May 2003.
[7] ITU-T. Recommendation z.120: Message sequence chart (msc). In *Formal description techniques (FDT)*, Geneva, Switzerland, 1997.
[8] H. J. and M. B. The jdom project www.jdom.org.
[9] T. Kistler and H. Marais. Webl - a programming language for the web. In *Proceedings of the 7th International World Wide Web Conference*, pages 259–270, Computer Networks and ISDN Systems 30, 1998.
[10] M. T. Ltd. Sax: The simple api for xml www.megginson.com/sax.
[11] D. Raggett. Clean up your web pages with html tidy. *Poster 7th International World Wide Web Conference www.w3.org/People/Raggett/tidy/*.
[12] M. P. Singh. Deep web structure. *Internet Computing*, 6(5):4–5, Sept.-Oct. 2002.
[13] Sun. Package java.net. In *JavaTM 2 Platform Standard Edition*, www.sun.com/java.
[14] W3C. Hypertext markup language (html and xhtml). *www.w3.org/MarkUp/*.
[15] W3C. Libwww - the w3c protocol library. In *www.w3.org/Library/*.
[16] W3C. Resource description framework (rdf). www.w3.org/RDF.
[17] W3C. Xsl transformations (xslt) version 1.0. *W3C Recommendation 16 November 1999*, 1999.
[18] W3C. Document object model (dom) level 2. *W3C Recommendation 13 November, 2000*, 2000.
[19] W3C. Xml pointer language (xpointer). *W3C Working Draft 16 August 2002*, 2002.
[20] W3C. Web ontology language (owl) reference version 1.0. In *W3C Working Draft 21 February 2003*, http://www.w3.org/2001/sw/, 2003.
[21] W3C. Xml path language (xpath) 2.0. *W3C Working Draft 02 May 2003*, 2003.
[22] W3C. Xquery 1.0: An xml query language. *W3C Working Draft 02 May 2003*, 2003.
[23] L. Wall. Perl language, v5.004. In *Freely available software package, June 1997*, ftp://ftp.perl.com/pub/perl/src/CPAN/5.0/perl5.004.tar.gz.

Extending the Rocchio Relevance Feedback Algorithm to Provide Contextual Retrieval

Chris Jordan and Carolyn Watters

Dalhousie University, Faculty of Computer Science, 6050 University Avenue, Halifax,
Nova Scotia, Canada, B3H 1W5
{cjordan, watters}@cs.dal.ca

Abstract. Contextual retrieval supports differences amongst users in their information seeking requests. The Web, which is very dynamic and nearly universally accessible, is an environment in which it is increasingly difficult for users to find documents that satisfy their specific information needs. This problem is amplified as users tend to use short queries. Contextual retrieval attempts to address this problem by incorporating knowledge about the user and past retrieval results in the search process. In this paper we explore a feedback technique based on the Rocchio algorithm that significantly reduces demands on the user while maintaining comparable performance on the Reuters-21578 corpus.

1   Introduction

Vast amounts of information are now widely accessible on the Web. At the same time, users are finding it harder and harder to satisfy specific information needs. Search engines provide a one-stop approach and are heavily relied on to access this information [2]. A shortcoming of the generic search engine is that it does not use knowledge about its users or about the data sources it covers. Users, however, may have significantly different preferences and needs even when using similar queries due to their education, interests, and previous experiences. Environmental factors such as these form a context [12] from which a query is issued. Incorporating this information into the search process will improve retrieval results at the individual level.

Typical search engines [2] rely solely on the user's query to select information for them. This is challenging as users normally use queries that consist of 1 to 3 terms and as such typically contain very little contextual information [11]. Not surprisingly, these queries are prone to ambiguity thus resulting in the retrieval of irrelevant documents for the user. Using characteristics about the user or specific feedback from them to modify the search query creates a context for those queries which can help remove ambiguities.

The Rocchio algorithm [3], which uses user feedback on the relevancy of retrieved documents, has been shown to improve search query results. Terms that occur in the retrieved items that are rated by the user are used to modify the query to, essentially, try to retrieve documents that are more relevant. A drawback of the Rocchio method is that users are required to cooperate in rating retrieved items as relevant or not through multiple iterations.

J. Favela et al. (Eds.): AWIC 2004, LNAI 3034, pp. 135–144, 2004.
© Springer-Verlag Berlin Heidelberg 2004

This paper will examine a new approach to automatic query modification for contextual retrieval, based on the Rocchio relevance feedback algorithm, called the Extended Rocchio algorithm. It will be shown that this approach improves document retrieval performance over standard Vector Space Retrieval (VSR) and has results comparable to the Rocchio algorithm while minimizing user interaction.

2   Background and Related Work

Filtering [3], recommending [14][15], and query modification [11] techniques have been used successfully in document retrieval systems to exploit knowledge about users to improve retrieval performance. Filtering and recommender systems use a profile of user interests to select relevant items from a retrieved document set or to generate a query that will retrieve an appropriate one. Query modification, however, responds to *ad hoc* queries presented by the user to improve the retrieved results for that user. Filtering, recommending and query modification all use profiles and document representations that are defined as sets of terms, weighted or not weighted. In this paper we concentrate on weighted terms consistent with the widely used Vector Space Model (VSM) [3]. Consequently, both profiles and documents are represented by vectors of term weights, where the term weight indicates the importance of that term in that profile or document.

Profiles are typically generated either directly by the user or by an analysis of documents rated by them [9]. User profiles can be most easily built by asking the user to fill out some form of questionnaire regarding their interests. User profiles can also be constructed from the content of documents that have been rated in some type of relevance feedback. These profiles can then be used in the search process to augment the query or to rank the retrieved documents. As well, they can be used in a collaborative process to identify groups of users with similar interests [16].

Profiles of interest often rely on feedback from users to rate the relevancy of items that have been retrieved for them. There are two general ways of doing this: direct and indirect [7]. Direct approaches outright ask users for input giving them the opportunity to rate the relevancy of retrieved items after each query. Indirect approaches gather information by tracking user interactions covertly often using server logs or keystroke analyses. Spink [19] has shown that Web users typically are engaged in three separate information tasks during each query session; profiles for this environment must be capable of handling multiple simultaneous user interests.

Given vectors of term weights for both documents and profiles there are two general approaches to using these vectors in the retrieval process; comparison of term vectors and machine learning. The term vector approach uses the term frequency/inverse document frequency (TF/IDF) value [3]. WebMate [6], for example, uses a single tier architecture where profiles can contain a maximum of N term vectors. Documents that are rated relevant by the user are converted into feedback term vectors. If the number of vectors in the profile is less than N then feedback vectors are add as new term vectors to the profile. Otherwise the two most similar vectors in the profile are merged together. Alipes [20], a similar system, allows negative relevancy judgments in addition to positive ones, in a three tier architecture representing short term positive, short term negative, and long term interests.

Machine learning techniques are frequently employed to build and use profiles of interest. News Dude [5], for example, uses a two tiered architecture to map short and long term interests respectively in a user profile. The short term interests are derived from the k previously rated documents. News stories are then classified as interesting or not by running a nearest neighbor algorithm on these k documents. If a story can not be classified using the short term tier then it is passed to the long term tier where it is classified using a Naïve Bayesian classifier. Mooney [15] developed a system called Libra to recommend books to users from a snapshot of Amazon's online catalogue using a single tier Naïve Bayesian classifier.

Rocchio's algorithm [3] is a query modification method using relevance judgments and has been used extensively in the retrieval of documents. The user provides relevance feedback on an initial set of retrieved results for a given query. This feedback is used to alter the query to better represent their current information need and return improved retrieval results. The algorithm is generally stated as:

$$Q_{i+1} = \alpha*Q_i + \beta*D_{pos}/n_{pos} - \gamma*D_{neg}/n_{neg} \qquad (1)$$

Where Q represents a query, D_{pos} represents the set of returned documents rated as relevant, D_{neg} represents the set of returned documents rated as not relevant, n is the cardinality of D, and α, β, and γ are constants that regulate the weight each component has on the formation of the new query. Typically $\alpha=1$ and $\beta + \gamma = 1$. The shortcoming of this algorithm is that it works only on a per query basis, so each time a user issues a new query a new model has to be constructed. Allan [1] showed, however, that feedback gathered over time will still have positive effects on performance using an incremental relevance feedback approach. In [13] Rocchio was used adaptively to predict what document categories users are interested in. The Extended Rocchio algorithm presented in this paper builds on these results.

The Rocchio algorithm has been used previously for text classification [8][17] on the Reuters-21578 corpus [22]. The variants of the Rocchio algorithm used in these papers indicated that they are useful in text classification even though they are outperformed slightly by machine learning techniques. A significant advantage of the Rocchio algorithm is that it has linear run time complexity. A distinction between text classification and contextual retrieval is that in classification a training set of documents is used to define term vectors for the categories in the corpus; these term vectors are then used to classify the documents in the test set. These learned term vectors can be thought of as derived queries. In contextual retrieval however, the user creates initial queries, which are improved by the incorporation of information based on relevance feedback.

Concept hierarchies have been used to add contextual information to queries. ARCH [18] uses concept term vectors based on the Yahoo concept hierarchy for query modification. Rocchio's algorithm was employed using concepts term vectors instead of document term vectors; this approach does show promise however the reported results are based on a small population. Concept term vectors in [13] are utilized in a general profile that is accessed by all users; an adaptive Rocchio algorithm is also made use of to generate individual user profiles.

3   Approach

The relevance feedback that users give in the Rocchio algorithm is used to fine tune a particular query. We theorize that this feedback represents the context from which the query was issued. In this work we proposed an Extended Rocchio algorithm that preserves this contextual information by constructing a profile of term vectors using the TF/IDF model. In this way, multiple query contexts can be profiled for the user instead of only one as in the traditional Rocchio algorithm. Each term vector represents a particular context that the user may issue queries from. For example, a user having two interests, automobiles and the stock market, would have a profile that contains two term vectors as they represent two different contexts that the user issues queries from. As the user rates documents as relevant or not new contextual information is introduced into the profile by the addition of new term vectors and the modification of existing ones.

There are three steps in this approach:

1. **Query Modification:** When a user issues a query, the query terms are compared to the profile term vectors. The similarity is calculated using the formula for the cosine of the angle between two vectors [3]:

$$Sim(Q,V) = \frac{Q \bullet V}{|Q| \times |V|} \qquad (2)$$

   Q and V represent the query and a profile term vector respectively. If there does not exist a term vector with a great enough similarity then no query modification takes place.

   If the most similar term vector, V, in the profile has a similarity greater than a threshold σ, a modified query, Q_{mod}, is generated by combining the initial query with this vector; the average weight is used for the terms that the vector and query have non-zero values for.

2. **Relevance Feedback:** This modified query is used to perform the document retrieval. The user can then give feedback by rating a subset of the retrieved results. The rated documents are used to form three term vectors:
   a)   Term vector P contains the average term weights for terms used in the relevant documents that do not occur in the original query, Q.
   b)   Term vector N contains the average term weights for terms used in negatively rated documents that do not occur in the query, Q.
   c)   Term vector F contains the terms in V that are not in P, N, or Q.
   P and N do not include terms in the original query Q as it assumed that since the user chose those terms they accurately represent the user's information need and should remain in the query. An additional reason for handling query terms separately is that it helps preserve the similarity between V and Q; this is important if this query is reissued by the user in step 1.

3. **Profile Modification:** The term vectors created in step 2 are used to modify the profile. If the original query was not modified in step 1 then a new term vector is added to the profile using the Rocchio relevance feedback algorithm:

$$V_{new} = \alpha*Q + \beta*P - \gamma*N \qquad (3)$$

Otherwise, V is replaced using the formula below:

$$V = \alpha * Q_{mod} + \beta * P - \gamma * N + \Delta * F \tag{4}$$

Where α, β, and γ are constants analogous to the ones in the Rocchio algorithm. Δ is a constant that regulates the rate of decay of terms that are not used in a profile. It is important to have some form of decay in the profile to reflect the dynamic aspects of a user's context such as interest drift [10]. Decay allows contextual information that is out of date to be removed from the profile.

For the trials performed in this paper: α is set to 1; β is set to .75; γ is set to .25; σ is set to .25; and Δ is set to .5. These were arbitrarily determined based on trial and error with the data set. To speed up the similarity calculations, a minimum weight of 0.1 was set for terms in the profile and only the 5 most heavily weighted terms from each feedback vector created in step 2 are used in modifying the profile in step 3.

4 Dataset

The dataset used in this paper was the Reuters-21578, Distribution 1.0 [22], a set of Reuters financial news stories. For experimentation purposes, only two subsets of this corpus were examined, the TRAIN LEWISSPLIT subset of 13,625 documents and the TEST LEWISSPLIT subset of 6,188 documents. We used a standard vector space model (VSM) and a standard Rocchio relevance feedback system to provide a baseline for comparison to the Extended Rocchio system. The TRAIN subset was used in the Extended Rocchio approach to generate the user profile and the TEST subset was used for evaluation. Consequently, the comparison between the Extended Rocchio method and the baseline systems was done using only the TEST subset.

The documents are also tagged by simple categorization schemes, including TOPICS and PLACES which were used during the experimentation process. The TOPICS labels reflect subject matter and the PLACES labels are typically country names. Below is an abbreviated sample document from the corpus.
<REUTERS TOPICS="YES" LEWISSPLIT="TRAIN" CGISPLIT="TRAINING-SET" OLDID="5544" NEWID="1">
<DATE>26-FEB-1987 15:01:01.79</DATE><TOPICS><D>cocoa</D></TOPICS>
<PLACES><D>el-salvador</D><D>usa</D><D>uruguay</D></PLACES>
<TEXT><TITLE>BAHIA COCOA REVIEW</TITLE>
<BODY>...<BODY></TEXT></REUTERS>
The feature set of the corpus was first reduced by the use of a standard stop word list [21] followed by basic term stemming using Porter's algorithm [3]. For each document, a standard TF/IDF term vector was created from the BODY and TITLE but not the TOPICS or PLACES fields.

5 Experimental Trials

In the experimental trials we used the TOPICS and PLACES data to judge the relevancy of retrieved documents. We defined 45 sets of documents where all the members for a given set have a minimum of one TOPICS label and one PLACES label in common and at least 20 are in the TRAIN subset and 10 are in the TEST subset. Four of these sets are described in Table 1.

Table 1. Sample document sets used in the evaluation.(P = PLACES, T = TOPICS)

Desired P label	Desired T label	TRAIN subset			TEST subset		
		#docs with T	#docs with P	#with both	#docs with T	#docs with P	#with both
Canada	acq	1615	725	93	719	304	44
China	Grain	424	150	31	149	55	11
Usa	Wheat	8130	206	130	3918	71	39
Usa	crude	8130	385	166	3918	189	96

We then created two sets of 45 queries that targeted these document sets for the trials. The first set of queries consists of only a single PLACES label. Consequently there are ambiguous queries in this set as a PLACES label may be related to different TOPICS labels in the documents. For example, consider the last two documents sets described in the above table. The third set is described by "PLACES=Usa, TOPICS=wheat" and fourth by "PLACES=Usa, TOPICS=crude". The simple query "Usa" targets documents in both of these sets. This first set of queries is designed to be missing significant contextual information. Queries in the second set contain both a PLACES and a TOPICS label; this reduces the ambiguity by incorporating more contextual information.

The test queries have been purposely designed to be short for two reasons. The first is that it allows documents to have their relevancy judge based on their set defining labels. The second reason is that users traditionally only issue queries that consist of 1 to 3 terms [11]. Although it has been acknowledged that longer queries tend to improve retrieval performance [4], the use of short queries makes these trials representative of actual user behavior.

For these experimental trials an automatic method for relevance feedback was developed. When no feedback is given for a particular query the results are equivalent to a VSM system. Depending on the query, there may not be any relevant documents in the top 10 retrieved results. While judging only negative documents does help improve the results, more significant improvements are attained when a document is rated to be positive because there are typically far fewer relevant documents than irrelevant ones. The approach adopted in this work is as follows:

1. The first document retrieved from the search that meets the PLACES and TOPICS label criteria is marked as relevant.
2. The search is performed again using the term vector of this document as feedback.
3. The top five results from this search are then judged as relevant or not based on the label criteria. The query is modified by the system.
4. The search is executed one final time.

For the Rocchio benchmark, the affect of the Rocchio relevance feedback system is measured after this fourth step. For the Extended Rocchio system a profile is created and modified from feedback on the TRAIN subset. A new profile is used for every query to remove the effect of the order that the queries are in during the experiment. The retrieval performance of the Extended Rocchio system is measured by using these profiles in combination with their respective initial query on the TEST subset; relevance feedback is only given on the TRAIN subset.

6   Results

Trail 1: The queries in the first set are simply PLACES labels. A few examples of the queries in this set are "Canada", "China", and "Usa". Table 2 shows the average precision in the top 5 and top 10 retrieval results for each query.

Table 2. Retrieval performances using a PLACES label as the query (average precision).

TRAIN subset				TEST subset					
VSM		Rocchio		VSM		Rocchio		Ext-Rocchio	
Top 5	Top 10	Top 5	Top 10	Top 5	Top 10	Top 5	Top 10	Top 5	Top 10
12.0	12.2	54.6	46.0	14.6	14.0	49.4	36.4	31.6	26.9

The results from a randomized block design, shown in Table 3, on both the performances over the Top 5 and Top 10 retrieval results indicate there is a significant difference between the systems with p < .001.

Table 3. Results from the randomized block design on the results from first set of queries.

	degrees of freedom	F	p value
Top 5	44	42.819	< .001
Top 10	44	8.706	< .001

Given the significant difference between the systems, a series of paired sample t tests were conducted. The outcome of these tests is shown in Table 4. These results indicate that the VSM system was significantly outperformed by both the Rocchio and Extended Rocchio systems. As well, the results also indicate that the Rocchio system significantly outperforms the Extended Rocchio system on the simple query set.

Table 4. Paired sample t tests on the results from first set of queries (VSM – Vector Space Model, R – Rocchio, ER – Extended Rocchio) degrees of freedom = 44

	Paired Differences					T	2 tailed p value
	mean	std. dev.	mean std. err.	95% CI of diff. Lower	Upper		
Top 5: R–VSM	1.73	1.50	.22	1.28	2.18	7.76	< .001
Top 5: ER–VSM	.84	1.26	.19	.47	1.22	4.49	< .001
Top 5: R–ER	.89	1.87	.28	.33	1.45	3.18	.003
Top 10: R–VSM	2.24	2.27	.34	1.56	2.93	6.64	< .001
Top 10: ER–VSM	1.29	2.11	.31	.66	1.92	4.10	< .001
Top 10: R–ER	.96	3.07	.46	.034	1.88	2.09	.042

Trail 2: The queries in the second set included both a PLACES and a TOPICS label, with any abbreviations expanded. A few examples of queries in this set are "Canada acquisitions mergers", "China grain", and "Usa wheat". As in the previous trial, the feedback for the Extended Rocchio system is given only on the TRAIN subset.

Table 5. Retrieval performances using more complex queries (average precision).

TRAIN subset				TEST subset					
VSM		Rocchio		VSM		Rocchio		Ext-Rocchio	
Top 5	Top 10	Top 5	Top 10	Top 5	Top 10	Top 5	Top 10	Top 5	Top 10
41.4	42.2	72.0	58.7	40.8	37.1	59.2	46.9	47.6	43.1

The randomized block design shown in Table 6 illustrates that there is a significant difference in performance between systems.

Table 6. Randomized block design on the results from the second set of queries

	degrees of freedom	F	p value
Top 5	44	15.152	< .001
Top 10	44	8.437	< .001

Paired sample t tests indicated that the VSM system was significantly outperformed by both the Rocchio and Extended Rocchio systems for the more complex query set. However, there is no significant difference between the Rocchio and Extended Rocchio in their performance on the Top 10 results with p = .142.

Table 7. Paired sample t tests for second set of queries (VSM – Vector Space Model, R – Rocchio, ER – Extended Rocchio) degrees of freedom = 44

	Paired Differences					t	2 tailed p value
	mean	std. dev.	mean std. err.	95% CI of diff.			
				Lower	Upper		
Top 5: R–VSM	.91	1.20	.18	.55	1.27	5.08	< .001
Top 5: ER–VSM	.33	.98	.15	.0398	.63	2.29	.027
Top 5: R–ER	.58	1.18	.18	.22	.93	3.29	.002
Top 10: R–VSM	.98	1.74	.26	.46	1.50	3.77	< .001
Top 10: ER–VSM	.60	1.37	.20	.19	1.01	2.93	.005
Top 10: R–ER	.38	1.70	.25	-.13	.89	1.49	.142

7   Discussion

Both the Rocchio and the Extended Rocchio algorithms significantly outperform the standard VSM for both the simple and complex queries. The Rocchio and Extended Rocchio are not, however, significantly different. The Extended Rocchio feedback system was able to achieve comparable performance to a traditional Rocchio system without requiring any user feedback after the training period. Furthermore, the Extended Rocchio system supports multiple simultaneous user interests.

The retrieval performances of the VSM and the Rocchio systems on the TRAIN subset are similar to their respective performances on the TEST subset indicating that the observed behaviors are not due to any abnormalities in the subsets. This strengthens the observation that the Extended Rocchio system maintains a positive effect on retrieval performance without requiring user feedback.

The feedback and evaluation scheme used in this paper was done in a very controlled environment. Obviously, there are some articles that represent a relevant document set better than others.

8   Conclusion

Query modification based on user feedback has been shown to be an effective means of improving retrieval performance. In this paper we show that the Extended Rocchio approach, which only uses feedback during a training phase, provides a performance improvement that is comparable to the traditional Rocchio algorithm, which requires user feedback at query time. The Extended Rocchio approach reduces the amount of relevance feedback that a user needs to provide. Furthermore, the Extended Rocchio method builds a profile that provides query modification for multiple user contexts.

The results from this initial experiment are promising. This will need to be followed up by studies using real users and other profile based query modification techniques to better understand the strengths and weaknesses of specific approaches. Using stereotypic information about the user such as age, occupation, and location should also be explored; contextual information of this type is static. This will provide a foundation for developing a hybrid. In the experimental trials reported in this paper, the Δ constant for contextual information decay was not tested although clearly retrieval systems based on profiles of user contexts must respond to both short and long term changes to those contexts as user preferences and interests change over time.

The Extended Rocchio algorithm provides contextual retrieval through query modification of the original query based on the user's profile. This technique helps overcome the short query problem by adding contextually relevant terms contained within the profile. Although this approach shows promise, there is still much work to be done before it can be incorporate into a hybrid system.

Acknowledgements

We would like to thank Qigang Gao and Wade Blanchard, both at Dalhousie University, for their input into this work.

References

1. Allan, J.: Incremental Relevance Feedback for Information Filtering. Proc. of the 19th Annual Int. ACM SIGIR Conf. on Research and Development in Info. Retri. (1996) 270 – 278
2. Arasu, A., Cho, J., Garcia-Molina, H., Paepcke, A., Raghavan S.: Searching the Web. ACM Transactions on Internet Technology, Vol. 1, No. 1 (2001) 2–43
3. Baeza-Yates, R., Ribeiro-Neto, B.: Modern Information Retrieval. Addison Wesley (1999)
4. Belkin, N.J., Cool, C., Kelly, D., Kim, G., Kim, J.-Y., Lee, H.-J., Muresan, G., Tang, M.-C., Yuan, X.-J.: Query Length in Interactive Information Retrieval. Proc. of the 26th Annual Int. ACM SIGIR Conf. on Research and Development in Info. Retri. (2003) 205–212
5. Billsus, D., Pazzani, M.: A hybrid user model for news story classification. Proceedings of the Seventh International Conference on User Modeling (1999) 99–108
6. Chen, L., Sycara, K.: WebMate: A Personal Agent for Browsing and Searching. Proceedings of the Second International Conference on Autonomous Agents (1998) 132–139
7. Chan, P. K.: Constructing Web User Profiles: A non-invasive Learning Approach. Revised Papers from the Int. Workshop on Web Usage Analysis and User Profiling (1999) 39–55
8. Joachims, T.: A Probabilistic Analysis of the Rocchio Algorithm with TFIDF for Text Categorization. Proceedings of ICML-97 (1997) 143–146
9. Kobsa, A.: User modeling: Recent work, prospects and hazards. In: Schneider-Huchmidt, M., Kiihme, T., Malinowski, U.(ed.): Adaptive User Interfaces: Principles and Practice (1993) 111–128
10. Koychev, I., Schwab, I.: Adaptation to drifting user's interests. Proceedings of ECML2000/MLnet Workshop: Machine Learning in New Information Age (2000) 39–46
11. Kruschwitz, U.: An Adaptable Search System for Collections of Partially Structured Documents. IEEE Intelligent Systems, July/August (2003) 44–52
12. Lawrence, S.: Context in Web Search. IEEE Data Engineering Bulletin, Vol. 23, No. 3 (2000) 25-32
13. Liu, F., Yu, C., Meng, W.: Personalized web search by mapping user queries to categories. Proc. of the 11th Int. Conf. on Information and knowledge management (2002)
14. Middleton, S., DeRoure, D., and Shadbolt, N.: Capturing knowledge of user preferences: Ontologies in recommender systems. Proc. of the 1st Int. Conf. on Knowledge Capture (2001)
15. Mooney, R. J., Roy, L.: Content-based book recommending using learning for text categorization. Proceedings of the Fifth ACM Conference on Digital Libraries. (2000) 195 – 204
16. Resnick, P., Iacovou, N., Suchak, M., Bergstrom, P., Riedl, J.: GroupLens: An open architecture for collaborative filtering of Netnews. Proc. of ACM Conf. on Computer-Supported Cooperative Work (1994) 175–186
17. Schapire, R., Singer, Y., Singhal, A.: Boosting and Rocchio applied to text filtering. Proc. of the 11th Int. Conf. on Research and Development in Information Retrieval (1998) 215 – 223
18. Sieg, A., Mobasher, B., Lytinen, S., Burke, R.: Concept based query enhancement in ARCH. To appear in Proc. of the Int. Conf. on Internet Computing (2003)
19. Spink, A., Ozmutlu, H.C., Ozmutlu, S.: Multitasking information seeking and searching processes. Journal of the American Society for Information Science and Technology, Vol. 53, No. 8 (2002) 639–652
20. Widyantoro, D.H., Ioerger, T.R., Yen, J.: An Adaptive Algorithm for Learning Changes in User Interests. Proc. of the 8th Int. Conf. on Information and Knowledge Management (1999) 405–412
21. Glasgow IDOM - IR linguistic utilities: Stop word list. http://www.dcs.gla.ac.uk/idom/ir_resources/linguistic_utils/. Access: Oct 24, 2003
22. UCI KDD Archive: Reuters-21578 Text Categorization Collection. http://kdd.ics.uci.edu/databases/reuters21578/reuters21578.html. Access: Oct 24, 2003

Toward a Document Model for
Question Answering Systems

Manuel Pérez-Coutiño, Thamar Solorio, Manuel Montes-y-Gómez[†],
Aurelio López-López, and Luis Villaseñor-Pineda

Instituto Nacional de Astrofísica, Óptica y Electrónica (INAOE)
Luis Enrique Erro No. 1, Sta Ma Tonantzintla, 72840, Puebla, Pue, México.
{mapco,thamy,mmontesg,allopez,villasen}@inaoep.mx

Abstract. The problem of acquiring valuable information from the large
amounts available today in electronic media requires automated mechanisms
more natural and efficient than those already existing. The trend in the evolution of information retrieval systems goes toward systems capable of answering
specific questions formulated by the user in her/his language. The expected answers from such systems are short and accurate sentences, instead of large
document lists. On the other hand, the state of the art of these systems is focused –mainly– in the resolution of factual questions, whose answers are named
entities (dates, quantities, proper nouns, etc). This paper proposes a model to
represent source documents that are then used by question answering systems.
The model is based on a representation of a document as a set of named entities
(NEs) and their local lexical context. These NEs are extracted and classified
automatically by an off-line process. The entities are then taken as instance
concepts in an upper ontology and stored as a set of DAML+OIL resources
which could be used later by question answering engines. The paper presents a
case of study with a news collection in Spanish and some preliminary results.

Keywords: Question Answering, Ontology, Semantic Web, Named Entity Classification.

1   Introduction

The technological advances have brought us the possibility to access large amounts of
information automatically, either in the Internet or in specialized collections of information. However, such information becomes useless without the appropriate mechanisms that help users to find the required information when they need it. Traditionally,
searching information in non-structured or semi-structured sources been performed by
search engines that return a ranked list of documents containing all or some of the
terms from the user's query. Such engines are incapable of returning a concise answer
to a specific information request [4].

[†] This work was done while visiting the Dept. of Information Systems and Computation Polytechnic University of Valencia, Spain.

J. Favela et al. (Eds.): AWIC 2004, LNAI 3034, pp. 145-154, 2004.
© Springer-Verlag Berlin Heidelberg 2004

The alternative to information retrieval systems for resolving specific questions are Question Answering (QA) systems capable of answer questions formulated by the user in natural language. Research in QA has increased as a result of the inclusion of QA evaluations as part of the Text Retrieval Conference (TREC)[1] in 1999, and recently [5] in Multilingual Question Answering as part of the Cross Language Evaluation Forum (CLEF)[2].

The goal of QA systems is to respond to a natural language question stated by the user, replying with a concrete answer to the given question and, in some cases, a context for its validation. Current operational QA systems are focused in factual questions [1, 15] that require a named entity (date, quantity, proper noun, locality, etc) as response. For instance, the question *"¿Dónde nació Benito Juárez?"*[3] demands as answer *'San Pablo Guelatao'*, a locality of Mexico. Several approaches of QA systems like [8, 14] use named entities at different degree of refinement in order to find a candidate answer. Other systems like [3, 9] include the use of ontologies and contextual patterns of named entities to represent knowledge about question and answer contents. Thus, it is clear that named entities identification plays a central role in the resolution of factual questions.

On this basis, we propose in this paper a model for the representation of the source documents that are then used by QA systems. The proposed model represents text documents as a set of classified named entities and their local lexical context (nouns and verbs). The representation is automatically gathered by an off-line process that generates instances of concepts from a top level ontology and stores them as resources in DAML+OIL.

The rest of this paper is organized as follows; section two describes the proposed model, both at conceptual and implementation level; section three details the process of the named entities extraction and classification; section four presents a case of study answering some questions employing the model in a set of news documents in Spanish; finally section five exposes our conclusions and discusses further work.

2   Model Description

The aim of modeling source documents for QA systems is to provide a preprocessed set of resources which contain valuable information that makes easier to accomplish answer retrieval and extraction tasks. An important feature of the proposed model is that implies a uniform format for data sources, as mentioned in [1] "...it is also necessary that the data sources become more heterogeneous and of larger size..." Developing a document model makes possible that several heterogeneous data sources can be expressed in a standardized format, or at least feasible the transformation and mapping between equivalent sources.

To reach these goals, the following key assumptions were made to develop the proposed model:
1. The collection of documents that will be used by the QA system contains documents about facts like those published in news without domain restriction.

---

[1] http://trec.nist.gov/

[2] http://clef-qa.itc.it/

[3] Where was Benito Juarez born?

2. The model must reuse an upper ontology in order to allow further refinement and reasoning on the named entities.
3. The model must be encoded in some ontological language for the Semantic Web in order to allow future applications such as specialized QA engines or web agents that make use of the document representation, instead of the document itself, to achieve their goals.

The next subsection details the conceptual and implementation levels of the model.

2.1 Conceptual Level

Figure 1 shows the model. At the conceptual level, a document is seen as a factual text object whose content refers to several named entities even when it is focused on a central topic. Named entities could be one of these objects: persons, organizations, locations, dates and quantities. The model assumes that the named entities are strongly related to their lexical context, especially to nouns (subjects) and verbs (actions). Thus a document can be seen as a set of entities and their contexts. Moreover, each named entity could be refined by means of ontologies [6]. This is the aim of instantiating an upper level ontology, instead of developing an ontology from scratch.

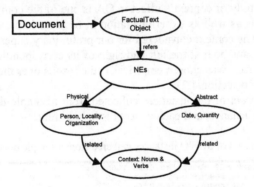

Figure 1. The proposed model.

The model is based on the Suggested Upper Merged Ontology (SUMO)[4] [7], an existing framework specifically designed to provide a basis for more specific domain ontologies. SUMO combines a number of top-level ontologies to achieve wide conceptual coverage, has a strong basis of semiotic and linguistic concepts already, and is being developed by an IEEE working group[5] that includes a number of experts from a variety of fields.

2.2 Implementation Level

As mentioned earlier the model is implemented as a set of instances of concepts in SUMO. The mapping between NEs and SUMO, as well as the used slots or axioms are shown in table 1.

---

[4] http://ontology.teknowledge.com:8080/
[5] http://suo.ieee.org/

The use of "refers" and "cooccurs" slots allow to refine the mapping of concepts between NEs and SUMO concepts. For instance, with an improved version of the extraction process, we could refer to a "City" instead of a "GeographicArea", or to a "Government" instead of an "Organization".

Table 1. Mapping between NEs and SUMO concepts.

NEs	SUMO Concept	Slot	Description
	FactualText	refers	This is the top concept of the model. Refers slot means that a factual text could make reference to other entities (like our NEs).
Person	Human	cooccurs	Human, Organization and GeographicArea could
Organization	Organization	cooccurs	be in co-occurrence with other entities (like verbs
Locality	GeographicArea	cooccurs	and nouns).
Date	TemporalRelation	refers	Date and Quantity are a special case because
Quantity	Quantity	refers	these entities are considered as abstract entities in SUMO. Thus their relation with other physical entities is established by the "refers" slot.

On the other hand context is mapped as the SUMO concepts "noun" and "verb" in accordance with the information gathered from the SL-tagger (refer to section 3). According to [1] the study of context's effect in QA is one of the complex issues that requires formal models as well as experimentation in order to improve the performance of QA systems. The context considered for our preliminary experiments consists of the four verbs or nouns both at the left and right of its corresponding NE. Despite the fact that this parameter was chosen empirically, the results over the test collection are encouraging (refer to section 4.2).

Table 2 shows a subset of the instances collected from a sample document. Each row corresponds to an instance, and each concept is in bold font.

Table 2. An extract of SUMO instances gathered from a sample document.

```
<sumo:FactualText rdf:about="#010698-1Lunes">
  <sumo:refers rdf:resource="#Cárdenas"/>
  <sumo:refers rdf:resource="#PNR"/>
  <sumo:refers rdf:resource="#Tamaulipas"/>
  <sumo:refers rdf:resource="#1931"/>
</sumo:FactualText>
<sumo:Human rdf:about="#Cárdenas">
  <sumo:cooccur rdf:resource="#presidente"/>
  <sumo:cooccur rdf:resource="#PNR"/>
  <sumo:cooccur rdf:resource="#echar"/>
  <sumo:cooccur rdf:resource="#mano"/>
</sumo:Human>
<sumo:Organization rdf:about="#PNR">
  <sumo:cooccur rdf:resource="#presidente"/>
  <sumo:cooccur rdf:resource="#echar"/>
  <sumo:cooccur rdf:resource="#mano"/>
  <sumo:cooccur rdf:resource="#Ersatz"/>
  <sumo:cooccur rdf:resource="#democracia"/>
</sumo:Organization>
<sumo:GeographicArea rdf:about="#Tamaulipas">
  <sumo:cooccur rdf:resource="#gobierno"/>
  <sumo:cooccur rdf:resource="#subir"/>
  <sumo:cooccur rdf:resource="#partido"/>
  <sumo:cooccur rdf:resource="#Partido_Social_Fronterizo"/>
</sumo: GeographicArea>
<sumo:TemporalRelation rdf:about="#1931">
  <sumo:refers rdf:resource="#echar"/>
  <sumo:refers rdf:resource="#mano"/>
  <sumo:refers rdf:resource="#Ersatz"/>
  <sumo:refers rdf:resource="#democracia"/>
```

```
    <sumo:refers rdf:resource="#vez"/>
    <sumo:refers rdf:resource="#selección/>
    <sumo:refers rdf:resource="#candidato"/>
    <sumo:refers rdf:resource="#gobernador"/>
</sumo: TemporalRelation >
<sumo:Verb rdf:about="#echar"></sumo:Verb>
<sumo:Verb rdf:about="#subir"></sumo:Verb>
<sumo:Noun rdf:about="#presidente"></sumo:Noun>
<sumo:Noun rdf:about="#gobierno"></sumo:Noun>
<sumo:Noun rdf:about="#partido"></sumo:Noun>
<sumo:Noun rdf:about="# Partido Social Fronterizo "></sumo:Noun>
<sumo:Noun rdf:about="#mano"></sumo:Noun>
<sumo:Noun rdf:about="#Ersatz"></sumo:Noun>
<sumo:Noun rdf:about="#democracia"></sumo:Noun>
<sumo:Noun rdf:about="#vez"></sumo:Noun>
<sumo:Noun rdf:about="#selección"></sumo:Noun>
<sumo:Noun rdf:about="#candidato"></sumo:Noun>
<sumo:Noun rdf:about="#gobernador"></sumo:Noun>
```

3   Extraction Process

We describe in this section the NE tagger used in order to extract the entities and their contexts that will be used to represent the documents. This NE tagger is also used to extract NEs in the questions which will help us exploit the representation model for question resolution. As mentioned earlier, this extraction process is performed off-line. Once we have extracted the entities and their contexts, these are taken as instances of an upper level ontology as described in section 2.2.

A NE is a word or sequence of words that falls in one of these five categories: name of persons, organizations, locations, dates and quantities. There has been a considerable amount of work aimed to develop NE taggers with human-level performance. However, this is a difficult goal to achieve due to a common problem of all natural language processing tasks: ambiguity; another inconvenience is that documents are not uniform, their writing style, as well as their vocabulary change dramatically from one collection to another.

The NE tagger used in this work is that proposed by [11]. This system is based on training a Support Vector Machine (SVM) [10,12,13] classifier using as features the outputs of a handcrafted system together with information acquired automatically from the document, such as Part-of-Speech (POS) tags and capitalization information. The goal of this method is to reduce the effort in adapting a handcrafted NE extractor to a new domain. Instead of redesigning the grammars or regular expressions, and revising the lists of trigger words and gazetteers, we need only to build a training set by correcting, when needed, the outputs of the handcrafted system.

The starting handcrafted system used is considered by Solorio and López (SL) tagger as a black box, in particular, the system developed by [2] was used. The system classifies the words in the documents into the following six categories: Persons, Organizations, Locations, Dates, Numeric Expressions, and "none of the above". Then each word in the documents has as features the output of the handcrafted system, their POS tag and their capitalization information (first letter capitalized, all letters capitalized, etc.). A previously trained SVM assigns the final NE tags using the features mentioned above. This process can be considered as a stacking classifier, in the first stage a handcrafted system assigns NE tags to the document, and then these tags (cor-

rected if necessary) are used as inputs to the SVM classifier which decides the final
NE tags.

In order to show an example of how this NE tagger performs, we present here a
comparison between the handcrafted system and the tagger from Solorio and López.
Table 3 shows the results of tagging questions that can be answered using the model
proposed here. In this table, we only show the named entities from the questions. As it
can be seen, the SL tagger improves the accuracy of the handcrafted system. In this
example, the SL tagger corrects 6 tags that were originally misclassified by the handcrafted system.

Table 3. Comparison between the handcrafted system (HS) and that of Solorio and López (SL).
Cases where the HS tagger misclassifies NEs that are correctly classified by the SL tagger are
in bold. The asterix (*) marks cases where the SL tagger misclassifies a NE correctly classified
by the HS tagger.

Named Entity	HS tags	SL tags	True NE tag
Unión_de_Cineastas_de_Rusia	Organization	Organization	Organization
Director_de_Aeroméxico*	Person	Organization	Person
Irán	**Organization**	**Location**	**Location**
Copa_Mundial_de_Fútbol	**Person**	**Organization**	**Organization**
Irán	**Organization**	**Location**	**Location**
Irán-Estados_Unidos*	Location	Organization	Location
Aeroméxico	**Person**	**Organization**	**Organization**
Aeroméxico	**Person**	**Organization**	**Organization**
Ruanda	Location	Location	Location
Mundial_Francia	Organization	Organization	Organization
Consejo_de_Ministros_de_Líbano	Organization	Organization	Organization
OTAN	Organization	Organization	Organization
Estados_Unidos	**Organization**	**Location**	**Location**
Accuracy	53%	84%	

4   Case of Study

This section presents a schema for the application of the proposed model to an experimental –and yet simple– QA system. In this case the searching process uses only
the information considered by the model.

The algorithm shows the appropriateness of the representation in searching for answers to factual questions. The following subsection describes the general algorithm
and its application over a sample collection of news in Spanish. Given the limitation
of space no implementation details are given.

4.1   The Algorithm

The algorithm is based in two key assumptions:

First, the kind of the question defines the class of NE to search. Generally speaking, factual questions do not rely on the predicate of the sentence, but on the subject,
the characteristics of the question, or on some other sentence element. In this way, by
the interrogative adverb (Wh-word) employed in the question, it is possible to infer
the role of the NE required as an answer. For instance, *"¿Quién es el presidente de*

México?"[6] requires to be answered with a NE of the class person (human). Of course not all interrogative adverbs define the kind of NE for the answer, e.g. *"¿Cuál es el nombre del presidente de México?"[7]*. For now, the algorithm is focused on partial interrogative questions whose answer role could be immediately identified by the interrogative adverb employed.

Second, from the question itself two kinds of information can be extracted: its NEs and the lexical context of the question. With the proposed model, all the NEs mentioned in a given document can be known beforehand. Thus the NEs from the question become key elements in order to define the document set more likely to provide the answer. For instance, in any of the sample questions above, the NE "Mexico" narrows the set of documents to only those containing such NE. At the same time, another assumption is that the context in the neighborhood of the answer has to be similar to the lexical context of the question. Once more, from the sample question, the fragment "even before his inauguration as president of Mexico, Vicente Fox..." contains a lexical context next to the answer which is similar to the question.

Following is the algorithm in detail:

1. Identify the type of NE-answer for a given question. We are limited by the set of NEs in the model (persons, organizations, locality, date & time, and quantity).
2. Extract NEs contained in the question and starting from them identify the appropriate document subset.
3. Retrieve all candidate NEs and their local lexical context (as detailed by the model) starting from those identified in step 2.
4. Compute the similarity between question context and those of the candidate NEs.
5. Rank the candidate NE in decreasing order of similarity.
6. Report the top NEs as possible answers

4.2 Results

This subsection shows the application of the algorithm just described on a small text collection of news in Spanish. The collection News94 consists of a set of 94 news (see table 4 for collection details). These documents contain national and international

Table 4. Main data of collection News94

Collection	Size	Number of documents	Average document size	Number of pages	Number of lexical forms	Number of terms
	372 Kb	94	3.44 Kb	124	11,562	29,611
Entities	**Date & Time**	**Locality**	**Organization**	**Person**	**Quantity**	**Others**
	266	570	1094	973	155	133

---

[6] Who is the president of México?
[7] What is the name of the president of Mexico?

news from the years 1998 to 2000. Regarding extracted information, the total of NEs obtained from this collection was 3191 (table 4 also shows totals by class).

The processing of the question: *"¿Quién era el presidente del PNR en 1931?"*[8] was done as follows:

1. Identify the class of the NE to search. Given that the interrogative adverb is *"quién" (who)*, the class is person (human).
2. Extract the NEs in the question. These are: PNR (Organization), present in the set of documents {0,13,86}; 1931 (Date), found in the set of documents {0}. As a consequence, the subset of documents is {0}.
3. Retrieve all NEs of class person (human) from the document '0'
4. Compute the similarity between the question context, that is {ser (be), presidente (president), PNR, 1931} and candidate NEs contexts. Table 5 shows the computed similarity.
5 y 6. {Cárdenas, Cárdenas_Presidente}

Table 5. Candidate NEs, their context and similarity

Context	NE	Sim.
{creador, 30, año, plebiscito, añoranza, embellecer, muerte}	Portes_Gil	0
{presidente, PNR, echar, mano}	Cárdenas	2
{prm, fundar, carácter, otorgar, ser, forma, permanecer, candidatura}	Cárdenas_Presidente	1
{arribar, 1964, pri, presidencia, Carlos, juventud, líder, camisa}	Madrazo	0
{Madrazo, arribar, 1964, pri, juventud, líder, traer}	Carlos	0
{pri, faltar, mano, gato}	Madrazo	0
{zurrar, Sinaloa, Madrazo, corto}	Polo_Sánchez_Celis	0
{Sinaloa, zurrar, Polo_Sánchez_Celis, corto, 11, mes, salir}	Madrazo	0
{pierna, cola, pri, salir, diputado, pelea, deber}	Polo_Martínez_Domínguez	0

In this example, "Cárdenas" is the correct answer, and the original text passage is shown in table 6.

Table 6. Passage with the answer to the sample question

"**Cárdenas** como presidente del PNR echó mano del Ersatz de democracia en 1931 por vez primera en la selección de candidatos a gobernadores"[9].

Table 7 shows a subset of the questions used in our preliminary experiments. A total of 30 questions were proposed by 5 assessors for this experiment. From these questions only 22 were classified as factoid and were evaluated. Results show that for 55% of the questions, the answer is found in the first NE, and that 82% of the questions are correctly responded within the top-5 NEs.

---

[8] Who was the president of the PNR in 1931?

[9] **Cardenas**, as president of the PNR made use of the Ersatz of democracy in 1931, for the first time in the selection of candidates for governor.

Despite of the informal evaluation of the algorithm and the small size of the collection, we found these results very encouraging, hinting the appropriateness of the proposed model and the likely robustness of the QA algorithm.

Table 7. Subset of testing questions.

Question	1st Answer	Correct Answer
¿Quién es el presidente de la Unión de Cineastas de Rusia? (Who is the president of the Moviemakers Union of Rusia?)	El Barbero de Siberia	Nikita Mijalkov
¿Quién ha impulsado el desmantelamiento del presidencialismo? (Who encouraged the dismantling of presidentialism?)	Zedillo	Zedillo
¿Cuándo calificó por última vez Irán para una Copa Mundial de Futbol? (When was the last time Iran classified for a Soccer World Cup?)	1978	1978
¿Quién es el presidente de Irán? (Who is president of Iran?)	Muhamad Khatami	Muhamad Khatami
¿Quién es la dirigente del sindicato de sobrecargos de Aeroméxico? (Who is the union leader of flight attendants of Aeromexico?)	Carlos_Ruíz_Sacristán	Alejandra Barrales Magdaleno
¿Cuántas personas fueron asesinadas en Ruanda durante 1994? (How many people were murdered in Rwanda during 1994?)	500,000	Más de 500 mil
¿Cuántos jugadores de futbol participarán en el Mundial de Futbol Francia 1998? (How many soccer player will participate in the World Soccer Cup of France 1998?)	------	704
¿Cuándo aprobó el senado la ampliación de la OTAN? (When did the senate approved the expansion of OTAN?)	30 de abril	30 de abril de 1998
Correct answer in the first NE	**55%**	
Correct answer within the top-5 NE	**82%**	

5   Conclusions

The proposed model can be an initial step toward document representation for specific tasks, such as QA as detailed. This representation is functional because captures valuable information that allows performing retrieval and extraction processes for QA in an easier and more practical way. Some important features of this model are that it considers a broader classification of NEs which improves the precision of the system; it also accelerates the whole process by searching only in the corresponding named entity class that is believed to contain the answer, instead of searching the answer in the whole document.

Besides, the representation is expressed in a standardized language as DAML+OIL –soon could be OWL–, in the direction of the next Web generation. This could yield to the exploitation of this document representation in multilingual settings for QA either in stand alone collections or the Semantic Web.

Preliminary results exploiting the representation of documents as proposed by the model were very encouraging. The context similarity assessment method has to be refined and additional information can be taken into account, e.g. proximity. We are also in the process of experimenting with large text collections and questions sets supplied by international conferences on Questions Answering systems such as TREC or CLEF. In further developments of this model we pretend to refine the classification of named entities in order to take full advantage of the ontology.

Acknowledgements. This work was done under partial support of CONACYT (Project Grant U39957-Y), SNI-Mexico, and the Human Language Technologies Laboratory of INAOE.

References

1. Burger, J. et al. *Issues, Tasks and Program Structures to Roadmap Research in Question & Answering (Q&A)*. NIST 2001.
2. Carreras, X. and Padró, L. *A Flexible Distributed Architecture for Natural Language Analyzers*. In Proceedings of the LREC'02, Las Palmas de Gran Canaria, Spain, 2002.
3. Cowie J., et al., *Automatic Question Answering*, Proceedings of the International Conference on Multimedia Information Retrieval (RIAO 2000)., 2000.
4. Hirshman L. and Gaizauskas R. *Natural Language Question Answering: The View from Here*, Natural Language Engineering 7, 2001.
5. Magnini B., Romagnoli S., Vallin A., Herrera J., Peñas A., Peinado V., Verdejo F. and Rijke M. *The Multiple Language Question Answering Track at CLEF 2003*. CLEF 2003 Workshop, Springer-Verlag.
6. Mann, G.S. *Fine-Grained Proper Noun Ontologies for Question Answering*, SemaNet'02: Building and Using Semantic Networks, 2002.
7. Niles, I. and Pease A., *Toward a Standard Upper Ontology*, in Proceedings of the 2nd International Conference on Formal Ontology in Information Systems (FOIS-2001), 2001.
8. Prager J., Radev D., Brown E., Coden A. and Samn V. *The Use of Predictive Annotation for Question Answering in TREC8*. NIST 1999.
9. Ravichandran D. and Hovy E. *Learning Surface Text Patterns for a Question Answering System*. In ACL Conference, 2002.
10. Schölkopf, B. and Smola A.J. *Learning with Kernels: Support Vector Machines, Regularization, Optimization, and Beyond*, MIT Press, 2001.
11. Solorio, T. and López López A. *Learning Named Entity Classifiers using Support Vector Machines*, CICLing 2004, LNCS Springer-Verlag, Feb. 2004, (to appear).
12. Stitson, M.O., Wetson J.A.E., Gammerman A., Vovk V., and Vapnik V. *Theory of Support Vector Machines*. Technical Report CSD-TR-96-17, Royal Holloway University of London, England, December 1996.
13. Vapnik, V. *The Nature of Statistical Learning Theory*, Springer, 1995.
14. Vicedo, J.L., Izquierdo R., Llopis F. and Muñoz R., *Question Answering in Spanish*. CLEF 2003 Workshop, Springer-Verlag.
15. Vicedo, J.L., Rodríguez, H., Peñas, A. and Massot, M. Los sistemas de Búsqueda de Respuestas desde una perspectiva actual. Revista de la Sociedad Española para el Procesamiento del Lenguaje Natural, n.31, 2003.

Designing Ontological Agents: an Alternative to Improve Information Retrieval in Federated Digital Libraries

María A. Medina[1], Alfredo Sánchez[2], Alberto Chávez[2], Antonio Benítez[2]

[1] Universidad Tecnológica de la Mixteca,
Huajuapan de León, Oaxaca, México
mmedina@nuyoo.utm.mx
http://www.utm.mx/~mmedina/index.html
[2] Universidad De Las Américas – Puebla
Cholula, Puebla, México
{alfredo, sp098974, sc098381}@mail.udlap.mx

Abstract. Search engines base their operation just in keywords management; some of them are ambiguous, consequently, a lot of irrelevant results are produced. To take into account the meaning of keywords, we describe the architecture of a multi-agent system in charged of information retrieval tasks in digital libraries. The main components are termed ontological agents. They are software entities that make use of ontologies to expand queries and to avoid as much ambiguity as possible of keywords. Ontologies are also used to identify relevant sources of information. The design of these agents is based on Gaia methodology.

1 Introduction

The advent of World Wide Web as a widely used space to publish documents, as well as the expansion of Internet have been key factors in the huge growth of information sources. We are interested in digital libraries because they are invaluable repositories of reliable and structured information.

To retrieve relevant information resources from several digital libraries, users need to address each repository and to be familiarized with each interface and correct syntax to express queries. After each search mechanism produces a set of partial results, users have to select just some of them. Distributed information retrieval is not new and it has been analyzed from diverse point of views. A lot of tools support this time-consuming task. It is common to delegate it to software or human agents.

On the other hand, ontologies emerge naturally to deal with semantic heterogeneity of this task [Pomerantz & Silverstein 2001]. The paper proposes the use of ontologies in a multi-agent architecture to improve information retrieval in digital libraries. The use of ontologies is twofold: ontologies can help to expand queries and to deal with keywords ambiguity, besides they can be considered an approach to identify relevant information sources. In order to avoid ad hoc development of agent-based software, we use Gaia methodology.

J. Favela et al. (Eds.): AWIC 2004, LNAI 3034, pp. 155-163, 2004.
© Springer-Verlag Berlin Heidelberg 2004

The paper is organized as follows: Section 2 describes previous work. Section 3 presents an interoperability protocol used by the digital libraries. Section 4 describes the design of ontological agents and section 5 includes related work. Conclusions are presented in Section 6.

2 Previous Work

In order to understand the design of ontological agents, it is necessary to know the context in which they are integrated. This is the Virtual Reference System [Sánchez et al. 2001]. In the further, the term VRef will be used. This is an environment where users post their queries in natural language. A staff of reference librarians and a set of software agents are in charged of searching digital or physical resources. We have termed these software entities *reference agents,* they retrieve information from the UDLAP[1] digital library [Medina et al. 2002], [Medina et al. 2003].

VRef has a knowledge base maintained and enriched with previous interactions. It enables make use of references suggested by reference librarians or by reference agents due to a mechanism that implements similarity between queries. This environment has been operating for almost two years. We are extending it to have access to a set of federated digital libraries using the Open Archives Initiative Protocol for Metadata Harvesting, which is briefly described in the next section.

3 Interoperability Protocol for the Digital Libraries

The set of digital libraries makes use of Open Archives Initiative Protocol for Metadata Harvesting, (abbreviated OAI-PMH). This protocol defines a standard, an open interface to implement interoperability based on the harvesting approach of metadata [OAI 2001]. Collections are from multiple disciplines and the type of documents is also varied. For example, articles in process of revision, technical reports or theses. The main objectives of this protocol are the following:

– To enable publication of metadata and full text of documents
– To standardize low level mechanisms to share content
– To build services of data management
– To provide mechanisms to support technical processes of organizations

OAI-PMH participants can be classified as data providers or service providers. The main function of the former ones is to publish their metadata represented using unqualified Dublin Core at least or XML [Weibel et al. 1998]. These metadata are classified behalf registers, a register is used for each document in a collection. A pair formed by the identifier of a registry and the identifier of the data provider is used to identify a document of the initiative. On the other hand, service providers collect data

---

[1] UDLAP is the short name of Universidad De Las Américas Puebla

of data providers and offer added value services. They use requests to obtain the data. Figure 1 shows these requests.

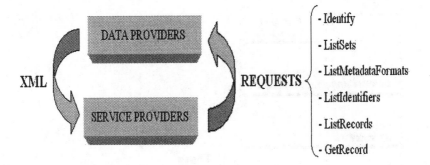

Fig 1. Participants and request of OAI-PMH protocol

This protocol has been incorporated in many important research projects. According to [Van de Sompel & Lagoze 2001], this popularity is due to the availability of tools to build OAI-PMH repositories and harvesters.

4 Designing Ontological Agents

Agent technologies are considered a natural extension of current component-based approaches. They constitute a natural way to model complex systems, (complexity emerges from the interactions among multiple, distinct and independent components). Agents are also perceived as an abstraction tool or a metaphor to design distributed systems [Luck et al. 2003]. We propose a multi-agent architecture composed by reference agents, mobile agents and ontological agents. The architecture pretends to improve retrieval information tasks in a set of digital libraries. We decided to extend VRef capabilities to access these resources. You can find a detailed description of these mobile agents in [Sánchez et al. 2002].

The architecture operates as follows: a reference agent reads a query and gets the keywords. Then, an ontological agent uses a general ontology of natural language to expand the query suggesting synonyms, hypernyms and hiponyms, [Fellbaum 1998]. Once a user chooses the appropriate alternatives, the ontologies of each collection are used to determine relevant sources of information. There is a specific ontology for each digital library. After that, the query is passed to a mobile agent in charged of visiting the identified sources of information. A mobile agent is used for each source. Finally, a reference agent collects the partial results, duplicate results are eliminated and a descent ordered list according to a ranking is shown in VRef. To control the growth of the knowledge base in VRef, we have limited the size of this list to ten elements. Figure 2 summarizes these tasks.

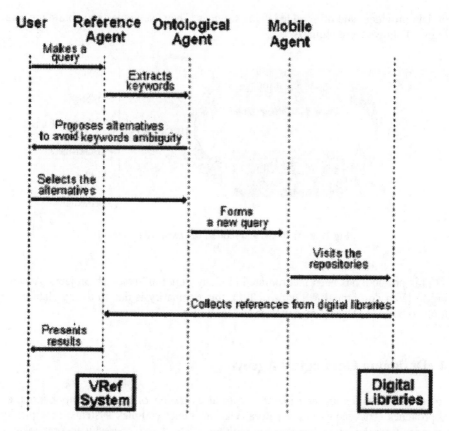

Fig. 2. Task diagram to retrieve information from a set of federated digital libraries.

To design ontological agents, we have use Gaia methodology. This is a top-down methodology for agent-oriented analysis and design. It is based on the concept of role. A multi-agent system is considered a computational organization formed by the interaction of various roles. Concepts are classified as *abstract concepts,* (roles, permissions, responsibilities, protocols, activities, liveness properties and safety properties), and *concrete concepts,* (agent types, services, acquaintances). The conceptual structure of Gaia consists of the next stages: requirements statement, analysis and design [Wooldridge 2000].

The first stage enables us to model and specify ontological agents in a conceptual level. It supports the description of the semantics without concerning implementation details. We adopted the requirements of a federated system: scalability and adaptability [Busse et al. 1999]. In addition, analysis stage consists of identification of roles, identification and documentation of protocols, and elaboration of roles model that is represented in the following tables.

Table 1. Role to process query

Role Schemata: *ProcessQuery*
Description: It gets keywords from a query expressed in natural language.
Protocols and activities: EliminateStopWords
Permissions: To read a query

Responsibilities:
    Aliveness: a query is available
                    Safety: a query must have at least one word

Table 2. Role to expand the query.

Role Schemata: *ExpandQuery*
Description: It involves ensuring as much ambiguity as possible from the keywords and the use of synonyms, hypernyms.
Protocols and activities: ShowNewWords, FormANewQuery
Permissions: To suggest other keywords

Responsibilities:
    Aliveness: keywords were extracted from the query
    Safety: suggest new words when ambiguity is detected

Table 3. Role to describe sources of information

Role Schemata: *DescribeSources*
Description: It uses ontologies to describe a source of information.
Protocols and activities: RepresentASource, ChooseASource
Permissions: To use an ontology

Responsibilities:
    Aliveness: an ontology is available
    Safety: complete or partial translations between ontologies

Table 4. Role to visit different sources of information

Role Schemata: *VisitSources*
Description: It has access to a source of information
Protocols and activities: RetrieveSources, SendSources
Permissions: Search sources

Responsibilities:
    Aliveness: there is a set of sources
    Safety: to have access to a source

Table 5. Role to collect results

Role Schemata: *CollectResults*
Description: It collects the results of each source of information
Protocols and activities: JoinResources, FiltrateResources
Permissions: Accept results

Responsibilities:
  Aliveness: available resources
  Safety: establish a minimum set of resources

We have identified four protocol definitions: KeywordsAgree, Identification-RelevantResource, RetrieveResources, PresentResources. They are represented in the templates of Figure 3. Top cell has the name of the role, middle cells are used for initiator and responder respectively, while bottom cell has processing attributes.

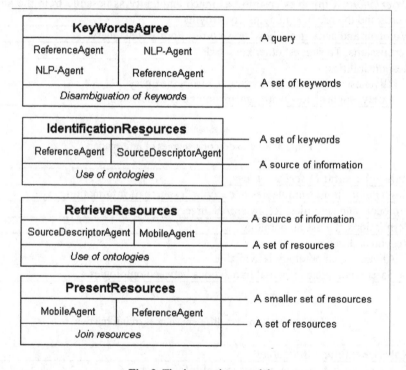

Fig. 3. The interactions model

An agent tree is another common representation. Figure 4 shows the respective one. Edges represent relationships between agents and leaf nodes denote roles. During this stage was decided to define two types of ontological agents we have termed: NLP-Agent and SourceDescriptorAgent. The service associated to the former is the extension of the query; the later manages a specific ontology that stores the concepts of each digital library. Finally, Figure 5 represents acquaintance model, this is used to represent the types of agents.

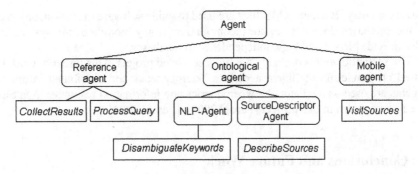

Fig. 4. Agent tree type.

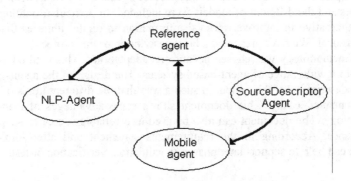

Fig. 5. Representation of the acquaintance model.

5 Related Work

The problem of having access to heterogeneous sources of information has been analyzed from diverse points of view. Research efforts continue, some of the most relevant ones are briefly described in this section.

FIPA (Foundation for Intelligent Physical Agents) fosters agent-based applications. It provides specifications to support interoperability between agents and a special specification to manage ontologies. This specification is implemented in an Ontology Agent (abbreviated as OA). Some of the services of an OA are: searching and accessing public ontologies, maintaining a set of ontologies and translation mechanisms. It is able to answer queries about relationships between terms. At FIPA, it is not mandated that every OA will be able to offer these services. The implementation of these services is left to developers. [FIPA 2001].

A method based on ontologies to federate documental databases is proposed in [Saavedra 2003]. This method accomplishes with the requirements of scalability, adaptability. Ontologies are used to integrate database schema and to build a friendly user interface at run time. The concepts that can be retrieved from the federation are represented in a structure called *concept tree*. Users select these trees when they introduce a query. Because XML files are used to guide software execution, any change in the databases does not require recompilation of any module of the system. XML files provide physic and logic independence of databases.

The semantic web is probably the biggest related project. This research work is focused on providing intelligent access to heterogeneous and distributed information. Agents are used as mediators between queries and information resources. Ontologies are a key concept in this project [Fensel 2000], [Fensel 2001].

6 Conclusions and Future Work

In this paper, we have described architecture of agents using Gaia methodology. All the stages and the different of models were included. In particular, ontological agents are an alternative to improve retrieval information in digital libraries that use OAI-PMH protocol. We have presented a brief description of this protocol.

Gaia methodology was chosen because its adaptability. This methodology can be applied to a wide range of agent-based systems. The design of the agents proposed a detailed description of the system in such a way that the different kinds of agents can be implemented easily. This document shows some advantages of using a design methodology. The document can also be used as a reliable source to support system maintenance. According to the requirements statement and after implementation phase, it can help to support later phases as validation, verification or test.

References

1. Chandrasekaran, B.; Josephson, R. What are ontologies, and why do we need them? In IEEE Inteligent systems. 14, 20-26. (1999)
2. Busse S., Kutsche R., Lesser U., Weber H. Federated information systems: concepts, terminology and architectures. Technical Report 99-9. TU Berlin. April. (1999)
3. Farquhar, A., Fikes, R., Pratt, W., and Rice, J. Collaborative ontology construction for information integration. Technical Report, Stanford University. (1995)
4. Fensel D. The semantic web and its languages. IEEE Computer Society 15, 6 (November /December), 67-73. (2000)
5. Fensel D. Ontologies: A Silver Bullet for Knowledge Management and Electronic Commerce. Springer. (2001)
6. FIPA Foundation for Intelligent Physical Agents.FIPA Ontology Service Specification. March. (2001)
   Available on: http://www.fipa.org/specs/fipa00086/XC00086D.html
7. Luck M., McBurney P, and Preist C. Agent technology: Enabling next generation computing: A roadmap for agent-based computing. AgentLink Report (2003).
   Available on: http://www.agentlink.org/roadmap.
8. Medina, M. A., Sánchez, J. A. Agents at the reference desk: Serving information needs and constructing knowledge for wide communities of users. Memorias del XII Congreso Internacional de Electrónica, Comunicaciones y Computadoras (Conielecomp 2002, Acapulco, México, Feb.), 74-78 (2002)

9. Medina Ma. Auxilio, Chávez-Aragón A. Inclusion of Reference Agents in a Virtual Reference Environment. Fourth Mexican International Conference on Computer Science (ENC 2003 , Apizaco Tlaxcala, September 10) (2003)
10. Open Archives Initiative. http://www.openarchives.org. (2001)
11. Pomerantz, J., & Silverstein, J. The Importance of Ontology: Standards for a Referral Tool. Paper presented at the 3rd Annual VRD Conference: Setting Standards and Making it Real, November, Orlando, FL. (2001)
    Available on: http://www.vrd.org/conferences/VRD2001 /proceedings/silverstein.shtml.
12. Saavedra A. Arquitectura para federación de bases de datos documentales basada en ontologías. Disertación doctoral. Universidade Da Coruña. Departamento de Computación. Enero. (2003)
13. Sánchez, J. A., García, A. J., Proal, C., Fernández, L. Enabling the collaborative construction and reuse of knowledge through a virtual reference environment. Proceedings of the Seventh International Workshop on Groupware, (Darmstadt, Germany, Sept. 6-8). IEEE Computer Society Press, Los Alamitos, California. 90-97. (2001)
14. Sánchez, J. A., Nava Muñoz, S., Fernández Ramírez, L., Chevalier Dueñas, G. Distributed information retrieval from web-accessible digital libraries using mobile agents. Upgrade 3, 2 (April), Special Issue on Information Retrieval and the Web, simultaneously published y Informatik/Informatique 8,3 June, 37 - 43. (2002)
    Available on: http://www.upgrade-cepis.org, (Informatik/Informatique is the magazine of the Swiss Informatics Society, http://www.svifsi.ch/revue).
15. Van de Sompel H., Lagoze C. Notes from the interoperability front: a progress report on the open archives initiative. Proceedings of the 6th European Conference on Research and Advance Technology for Digital Libraries (ECDL 2002, Rome, Italy, September), 144-157 (2001)
16. Weibel, S., Kunze, J., Lagoze, C. y Wolfe, M. Dublin Core metadata for resource discovery. Internet RFC-2413 (1998)
    Available on: ftp://ftp.isi.edu/in-notes/rfc2413.txt.
17. Wooldridge, M., Jennings N. Kinny D. The Gaia Methodology for Agent-Oriented Analysis and Design. Autonomous Agents and Multi-Agent Systems, 3, 285-312. Kluwer Academic Publishers. The Netherlands (2000)

Query Clustering for
Boosting Web Page Ranking

Ricardo Baeza-Yates[1], Carlos Hurtado[1], and Marcelo Mendoza[2]

[1] Center for Web Research
Department of Computer Science
Universidad de Chile
{rbaeza,churtado}@dcc.uchile.cl
[2] Department of Computer Science
Universidad de Valparaiso
marcelo.mendoza@uv.cl

Abstract. Over the past few years, there has been a great deal of research on the use of content and links of Web pages to improve the quality of Web page rankings returned by search engines. However, few formal approaches have considered the use of search engine logs to improve the rankings. In this paper we propose a ranking algorithm that uses the logs of search engines to boost their retrieval quality. The relevance of Web pages is estimated using the historical preferences of users that appear in the logs. The algorithm is based on a clustering process in which groups of semantically similar queries are identified. The method proposed is simple, has low computational cost, and we show with experiments that achieves good results.

1 Introduction

A fundamental task of Web search engines is to rank the set of pages returned to a user's query in a way such that most relevant pages to the query appear in the first places of the answer.

Early search engines used similarity measures between queries and text in Web pages to rank pages. Variations of the vector model [2] were used for this purpose. However, these approaches did not achieve good results, because the words in a document do not always capture properties such as semantics, quality, and relevance of the document, in particular when the size of the Web reached half a billion pages. A further generation of ranking algorithms appeared in the late nineties. They take into account not only the text of Web pages, but also Web hyperlinks. These algorithms explore the fact that links in the Web represent a source of human annotations about the quality of pages. Between them, the most popular are Most-Cited [16], PageRank [8], and HITS [7]. Variations of these algorithms have been described and classified by Lawrence and Giles [9] and Marendy [11].

Web links, as a source of human annotations for ranking algorithms, have some drawbacks. First, they are in general made by experts which are the people

J. Favela et al. (Eds.): AWIC 2004, LNAI 3034, pp. 164–175, 2004.
© Springer-Verlag Berlin Heidelberg 2004

that design Web pages and can place links in the Web. Not always the recommendations of experts are as good as one may think. Frei and Schäuble [5] argue that opinions of common users are more consistent than the ones of experts. Based on empirical evidence, Ress and Schultz [13] and Lesk and Salton [10] conclude that when the opinions of common users are context independent, they do not have the bias inherent to a group of experts. Second, links do not necessarily reflect the dynamism of human preferences in the Web. It is natural for older sites to have more links coming to them than new sites. Web sites that become obsolete for users may keep links and high ranks in search engines, after long periods of time. Third, it is not easy to capture meaningful connections between pages from links. In many cases, Web resources are not oriented to a single subject, in which cases links represent ambiguous connections whose semantic may not be clear.

1.1   Problem Statement

Search logs keep track of queries and URL's selected by users when they are finding useful data through search engines. Current search engines use search logs in their ranking algorithms. However, there is not much public information on the methods they use to do so. The vast majority of ranking algorithms in research papers consider only text and Web links, and the inclusion of logs in the equation is a problem scarcely studied.

Algorithms that use logs such as DirectHit[3] have appeared on the Web. They use previous session logs of a given query to compute ranks based on the popularity (number of clicks) of each URL that appears in the answer to a query. However, this approach only works for queries that are frequently formulated by users, because less common queries do not have enough clicks to allow significant ranking scores to be calculated. For less common queries, the direct hit rating provides a small benefit. A solution to this problem is to cluster together similar queries to identify groups of user preferences of significant sizes from which useful rankings can be derived. This is the approach we present in this paper. However, there is still little formal research on the different problems that arise when doing so in the context of web queries. Problems such as the definition of an adequate notion of similarity for Web search queries, and the design of an adequate clustering process in this setting are still open.

1.2   Contributions

In this paper we present a ranking algorithm in which the computation of the relevance of pages is based on historical preferences of other users, registered in query-logs. The algorithm is based on a new query clustering approach, which uses a notion of query similarity that overcomes the limitations of previous notions (see Section 2). In our algorithm, the degree of similarity of two queries is given by the fraction of common terms in the URL's clicked in the answers

---

[3] Now Ask Jeeves http://www.askjeeves.com

of the queries. Our similarity measure allows to capture semantic connections between queries, that cannot be captured by query words. In addition, the notion does not yield sparse similarity matrices, which are usually generated by other notions of query similarity.

Finally, we present an experimental evaluation of the proposed algorithm. The algorithm is trained with logs from a popular search engine for the Chilean Web (TodoCL). The results show that our ranking algorithm improves the retrieval precision of this search engine.

2 Related Work

Some previous works (e.g. DirectHit, PageRate [4], MASEL [17]) have studied the problem of using Web logs in ranking algorithms. Click-through data is also used by search engines to evaluate the quality of changes to the ranking algorithm by tracking them. Baeza-Yates [1] presents a survey on the use of Web logs to improve different aspects of search engines.

Wen *et al.* [15] propose to cluster similar queries to recommend URLs to frequently asked queries of a search engine. They use four notions of query distance: (1) based on keywords or phrases of the query; (2) based on string matching of keywords; (3) based on common clicked URL's; and (4) based on the distance of the clicked documents in some pre-defined hierarchy. Befferman and Berger [3] also propose a query clustering technique based on a distance notion (3). From a study of the log of a popular search engine, Jensen *et al* [6], conclude that most queries are short (around 2 terms per query) and imprecise, and the average number of pages clicked per answer is very low (around 2 clicks per query). Thus, notions (1)-(3) are difficult to deal with in practice, because distance matrices between queries generated by them are very sparse, and many queries with semantic connections appear as orthogonal objects in such matrices. Notion (4) needs a concept taxonomy and requires the clicked documents to be classified into the taxonomy as well.

Additional related work is on a technique for building recommender systems called *collaborative filtering* [12]. The task of collaborative filtering is to predict the utility of items to a particular user, called the active user, based on a database of votes from a sample or population of other users. Given a user searching for information, the idea is to first find similar users (via a k-neighborhood search or clustering process) and then suggest items preferred by the similar users to the active user. Since users are difficult to identify in search engines, we aggregate them in queries, i.e., sets of users searching for similar information. Thus the active user in our context is the input query. The items are respectively Web pages and queries in the answer ranking and query recommendation algorithms.

Zhang and Dong [17] propose the MASEL (Matrix Analysis on Search Engine Log) algorithm which uses search engine logs to improve the ranking of an image search engine. Clicks are considered positive recommendations on pages. The basic idea is to extract from the logs, relationships between users, queries, and pages. These relationships are used to estimate the quality of answers, based on the quality of related users and queries. The approach relies in the identification of users of the search engine in different sessions, a task difficult to achieve in practice. Our approach instead focuses on queries by aggregating user preferences into queries, and then into clusters of queries.

3   Ranking Algorithm

The available data is a set of user logs from which we extract query sessions. Figure 1 shows the relationships between the different entities that participate in the process induced by the use of a search engine. Our approach focuses in the semantic relationship between queries (that will be defined by a notion of query similarity) and the preferences/feedback of user about Web pages.

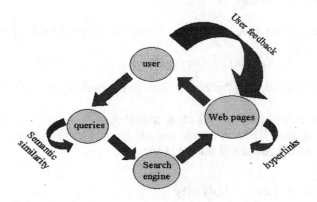

Fig. 1. Relationship between entities in the process of a search engine.

The ranking algorithm is based on a clustering process that defines neighborhoods of similar queries, according to user preferences. A single query (list of terms) may be submitted to the search engine several times, each of which defines a query session. In this paper, we use a simple notion of query session similar to the notion introduced by Wen *et al.* [15] which consists of a query, along with the URL's clicked in its answer:

$$QuerySession := (query, (clickedURL)^*)$$

The selected URL's are those the user that submitted a query clicked on until she/he submit another query. A more detailed notion of query session may consider the rank of each clicked URL and the answer page in which the URL appears, among other data that can be considerer for further versions of the algorithm we present in this paper.

3.1 Algorithm Sketch

Our ranking algorithm considers only queries that appear in the query-log. The algorithm operates in the following two phases:

1. Preprocessing phase at periodical and regular intervals:
   - Queries and clicked URLs are extracted from the Web log and clustered using the text of all the clicked URLs.
   - For each cluster C_i, compute and store the following; a list Q_i containing queries in the cluster; and a list U_i containing the k-most popular URLs in C_i, along with their popularity (number of clicks in the query log).
2. On-line searching phase: Given a query q, if that query appears in the stored clusters, we find the cluster C_i to which the query belongs. Then the ranking for q, $\mathtt{Rank}(q)$, is U_i, that is, we order the URLs according to their popularity. Otherwise, do nothing.

This ranking can then be used to boost the original ranking algorithm by using

$$\mathtt{NewRank}(u) = \beta \, \mathtt{OrigRank}(u) + (1 - \beta) \, \mathtt{Rank}(u) \tag{1}$$

In this expression, $\mathtt{OrigRank}(u)$ is the current ranking returned by the search engine.

Although is true that not all clicks are relevant to a query, during the clustering process those URLs in most cases will be outliers or fall into bad clusters. Then, those *wrong* clicks will not be used.

3.2 Notion of Query Similarity

In our framework, the similarity of two queries is essentially given by the similarity of the documents that users click in the answers of the queries.

Given a query q, and a URL u, let $\mathtt{Pop}(q, u)$ be the popularity of u (fraction of clicks coming from the log) in the answers of q. Let $\mathtt{Tf}(t, u)$ be the number of occurrences of term t in URL u. Our vocabulary is the set of all different words in the clicked URLs. *Stopwords* (frequent words) are eliminated from the vocabulary considered.

We define a vector representation for q, $\boldsymbol{q}$, where $\boldsymbol{q}[i]$ is the i-th component of the vector associated to the i-th term of the vocabulary (all different words), as follows:

$$\boldsymbol{q}[i] = \sum_{URLs \; u} \frac{\mathtt{Pop}(q, u) \times \mathtt{Tf}(t_i, u)}{\max_t \mathtt{Tf}(t, u)} \tag{2}$$

where the sum ranges over all clicked URLs. Note that our representation changes the inverse document frequency by click popularity in the classical tf-idf weighting scheme.

Different notions of similarity (e.g., cosine function or Pearson correlation) can be applied over the aforementioned vectorial representation of queries. In this paper we use the cosine function, which considers two documents similar if they have similar proportions of occurrences of words (but could have different length or word occurrence ordering).

The notion of query similarity we propose has several advantages: (1) it is simple and easy to compute; (2) it allows to relate queries that happen to be worded differently but stem from the same information need; (3) it leads to similarity matrices that are much less sparse than matrices based on previous notions of query similarity (see Section 2); (4) the vectorial representation of queries we propose yields intuitive and useful feature characterizations of clusters, as we will show in Section 4.1.

3.3   Clustering Queries

The clustering process is achieved by successive runs of a k-means algorithm, using the CLUTO software package[4]. The algorithm we used operates as follows. Initially, it randomly selects a set of objects (in our case queries) that act as seed centroids of initial clusters. During each iteration the objects are visited at random order, each object is moved to the cluster whose centroid is closest to the object, whenever this operation leads to an improvement of the overall clusters quality. This process is repeated until no further improvement is achieved. We refer the reader to [18] for details.

We chose a k-means algorithm for the simplicity and low computational cost of this approach compared with other clustering algorithms. In addition, the k-means implementation chosen has proved to have good quality performance for document clustering [18]. Since queries in our approach are similar to vectors of web documents, the requirements for clustering queries in our approach are similar to those for clustering documents.

The quality of the resulting clusters is measured by a score or criterion function, used by common vector-space implementations of the k-means algorithm [19]. The function measures the average similarity between the vectors and the centroids of the cluster that are assigned to. Let C_r be a cluster found in a k-way clustering process ($r \in 1..k$), and let c_r be the centroid of the rth cluster. The criterion function $\mathcal{I}$ is defined as

$$\mathcal{I} = \frac{1}{n} \sum_{r=1}^{k} \sum_{v_i \in C_r} sim(v_i, c_r) \qquad (3)$$

where the centroid c_r of a cluster C_r is defined as $(\sum_{v_i \in C_r} v_i)/|C_r|$, and n is the number of queries.

---

[4] CLUTO is a software package developed at the University of Minnesota that provides a portfolio of algorithms for clustering collections of documents in high-dimensional vectorial representations. For further information see http://www-users.cs.umn.edu/ karypis/cluto/.

4   Experimental Results

We performed experiments with a 15-day query-log of TodoCl, a popular search engine for the Chilean Web (.cl domain), having approximately 50,000 visits daily. In the experiments we compare the retrieval precision of our algorithm with the retrieval precision of the ranking algorithm of TodoCL. The ranking algorithm of TodoCL is based on a belief network which is trained with links and content of Chilean Web pages [14], and does not consider logs.

The 15-day log contains 6042 queries which have at least one click in their answers. There are 22190 clicks in answers (almost 3.7 per query), and these clicks are over 18527 different URL's. The experiments consider the study of a set of 10 randomly selected queries. The 10 queries were selected following the probability distribution of the 6042 queries of the log. Queries in search log distribute according to a power-law [1], our data shows the same. The first column of Table 1 shows the selected queries. The original Spanish terms in the queries have been translated.

Query	Custer Rank	Features
amebiasis	279	therapy (75%)
bride dress	179	fiances (84%)
electronic invoice	123	internet (95%)
free internet	289	free (85%)
hotel beach	73	hotel (95%)
plotters	487	printer (54%) parts (8%) toner (7%) note-books (7%)
secondary-school	127	secondary-school (37%) institution (30%) admission (9%)
soccer leagues	210	*vivefutbol* (39%) leagues (32%)
tourism offer	57	state (99%)
yoga	525	letter (33%) yoga (23%) tai-chi (9%)

Table 1. Queries selected for the experimental evaluation and their clusters.

4.1   Clustering Process

We determine the final number of clusters by performing successive runs of the k-means algorithm. Figure 2 shows the quality of the clusters found for different values of k, i.e., the number of clusters computed in each run. The figure also shows the quality gain in the successive runs. The quality score is an input of the clustering process, and determines the number of clusters found. In our experiments, we fix a quality score of 0.58 which was reached at $k = 600$ clusters. Figure 3 shows an histogram for the number of queries in each of cluster found.

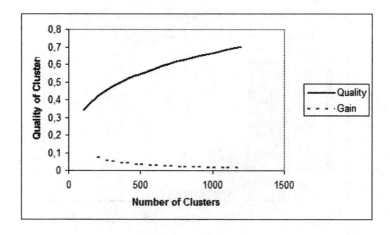

Fig. 2. Cluster quality vs. number of clusters

It took 22 minutes to compute the 600 clusters using a Pentium IV computer, with CPU clock rate of 2.4 GHz, 512MB RAM, and running Windows XP.

table 1 also shows statistics of the clusters to which the selected queries belong to. The second column shows the quality rank of each cluster, among the 600 clusters. The last column depicts the set of feature terms that best describe each one of the clusters. We have translated the original Spanish terms. Right next to each feature term, there is a number that is the percentage of the within cluster similarity that this particular feature can explain. For example, for the first cluster the feature "letter" explains 33% of the average similarity of the queries in the cluster. Intuitively, these terms represent a subset of dimensions (in the vectorial representation of the queries) for which a large fraction of queries agree. The cluster queries form a dense subspace for these dimensions.

Our results are very encouraging. Table 2 shows the queries that belongs to the clusters of queries *dress bride, free internet, yoga,* and *soccer leagues.* Many clusters represent clearly defined information needs of search engine users. Notice that the clusters contain queries which have different keywords but stem from the same information needs, and allows us to identify semantic connections between queries which do not share query words. As an example, the feature term *letter* of the cluster of query *yoga* reveals that users that search for web sites about yoga, also search for information about *astral letters.* Probably, some sites containing information about yoga contain references to astral letters. The term *vivefutbol* related to the query *soccer league* refers to a soccer site which is popular in the domain of the search engine. The term *therapy* suggests that the users looking at *amebiasis* are interested in therapies for this disease. Another example is the term *admission* related to query *secondary-school,* which shows that users searching for secondary-schools are mainly interested in admission information.

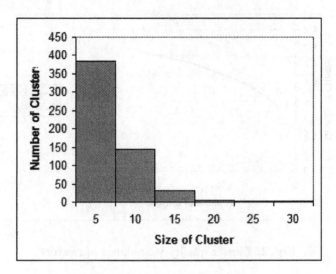

Fig. 3. Histogram of cluster sizes.

Query	Other Queries in Cluster.
dress bride	house of bride
	dress wedding
	dress bridegroom
	wedding cake
	wedding rings
free internet	phone company
	free internet connection
	free ads
	cibercafe santiago
	free text messages
	free email
yoga	tai chi exercises
	astral letter
	reiki
	birth register
soccer leagues	*ivan zamorano*
	soccer leagues chile
	soccer teams chile
	marcelo salas

Table 2. Queries in clusters.

4.2   Quality of the Ranking Algorithm

Figures 4 illustrates the average retrieval precision of TodoCL and the proposed ranking algorithms, for the top-10 answers of each of the the ten queries studied.

In order to evaluate the quality of the ranking approach based on query-logs we use $\beta = 0$ (Equation 1) in the proposed algorithm. The judgments of the relevance of the answers to each query were performed by people from our computer science department. The figure shows that the proposed algorithm can significantly boost the average precision of TodoCL. For the top-2 answers the two algorithms behave similarly since todoCl in general returns good answers at the top and users tend to click them. The improvement in the retrieval quality of the original algorithm becomes notorious when we consider answer sets of more than three documents, where the information carried by the clicks is very useful to discard documents that are of little interest to users.

For six of the ten queries studied, the proposed ranking algorithm clearly outperformed the retrieval precision of TodoCL. In two of them the original algorithm performed slightly better. A possible explanation for this is that some relevant URLs returned by TodoCL in the first places of these queries had text descriptors that were not attractive to users. In the remainder two queries both approaches had a similar performance.

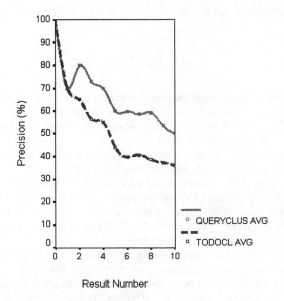

Fig. 4. Average retrieval precision for ten randomly selected queries.

5   Conclusion

We have proposed a method for boosting page rankings based on a clustering process over queries extracted from search engine logs. The method proposed is simple and has reasonable computational cost for periodical preprocessing. Our experiments show that it achieves good results in improving the retrieval precision of a popular search engine for the Chilean Web.

Our ranking algorithm considers only queries that appear in the query-log. We are working on extensions to deal with new queries submitted by users. Since these queries do not have log history, we have to solve the problem of determining the closest clusters to them. One approach to do this is to compute the similarity between query words and feature terms that characterize each cluster (such as cluster features of Table 1).

Another problem inherent to the use of query logs is that the clicked URLs are biased to the ranking algorithm of the search engine. We are currently working in how to reduce and adjust this bias. In addition, we are adapting the algorithm to the natural changes of the problem. Queries and URLs change in time, so the clusters should change too.

Acknowledgments

This research was supported by Millennium Nucleus, Center for Web Research (P01-029-F), Mideplan, Chile. M. Mendoza was partially supported by DIPUV-03 project.

References

1. R. Baeza-Yates. Query usage mining in search engines. *Web Mining: Applications and Techniques, Anthony Scime, editor. Idea Group*, 2004.
2. R. Baeza-Yates and B. Ribeiro-Neto. *Modern Information Retrieval*, chapter 3, pages 75–79. Addison-Wesley, 1999.
3. D. Beeferman and A. Berger. Agglomerative clustering of a search engine query log. In *KDD*, pages 407–416, Boston, MA USA, 2000.
4. C. Ding and C. Chi. Towards an adaptive and task-specific ranking mechanism in web searching (poster session). In *Proceedings of the 23rd annual international ACM SIGIR conference on Research and development in information retrieval*, pages 375–376, Athens, Greece, 2000. ACM Press. http://doi.acm.org/10.1145/345508.345663.
5. H. Frei and P. Schuble. Determining the effectiveness of retrieval algorithms. *Information Processing and Management*, 27(2):153–164, 1991.
6. M. Jansen, A. Spink, J. Bateman, and T. Saracevic. Real life information retrieval: a study of user queries on the web. *ACM SIGIR Forum, 32(1):5-17*, 1998.
7. J. Kleinberg. Authoritative sources in a hyperlinked environment. *ACM-SIAM Symposium on Discrete Algorithms (SODA)*, 46(5):604–632, 1998. http://www.cs.cornell.edu/home/kleinber/auth.pdf.
8. P. Lawrence, S. Brin, R. Motwani, and T. Winograd. The pagerank citation ranking: Bringing order to the web. *Stanford Digital Library Technologies Project*, 1998. http://citeseer.nj.nec.com/page98pagerank.html.
9. S. Lawrence and C. Giles. Searching the web: General and scientific information access. *IEEE Communications*, 37(1):116–122, 1999.
10. M. Lesk and G. Salton. Relevance assessments and retrieval system evaluation. *Information Storage and Retrieval*, 4(3):343–359, 1968.

11. P. Marendy.   A review of world wide web searching techniques. http://citeseer.nj.nec.com/559198.html, 2001.
12. M. Oconnor and J. Herlocker.   Clustering items for collaborative filtering.   Technical report, University of Minnesota, Minneapolis, MN, 1999. http://www.cs.umbc.edu/ ian/sigir99-rec/papers.
13. A. Rees and D. Schultz. A field experimental approach to the study of relevance assessments in relation to document searching. Technical report, NFS, 1967.
14. I. Silva, B. Ribeiro-Neto, P. Calado, E. Moura, and N. Ziviani. Link-based and content-based evidential information in a belief network model. In *Proc of the 23rd ACM SIGIR Conference on Research and Development in Information Retrieval*, pages 96–103, Athens, Greece, July 2000.
15. J. Wen, J. Nie, and H. Zhang. Clustering user queries of a search engine. In *Proc. at 10th International World Wide Web Conference*, pages 162–168. W3C, 2001.
16. B. Yuwono and L. L. Search and ranking algorithms for locating resources on world wide web. In *International Conference on Data Engineering*, pages 164–171. ICDE, 1996.
17. D. Zhang and Y. Dong. A novel web usage mining approach for search engines. *Computer Networks Elsevier*, pages 303–310, Abril 2002.
18. Y. Zhao and G. Karypis. Comparison of agglomerative and partitional document clustering algorithms. In *SIAM Workshop on Clustering High-dimensional Data and its Applications*, 2002.
19. Y. Zhao and G. Karypis. Criterion functions for document clustering. Technical report, University of Minnesota, Minneapolis, MN, 2002.

Fast Transforms in the Internet Document Retrieval

Piotr S. Szczepaniak [1, 2], Michał M. Jacymirski [1]

[1] Institute of Computer Science, Technical University of Lodz
Wólczańska 215, 93-005 Lodz, Poland
[2] Systems Research Institute, Polish Academy of Sciences
Newelska 6, 01-447 Warsaw, Poland

Abstract. Recently, Fourier and cosine discrete transformations have been proposed to improve document ranking. The methods are advantageous in that they allow the use of spatial information on the presence of a term rather than a count of the term frequency. Further improvement of the approach can be reached by application of fast realizations of discrete transforms. The latter can also obtain a neural implementation.

Keywords. Information retrieval, text representation, fast discrete transforms, neural computations

1 Introduction

The two methods for text representation, most frequently reported in the literature, are those of string kernels and vector space models. Operating on characters, string kernels [7,8] use low level information. Features are defined by the extent to which all possible ordered sequences of characters are represented in the document. Due to a modified usage idea, string kernels can be also applied to sequences of words [2]. Although, on one hand, this considerably increases the number of symbols to process, on the other hand it reduces the average number of symbols per document, and results in higher computational efficiency. Moreover, strings of words carry more high level information than strings of characters. Further modification of string kernels enables soft-matching and cross-lingual document similarity [2].

A vector space model is, in a nutshell, a representation of a textual document by a vector [15]. Since within every vector there is information on the number of times that each word appears in the document, document vectors can be easily compared either to each other or to query vectors. Unfortunately, the information about the spatial location of words is lost. Recently, Fourier and cosine discrete transformations have been proposed to improve document ranking [11,12]. Discrete transforms allow storing of term signals, and thus tracing of terms throughout the document. The comparison of query and document terms, based on such features as their magnitude and phase, is performed in the following four standard steps:
- Preparation of word signals;
- Pre-weighting;
- Determination of the discrete transformation;
- Document relevance evaluation.

J. Favela et al. (Eds.): AWIC 2004, LNAI 3034, pp. 176-183, 2004.
© Springer-Verlag Berlin Heidelberg 2004

Each of the steps can involve different methods. For the sake of clarity and completeness of the presentation, the first two steps will be briefly described following the mentioned works of Park et al. [11,12], and then closer attention will be focused on the speed of determination of discrete transformations as well as on their neural implementation.

2 Word Signal

Following [11], let us group words into bins. Assuming w words and b bins within a considered document, one obtains w/b words in each bin. The elements of word vectors are numbers representing occurrence of a selected word within successive bins of the document. Then, for a quick retrieval of word vectors an inverted index should be created. The weighting of document vectors may be performed in different ways, for example

$$w_{n,t,d} = 1+\log_e f_{n,t,d}$$

or

$$w_{n,t,d} = (1+\log_e f_{t,d})\left(\frac{f_{n,t,d}}{f_{t,d}}\right)$$

where $w_{n,t,d}$ and $f_{n,t,d}$ are the weight and count of term t in spatial bin n of document d, respectively, and $f_{t,d}$ - the count of term t in document d.

The weights are then applied as input signals for a chosen discrete transform, i.e. either the cosine or the Fourier one.

Let the Fourier transform be applied:

$$F_{k,t,d} = \sum_{n=0}^{N-1} w_{n,t,d} \exp\left(-\frac{j2\pi kn}{N}\right), \quad k = 0,1, ..., N-1.$$

It transforms the input signal from the time or spatial domain to the frequency domain, and consequently, instead of considering the weight of term t in bin n of document d, it is possible to consider the k-th frequency component $F_{k,t,d}$ in this document.

3 Fast Transforms

3.1 Base Computational Scheme

Let the elements of a given sequence $\vec{x}_N$ be real numbers. Any linear transformation

$$y_N = A_N x_N \tag{1}$$

is uniquely determined by the elements of matrix A_N, where $x_N^T = [x_0 x_1 ... x_{N-1}]$ and $y_N^T = [y_0 y_1 ... y_{N-1}]$ – samples of input and output signals, respectively; A_N – $N \times N$ matrix determining the transformation; T– transposition.

This general definition of transformation covers all types of orthogonal discrete transformations, in particular those of Fourier, Hartley, Walsh, Hadamard, cosine and sine [1,9,14,19]. For the discrete Fourier transformation (DFT) we have [1]:

$$F_N(n,k) = \exp(-j2\pi n k / N); \quad n,k = 0,1,...,N-1 \qquad (2)$$

Generally, the DFT enables processing of complex sequences, which evidently must results in redundancy when real sequences are processed. The solution proposed recently is the application of the discrete Hartley transformation (DHT) which has the property of symmetry. In the DHT, the direct and inverse transformations coincide up to the constant multiplier $1/N$, cf. [1]

$$H_N^{-1}(n,k) = \frac{1}{N} H_N(n,k), \; H_N(n,k) = \cos(2\pi n k / N) + \sin(2\pi n k / N); \quad (3)$$

$$n,k = 0,1,...,N-1.$$

Four basic variants of the discrete cosine C_N^X and sine S_N^X transformations [14,18] are employed in the signal processing practice. For example, the second (C_N^{II}, S_N^{II}), the third (C_N^{III}, S_N^{III}) as well as the fourth (C_N^{IV}, S_N^{IV}) of their variants are most frequently used in data compression. Note that they are mutually inversive:

$$C_N^{II}(n,k) = \cos(\pi(2n+1)k/(2N)),$$

$$S_N^{II}(n,k) = \sin(\pi(2n+1)(k+1)/(2N)),$$

$$C_N^{III}(n,k) = p_n \cos(\pi n(2k+1)/(2N)),$$

$$S_N^{III}(n,k) = q_n \sin(\pi(n+1)(2k+1)/(2N)),$$

$$C_N^{IV}(n,k) = \cos(\pi(2n+1)(2k+1)/(4N)),$$

$$S_N^{IV}(n,k) = \sin(\pi(2n+1)(2k+1)/(4N)),$$

where $n,k = 0,1,...,N-1$, $p_0 = 1/N$, $p_n = 2/N, n \neq 0$, $q_{N-1} = 1/N$, $p_n = 2/N, n \neq N-1$.

Generalisation of the results presented in [4,6,16,17] leads to the sequence of operations shown in Fig.1; they allow calculation of all the mentioned transformations.

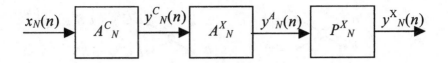

Fig.1. The generalized scheme of direct DCT and DFT (also DST and DHT) calculation

Block A_N^C is common to all the transformations; A_N^C performs an intermediate calculation and its result $y_N^C(k)$ is identical for all the considered transformations. In block A_N^X the transition from the intermediate transformation $y_N^C(k)$ to the required $y_N^{CII}(k)$, $y_N^{SII}(k)$, $y_N^{CIV}(k)$, $y_N^{CIV}(k)$, $y_N^F(k)$ or $y_N^H(k)$ is carried out. In block P_N^X depending on the kind of transformation, the rearrangement of data is performed. Block P_N^X is obviously redundant for grouping and classification tasks, and consequently for the problem considered in this paper.

It is worth mentioning that blocks A_N^C and A_N^X apply fast algorithms. In Fig.2 the flow diagram of the fast algorithm for $N = 8$ is presented while in Fig.3 its base operations are explained. The particular values of C_N^k and S_N^k are specific for a chosen transformation.

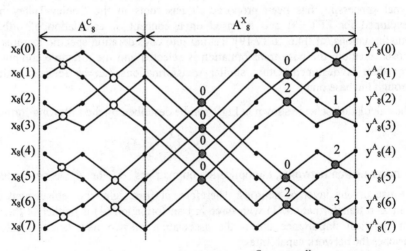

Fig.2. Diagram of 8-point blocks A_N^C and A_N^X

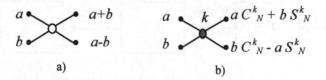

Fig.3. Base operations: a) summation/subtraction, b) vector rotation

For inverse transformations, a similar scheme is valid [6] with the only differences lying in the order of elements and the values of coefficients in the vector rotation formulae. The main advantage of the base computation procedure is the unification of algorithms for various methods. Moreover, all the blocks are realized with the use of fast algorithms [4,6,17,18], which ensures high efficiency.

3.2 Neural Interpretation

As known (cf.[9]), transformations (1) can be realized directly in a linear neuron network with one layer consisting of N neurons with N inputs and one output. Training of such a network consists in a selection of elements in A_N. For example, the network task in data coding is to choose Q coefficients, where Q is essentially smaller than N. Generally, network training requires determination of $2N^2$ elements and proves to be a time-consuming process.

To eliminate this imperfection, a new approach to the design of neural networks for signal processing has been proposed. It has roots in the Cooley-Tukey method developed for FFT [3] and is based on a concept of calculation of orthogonal transformations, cf. [4,6,16,17,19]. Taking into consideration specific features of the chosen method, the base transformation is selected and the effective computational procedure is designed. Other similar transformations can be realized indirectly, through the base one.

The calculation scheme shown in Fig.1 can be described by the following formula

$$y_N^X = P_N^X A_N^X A_N^C x_N. \tag{4}$$

In linear neuron networks, multiplication on matrices A_N^X or A_N^C is performed with the use of one layer of neurons. Therefore, at first sight, the replacement of one matrix in transformation (1) with three in transformation (4) is neither of theoretical nor practical importance unless the association of two new layers substantially enriches the network capabilities.

In general, anything feasible in a network with two, three or more layers can be realized in one layer as well with the same outcome. However, when the properties of matrices A_N^X and A_N^C are taken into account, such a replacement appears well justified.

Firstly, the neuron structure becomes essentially simpler due to the possibility of replacing the vector rotation by two neurons with two inputs and one output, see Fig.4, where $w_1^{(i)}$ and $w_2^{(i)}$ denote weights of the i-th neuron e_i, i=1,2. Obviously, the training of such a neuron becomes more effective than that of a standard neuron with N inputs and one output.

Secondly, multiplication of matrices A_N^C and P_N^X does not need any training (in the considered case, P_N^X can even be omitted). It can be performed using standard, well-known methods, including parallel computers. Thus, the training has been reduced to the determination of matrix A_N^X, most elements of which are equal to zero. Consequently, the training has to be applied only to $N \cdot log_2 N$ two-input neurons, instead of to N neurons with N inputs, which results in a considerable saving of computation time.

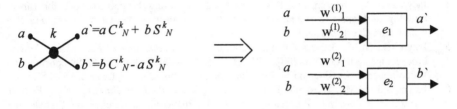

Fig.4. Replacement of vector rotation by two neurons e_1 and e_2

It has been shown so far that six transformations, namely DCT and DST of the second and fourth kind, as well as DHT and DFT, can be realized on the basis of the simplified neural architecture. Moreover, the training is fast and the accuracy is high. (Similarly, one arrives at a neural network which enables fast calculation of inverse transformations DCT, DST, DFT, DHT of the third and fourth variants.)

4 Summary

Internet has become an information source of unquestionable importance. Consequently, the aspiration to meet an obvious need for effective information retrieval by making improvements in the solutions offered by popular indexing engines is observed. The improvement is expected in both retrieval accuracy and speed. For accuracy - the method of text representation and analysis is critical; for speed – apart from hardware, critical is the processing method for the prepared textual data. When discrete transformations allowing for the spread of terms throughout documents are applied, then fast realizations of transformations are the solution for speed improvement.

Orthogonal discrete transformations can be implemented in their fast versions; neural realizations are also possible. The neural method described here assures effective learning of the network because the original task of the complexity of order $O(N^2)$ has been replaced by the task of order $O(N \cdot log_2 N)$ as this is the case for the known Cooley-Tukey algorithm [3]. The (supervised) learning may be performed using any standard method suitable for adjusting weights in linear networks with consideration of the layer network organization, which is not the usual situation in networks of this type. Moreover, the network is able to realize a wide class of known transformations. Consequently, it is flexible in adaptation to a new task.

References

1   Bracewell R.N. (1986): *The Hartley Transform*. Oxford University Press. New York.
2   Cancedda N., Gaussier E., Gooutte C., Renders J.-M. (2003): *Word-Sequence Kernels*. Journal of Machine Learning Research, 3, 1059-1082.
3   Cooley J.W., Tukey J.W. (1965): *An algorithm for the machine calculation of complex Fourier series*. Math. Comput., 5, no.5, 87-109.
4   Jacymirski M., Szczepaniak P.S. (2000): Fast Learning Neural Network for Linear Filtering of Signals. *Proceedings of the 5th Conference on Neural Networks and Soft Computing*, Czestochowa, Poland, pp.130-139.
5   Jacymirski M.M., Szczepaniak P.S. (2002): *Neural Realization of Fast Linear Filters*. Proceedings VIPromCom-2002: 4th EURASIP – IEEE Region 8 Symposium on Video/Image Processing and Multimedia Communications, Zadar, Croatia, 153-157.
6   Jacymirski M.M., Wiechno T.(2001): *A Novel Method of Building Fast Fourier Transform Algorithms*. Proceedings of the International Conference on Signals and Electronic Systems (ICSES'2001), Lodz, Poland, 415-422.
7   Lodhi H., Cristianini N., Shave-Taylor J., Watkins C. (2001): *Text classification using string kernel*. In: Advances in Neural Information Processing Systems, 13, MIT Press.
8   Lodhi H., Saunders C., Shave-Taylor J., Cristianini N., Watkins C. (2002): *Text classification using string kernels*. Journal of Machine Learning Research. 2, 419-444.
9   Lu F.-L. and Unbehauen R. (1998): *Applied Neural Networks for Signal Processing*, Cambridge University Press.
10 Martelinelli G., Ricotti L.P., Marcone G. (1993): Neural Clustering for Optimal KLT Image Compression, *IEEE Transactions on Signal Processing*, Vol.41, No. 4, pp.1737-1739.
11 Park L.A.F., Ramamohanarao K., Palaniswami M. (2002a): *Fourier Domain Scoring: A Novel Document Ranking Method*. IEEE Trans. on Knowledge and Data Engineering (submitted); http://www.ee.mu.oz.au/pgrad/lapark/fds_compare3.pdf
12 Park L.A.F., Ramamohanarao K., Palaniswami M. (2002b): *A Novel Web Text Mining Method Using the Discrete Cosine Transform*. In: T.Elomaa, H.Mannila, H.Toivonen (Eds.): *Principles of Data Mining and Knowledge Discovery*. (Proceedings of the 6th European Conference PKDD'2002, Helsinki, Finland) LNCS, vol.2431, subseries LNAI, Springer-Verlag, Berlin, Heidelberg, 385-396.
13 Szczepaniak P.S., Gil M. (2003): *Practical Evaluation of Textual Fuzzy Similarity as a Tool for Information Retrieval*. In: Menasalvas E., Segovia J., Szczepaniak P.S. (Eds.): *Advances in Web Intelligence*. First International Atlantic Web Intelligence Conference AWIC'2003, Madrid, Spain; Proceedings. Lecture Notes in Artificial Intelligence 2663, Springer-Verlag, Berlin, Heidelberg; pp.250-257.
14 Wang Z. (1984): Fast Algorithms for the Discrete W Transform and for the Discrete Fourier Transform, *IEEE Trans. ASSP*, 32, No.4., pp. 803-816.

15   Witten I.H., Moffat A., Bell T.C. (1999): *Managing gigabytes: compressing and indexing documents and images*. Morgan Kaufmann Publishers.

16   Yatsimirskii M.N. (1993): *Fast Algorithms for the Discrete Cosine Transformations*. Comput. Maths Math. Phys., **33**, no.2, pp.267-270; Pergamon Press Ltd.

17   Yatsymirskyy M.M., Liskevytch R.I. (1999): Lattice Structures for Fourier, Hartley, Cosine and Sine Transformations (*in Ukrainian*). *Modeling and Information Technologies*, No. 2, Institute of Modeling Problems in Power Engineering, Ukrainian Academy of Sciences, Kiev, Ukraine, pp. 173-181.

18   Enger S., Pŭschel M. (2001): Automatic Generation of Fast Discrete Signal Transforms. IEEE Trans. on Signal Processing, **49**, no. 9, pp. 1992-2002.

19   Yatsimirskii M.N. (2000): *Shifted in the Time and Frequency Domains Cosine and Sine Transforms Fast Algorithms with Homogeneous Structure*. Radioelektronika, Kiev, Ukraine, **5-6**, pp.66-75 (Radioelectronics and Communication Systems, Allerton Press Inc., New York).

Analysis of a Web Content Categorization System Based on Multi-agents

Pedro A.C. Sousa[1], João P. Pimentão[1], Bruno R.D. Santos[2], and A. Steiger Garção[2]

[1] Faculdade de Ciências e Tecnologia, Universidade Nova de Lisboa Caparica, Portugal
{pas,pim}@fct.unl.pt
http://www.fct.unl.pt
[2] UNINOVA Campus da FCT/UNL Caparica, Portugal
{brd,asg}@uninova.pt
http://www.fct.unl.pt

Abstract. This paper presents a Multi-Agent based web content categorization system. The system was prototyped using an Agents' Framework for Internet data collection. The agents employ supervised learning techniques, specifically text learning to capture users preferences. The Framework and its application to E-commerce are described and the results achieve during the IST DEEPSIA project are shown. A detailed description of the most relevant system agents as well as their information flow is presented. The advantages derived from agent's technology application are conferred.

1   Introduction

The proliferation of unwanted information is becoming unbearable, imposing the need of new tools to overcome the situation. Either through push mechanisms, such as Email spamming, or by pull mechanisms as presented in web sites, it is necessary to ensure that the individuals can access the relevant information, avoiding unwanted information; saving valuable time otherwise spent on processing more information than that is needed and to decide which information to retain or discard.

In consequence, tools to enhance the results of the current electronic procedures of acquiring data, substituting them by more efficient processes, are required. The "Framework for Internet data collection based on intelligent agents", hereon designated by "Framework", developed in UNINOVA, offers a user-friendly interface customized through a user's-personalized catalogue, which is automatically updated with information gathered from available web sites. The catalogue stores, in a pre-selected ontology, the data collected from different web sites, avoiding manual useless visits to several sites. The process of presenting the catalogue's-collected data is ergonomic and automates the user's most common tasks.

The autonomous data collection and semi-automatic catalogue updating is executed by a FIPA compliant Multi-Agent System (MAS), relieving the end-user from all the "hard work" (i.e. interfacing the web and the private databases). The agents increase their performances, taking advantage of text learning methods, dedicated to Internet information retrieval. The use of an Agent-based System was agreed due to its inherent scalability and ease to delegate work among agents. The

J. Favela et al. (Eds.): AWIC 2004, LNAI 3034, pp. 184-195, 2004.
© Springer-Verlag Berlin Heidelberg 2004

Framework being presented was intensively tested in the project DEEPSIA. All the examples presented in this paper were produced under DEEPSIA's context; i.e., the creation of personalised catalogues of products sold on the Internet.

2   The DEEPSIA Project

The project DEEPSIA "Dynamic on-linE IntErnet Purchasing System, based on Intelligent Agents", IST project Nr. 1999-20 283, funded by the European Union has the generic aim of supporting Small and Medium Enterprises (SME) usual day-to-day purchasing requirements, via the Internet, based on a purchaser-centred solution and tailored to meet individual needs.

Usually, Business-to-Business (B2B) e-commerce models focus on SMEs as suppliers, often within virtual shops or marketplaces, nevertheless, all SMEs are purchasers of goods and services. Depending on the size of the SME, this function may be performed by one person the owner/manager, or the purchasing manager – or may be open to a number of staff [1].

The procurement process is no exception in trying to find relevant information on an information-overloaded web, magnified by the myriad of new commercial sites that are made available everyday.

DEEPSIA's purpose is to provide a purchaser centred solution, available on the user's desktop and tailored to individual requirements, rather than a supplier centred marketplace.

The reduction of time in collecting data will be achieved by presenting the user with a catalogue of products organised under an ontology representing a set of relevant entries, thus avoiding having to browse through a wide range of web pages and links that are not related to his/her needs.

3   The Deepsia's Adopted Framework

DEEPSIA adopted a framework composed of three subsystems, responsible for performing specific tasks, and interacting with each other through data and information flows.

Depicted in Fig. 1 the Framework's subsystems are: a Dynamic Catalogue (DC), responsible for data storage and presentation; a Multi-Agent System (MAS), responsible for autonomous data collection, and semi-automatic catalogue process update; and an optional Portal and Agents Interface System (PAIS), responsible for interfacing directly with the web data suppliers.

3.1   Dynamic Catalogue

The Dynamic Catalogue is the user interface, which is responsible for presenting the information collected by the MAS based on the user's preferences. The dynamic on-line catalogue communicates with the MAS in order to provide the end-users with

186   Pedro A.C. Sousa et al.

all the required information. The catalogue holds not only the information about the data selected by the agents on the web, but also the information about the sites contacted, the ontology in use (configurable by the user) and all user requirements regarding the data gathered and stored. The electronic catalogue's data is stored in a database (DB) and it is made available through a web-browsing interface. For concept storage, ontology and conceptual graph approaches were selected in order to create a user-friendly interface [2].

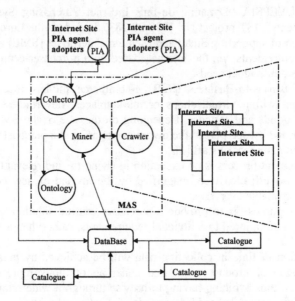

Fig. 1. Conceptual description of the most relevant components (represented by rectangles) and software Agents (represented by circles) that compose the Framework.

For the customisation of the architecture to the project, the DEEPSIA's consortium selected the Universal Standard Products and Services Classification (UNSPSC), from ECCMA [3]. The dynamic catalogue is filled with information provided using two search mechanisms: The Direct Search and the Autonomous Search.

The PAIS implement the direct search system, using Portal Agent Interfaces (PIA), adopted by the commercial web sites and a Collector Agent, which is the multi-agents' systems interface to manage the PIAs.

The PIA is responsible for creating an interface between one specific web supplier's portal (Internet Site PIA agent adopters) and the MAS. The PIA is a facilitator agent installed in the web supplier's site. With this agent, the web supplier creates a dedicated interface to interact with the MAS, thus enabling direct querying to their sites' private databases. It is not mandatory for this agent to be adopted by the web suppliers, since the MAS is able to collect information based on the autonomous search strategy. Nevertheless, its inclusion provides the web suppliers with a much more integrated and flexible interface and enables the possibility of direct querying to web suppliers' DB, i.e. the MAS is able to query the web supplier about specific information.

For the autonomous search an MAS was defined. The tasks performed by the different agents, include between others: message processing, name resolution service, web page discovery, etc. These agents are not described in this paper since their role is quite common and it is not relevant in the context of information retrieval.

The agents responsible for performing the autonomous search can be identified in the , following the path that goes through the Web Crawler agent (WCA), the Miner agent (MA), and the database (DB), with the connection with the Ontology agent. The WCA has the responsibility of crawling and identifying pages with the user's interest themes. The MA has the responsibility to identify the relevant concepts included in the pages selected by the WCA, with the support of the Ontology Agent (that stores all the concepts that the system recognises), and send the concepts, together with the ontology classification, to the user's catalogue.

The Ontology agent is responsible for ontology management and for classifying the concepts found. The Ontology agent answers to queries from the miner for product classification purposes.

Applying the Autonomous Search Mechanism to product promotions' identification scenario (one objective of DEEPSIA), it will result in the following tasks division. A WCA is the responsible discovering and deciding if a page is a product promotion page or not. The MA is responsible for the product identification and for determining the promotion's associated conditions (price, quality, etc).

3.2   The Web Crawler Agent (WCA)

The WCA automatically fetches web pages looking for pre-selected themes defined by the user. The search starts by fetching a seed page, and then all the pages referenced by the seed page, in a recursive approach. Therefore, each time the end-user finds a new site containing the selected theme, he/she can send its URL to the WCA in order to start a deep search for useful information starting at that location.

In the on-line process, the WCA agent uses the last DSS sent by the Tutor, in order to classify and assign a trust factor to each page found.

The trust factor assigned is based on the performance estimated to the DSS in use by the WCA. After the classification process the pages are sent to the Miner agent.

3.3   The Miner Agent (MA)

The MA is responsible for the analysis of the web pages found by the WCA. Once found and classified by the WCA, the MA analyses each page and the relevant information presented on the page will be selected for storage on the catalogue's database. The main challenge for this agent is the selection of the data to be loaded into the catalogue. In fact, it is expectable to find a huge amount of non-significant data that must be avoided in order to produce easy-to-read and directly comparable catalogues. There are two fundamental problems to overcome, concept identification and concept classification. In the on-line process the MA uses a forward inference decision support system for concept identification and a reverse index keyword system for concept classification. The rules instantiated in both systems are maintained by the Tutor Agent. Despite the classification given to each page by the WCA, the MA will overwrite this value according to the quality of the information found during the analysis process.

4   The Tutor Agent (TA)

The Tutor Agent's role is to support the user to perform all the text learning techniques, in an off-line process, in order to create Decision Support Systems (DSS) for the WCA and the MA. To keep the Agent's simplicity, all the learning processes (feature selection, classifiers creation, DSS-Decision Support System definition) are performed by the special Tutor Agent, (omitted from Fig. 1 to improve readability). Their achieved results are mapped to XML and then communicated, using FIPA compliant agent messages, to the respective agents (the Crawler and Miner) [4]. The basic behaviour of all agents is based on a bootstrap knowledge, complemented in time, by the Tutor Agent whenever new conclusions are achieved.

4.1   Web Crawler Agent DSS

For the WCA, the TA's role is to support the user in performing the classical learning tasks of:

Corpus creation: the creation of a database of samples to perform supervised learning. As in all supervised learning process, knowledge is extracted from a set of classified observations (the corpus) that are previously stored [5]. The corpus, used for the experimental results was created during the DEEPSIA project. The corpus was built using one hundred commercial web sites, from an arbitrary Internet site selection. The corpus included a total of 3579 documents, tagged as selling or non-selling samples. Unlabelled documents, or double document tagging (i.e. one document classified in both categories) were not allowed. The corpus included 2528 selling documents and 1051 non-selling documents.

Feature selection: identification of the most relevant words to be selected for the vector in order to reduce the vector's size, usually superior to 30.000 dimensions (one dimension for each word found in the dictionary). The first step consisted in removing all the features included in the stop list DTIC/DROLS. This list retains most of the words in the standard Verity Stop List and adds the words from the DTIC/DROLS stop word list (the full list can be found at http://dvl.dtic.mil/stop_list.html). The second step consisted in performing feature selection (over all words still included in the corpus) using feature's Mutual Information [6], Conditional Mutual Information and Chi-square. Just the most expressive features are selected to be included in the vector for document representation. The exact number of features to be selected (the k-trash-older) is dynamically de-fined depending on the system's performance.

Creation of classifiers: the creation of several possible classifiers in order to produce alternative classification procedures. The classifiers are produced using the pre-selected features vector. The methods studied were the K nearest neighbour, K weighed – NN [7], C4.5 [8] and Bayesian classifier [9].

Setting up a Decision Support System: the creation of rules in order to perform the classification task. The setting up of the DSS is defined based on the available classifiers and the analysis of their performance. The currently selected DSS is the rule of majority applied to the classifications assigned by the selected classifiers.

Creation of the Equivalent Decision Support System (EDSS) for Performance Optimisation. In order to enhance the system global performance an effort was made on the creation of an EDSS, which was presented in [1].

4.1.1   Methodology for Performance Estimation

The corpus was used based on the strategy division presented in Fig. 2, design training, design validation and test set. The Design training Set is used during the learning process. The Design validation Set is exclusively used, if required, for validation within the process of classifier creation. Finally, the Test Set can only be used to evaluate the performance of the system once the classifier is produced and cannot be used to influence the process.

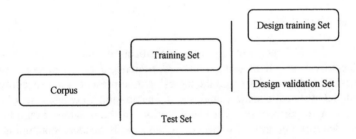

Fig. 2. Corpus logical division for all the different leaning processes

For evaluating the effectiveness of the category assignments by the inducted DSSs, the recall, precision and F_1 measures were used. Recall (R) is the obtained dividing the correct selling assignments by the total selling documents. Precision (P) is obtained dividing the correct selling assignments, by the total selling assignments [10; 11]. The F_1 measure, presented by van Rijsbergen in [12], combines precision and recall in the following equation:

$$F_1 = \frac{2RP}{R+P} \tag{1}$$

The measures used were computed to the document selling assignment, and the values obtained are an average of the values calculated using the k-fold cross-validation [13]. In k-fold cross-validation, the corpus is divided into k subsets of (approximately) equal size. The classifier is inducted k times, each time leaving out one of the subsets from training, and using only the omitted subset to compute the presented measures. In DEEPSIA k=10 was used.

4.1.2   Induction of Classifiers and DSS Definition

The text learning process and DSS definition is not the focus of this paper, therefore only the final results are presented.

Regarding feature selection methods, the best method used was the Conditional Mutual Information (CMI), because of its capability to eliminate correlated features. Genetic Algorithms were used for CMI determination to overcome its computational complexity with a remarkable performance, even if they do not guarantee the best solution.

Regarding classifier induction, several classes of methods were under intensive analysis: nearest neighbour, K weighed – NN, C4.5 and Bayesian classifier. All the classifiers were inducted using the CMI features ranking. The best results were achieved with the decision trees inducted using the C4.5 algorithm.

Regarding the Decision Support System development the best results were achieved using nine C4.5 decision trees induced using different training sets over the original corpus. The trees were aggregated using the majority rule.

Finally, the created EDSS increased the system performance reducing the number of used decision trees.

4.2   Miner Agent DSS

The DSS of the MA performs concept identification and concept classification. Concept identification is done using a forward inference decision support system with if-then rules. The rules are based on the pages' textual presentation procedures. Based on detailed and systematic sample analysis, it was possible to create a set of rules that enables the MA to perform concept identification. In the previous example it would consist on determining the existence of a table with headers containing specific tokens. Concept identification rules are stored in the Tutor agent's knowledge base; which then updates the MA's behaviour by sending, using XML, the new rules encapsulated in FIPA compliant agent messages. To accomplish this task Machine Learning techniques were not employed.

After the concept's identification, the concept needs to be classified in order to assign it to a given section of the catalogue, i.e. concept classification. The concept classification is done based on a reverse index keyword mechanism. The keywords are automatically suggested by the MA based on the identification rules of the previous task and on hyperlink interpretation[14].

In DEEPSIA, the keywords produced by the identification rules are a composition of the product fields identified: (product description and product reference) derived by the forward inference rules. This set of rules is usually site independent.

Besides the previous keywords, hyperlink interpretation also enables keyword generation. The latter, are produced taking advantage of the fact that an important number of e-commerce sites dynamically compose their web pages. This set of rules is usually site dependent. A brief analysis of the hyperlink http://ess.shopping.sapo.pt/ shop/searchresults.asp?CategoryID=2536 can easily exemplify the rules used for interpretation. The page, obviously, belongs to the shopping "SAPO" and is selling a product with the CategoryID 2536, since this number follows the identifier CategoryID=. Therefore, the first rule for future analysis of SAPO's links should be "find CategoryID= and use the following number for product classification".

After this rule instantiation, for all future SAPO shops the MA will try to find the "CategoryID=" in the hyperlink and select the following numbers as a keyword for product identification. Since, these products are usually stored in a database and the categories do not change overtime, after storing the relation of that keyword to the Ontology node where it fits, the future products will be correctly identified.

The knowledge base of the MA can be continuously updated, which allows it to focus the data acquisition process towards the set of resources and resource categories that are usually requested by the users of the service.

5   The Web-Based Prototype

The developed prototype is a Web based application, with two distinct user profiles: Regular User and Power User. The Regular User profile gives the user access to the system through the catalogue. This is the interface for the final user that does not have specific Information Technology skills. The Power User profile gives the user access to the components of the Framework through a dedicated interface enabling the observation of the system's progress. This interface is devoted to advanced Information Technology users and it is available just for internal system demonstration purposes.

In order to enable this approach, the user interfaces were developed separated from the respective controlled modules and agents. This means that the components do not have built-in user interfaces, but only querying interfaces with a defined protocol. This allows the component usage in different contexts (e.g. in the specific case of the prototype, in the Regular User and in the Power User profiles) for the same platform of agents. The tool was developed in JAVA [15] using a JADE platform [16].

In both user profiles, different users have different logons that correspond to different resources allocation, thus enabling individual use of the system. Therefore, independently of the profile, different users will have access to different logical databases, personal catalogues and all the necessary agents to create a personalised instance of the multi-agent system. Therefore, after login, the user will be assigned, if available, all the resources to collect information and to build their personal customised catalogue. The resources will be available to the user for a 24 hours period.

In Fig.3 it is possible to identify, the information flow and the resources allocated to the users in the autonomous search context.

5.1   Information Flow

Given a seed root web page, the WCA initiates the process of site content categorization, see Fig.3 a). For every page of the web site, the WCA uses its current DSS to determine the class of the page (relevant/irrelevant for the theme under analysis). The WCA sends all the pages categorized as relevant for the user, to the MAs that have stated their capability to process the specific theme, see Fig.3 c). After this moment, the pages are available for the MA to perform concept identification.

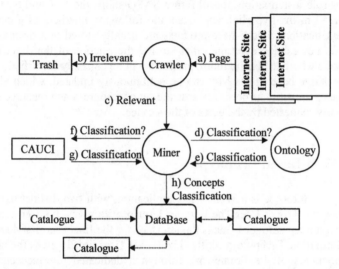

Fig. 3. User's personal resource set allocation solid arrows represent ACL messages and dotted arrows represent system information

For each message received the MA performs the following process: i) Page analysis using the concept identification rules, to identify the user's interesting concepts, which, in the case of DEEPSIA, are the available products. ii) For every concept identified, the MA collects concept information using the concept's classification rules, stored in the Ontology, by querying the Ontology agent, see Fig. 3 d) and e). iii) Depending on the ontology agent answer, the MA sends the concept information directly to the catalogue or to the user interface for computer-aided user's concept identification, see Fig. 3 f) to h).

From all the resources visible in Fig. 3, the WCA, the MA and the Catalogue, are allocated as a block to each individual user since they are user context dependent. The other components are shared since they are stateless.

5.2   Deployment

The prototype was demonstrated as a Brazilian/European effort. The distributed platform was installed in all the countries involved in the project (Belgium, Brazil, Poland, Portugal, Spain) and the task oriented agents separated by countries. The Crawlers and Miners were located in Portugal, Brazil and Belgium; the PIA in Spain; the Catalogue and the respective interface agents in Poland. The platform used the Internet connectivity and the sites processed (scanned by the demo) were one hundred European commercial sites randomly selected. This prototype configuration proved its ability to work in a widely distributed environment with the standard Internet infrastructure since no dedicated links were established. The platform's deployment was facilitated due to the use of an Agent-based system because each agent is an autonomous application that uses a standard protocol of communication, which makes the platform distribution quite easy as the actual location of the agent is totally irrelevant for the operation of the platform.

The inherent scalability of an Agent-based system is also a powerful tool in order to provide a better service to the platform's users, because it is possible to replicate several instances of an agent that provides a given service. The location of an agent can be irrelevant for regular use of the platform but it can be extremely important if we need to optimize the service provided. For example, we can deploy WCA's in different countries and force these agents only to crawl in its regional environment. That way the downloading of pages' bottleneck will be drastically reduced as only the interesting pages will be transferred to the MA for content extraction. The service can be improved by using different learning techniques and different training sets for different agents, which will empower the agents with a speciality, in terms of content categorization or extraction.

6 Why Agent Technology?

The agent technology is not a generic panacea to be applied to every day problems. Between others, the general complexity of the paradigm, the imposed communication and computational overhead, and the usage of a real distributed programming approach must be taken into account at the decision's moment. Furthermore, the lack of a sound theory and standards to support the analysis' and implementation process, together with the inexistence of robust, scalable and secure agent development platforms and agent deployment platforms are real obstacles to produce fast, reliable, and secure systems.

Therefore, the usage of agent's approach must be carefully analyzed and specially applied to real distributed, modular, decentralized decision making and ill-structured problems. Then the advantages will overcome the disadvantages and the achieved solutions are flexible, natural and elegant.

The nature of the problem under study is difficult to deal with, using traditional software engineering techniques. Even the traditional distributed approaches are difficult to applied because of the decentralized decision making and the geographical distribution. Therefore, the agent approach seamed suitable at the beginning of the project.

In fact, the agents' paradigm confirmed this assumption throughout the project execution coping efficiently with the day-by-day problems and situations.

The agents' modular approach enables a flexible source encapsulation increasing reusability, and fast and easy error detection and correction. The fact that every agent implements an independent decision maker allowed the implementation of a natural decentralized decision system. The straightforward capability to introduce, eliminate, or change agents, or agent types, adapted to the problem's ill-structure facilitated the development and implementation, since the error reflexes, or unexpected behaviors resulting from changes are self-contained and avoided secondary reflexes.

The agents' intelligence is the result of applying learning techniques, specifically the supervised text learning and the if-then-else rules.

7   Conclusions

The "Framework for Internet data collection based on intelligent agents" is a generic approach; its context definition is done using the training process of the Crawler and of the Miner agents. Depending on the class, the ontology and the rules definition, the system may be adapted to distinctive objectives and we hope time and experience will continue to support our expectations.

The framework was under extensive tests in the DEEPSIA's project, and the achieved results were very positive and above the consortium's expectations. Although the used corpus is dedicated to e-procurement, the global results achieved are encouraging and the framework is now under testing with other corpus.

The use of different learning techniques and DSS was a priority from the beginning of the project as the joint effort of all learning techniques increases drastically the performance of the platform, taking advantage of the particularities of each technique concerning its success ratio in terms of quantity and aim.

The Framework has shown to be fit for the application in the DEEPSIA scenario. During the project, we reached the conclusion that SMEs, would rather prefer to monitor a set of pre-selected sites (their usual suppliers), than to search the whole World-Wide-Web trying to identify new web sites (most of them not relevant to the business of the company). In this environment the DEEPSIA solution is quite effective. Since the corpus from where the DSSs are inducted is created with the pages from the user's selected sites, the corpus is roughly equal to the universe; therefore the estimated precision and recall values achieved are very similar to the real values.

For further information about the project, the latest achievements and access to the prototype please consult the DEEPSIA's web site on www.deepsia.org.

Generically speaking, the architecture contributes to a new solution for information retrieval based on text learning techniques.

The usage of agents was fundamental to achieve the results in a short period.

The association of both technologies, agents and leaning, enabled promising results and the creation of a generic approach applicable in different environments. Its usage in Finance and Military fields are already under analysis with similar results.

References

1. Sousa, P. A. C., J. P. Pimentão, et al. 2002. A framework for Internet data collection based on intelligent Agents: The methodology to produce equivalent DSS. Smart Engineering System Design: Neural Networks, Fuzzy logic, Evolutionary programming, data mining, and complex systems, St. Louis, USA, ASME.
2. Tan, T. 1993. The development of Intelligent Conceptual storage and retrieval system. Sunderland, UK, University of Sunderland.

3. ECCMA 2002. ECCMA web site. 2002.
4. FIPA00061 2000. FIPA ACL Message Structure Specification. Foundation for Intelligent Physical Agents.
5. Mitchell, T. M. 1996. Machine Learning, McGraw-Hill International Editions.
6. Yang, Y.&J. P. Pedersen 1997. A Comparative Study on Feature Selection in Text Categorization. ICML'97 - Fourteenth International Conference on Machine Learning.
7. Yang, Y.&X. Liu 1999. A re-examination of text categorization methods. SIGIR'99.
8. Quinlan, J. 1993. C4.5: Programs for Machine Learning. San Mateo, Morgan Kaufmann.
9. Hastie, T., R. Tibshirani, et al. 2001. The elements of statistic learning, Data Mining, Inference, and prediction, Springer.
10. Junker, M., A. Dengel, et al. 1999. On the Evaluation of Document Analysis Components by Recall, Precision, and Accuracy. Fifth International Conference on Document Analysis and Recognition, Bangalore, India, IEEE.
11. Ault, T.&Y. Yanq 2001. kNN, Rocchio and Metrics for Information Filtering at TREC-10.
12. Rijsbergen, C. J. v. 1979. Information Retrieval. London, Butterworths.
13. Sarle, W. 2002. What are cross-validation and bootstrapping? 2003.
14. Ghani, R., S. Slattery, et al. 2001. Hypertext Categorization using Hyperlink Patterns and Meta Data. ICML'01 - The Eighteenth International Conference on Machine Learning.
15. Horstmann, C. 2003. Computing Concepts with Java Essentials, John Wiley & Sons, Inc.
16. Bellifemine, F., A. Poggi, et al. 1999. JADE - A FIPA-compliant agent framework. 4th International Conference and Exhibition on the Practical Application of Intelligent Agents and Multi-Agents, London, UK.

ImmoSoftWeb: a Web Based Fuzzy Application for Real Estate Management

Carlos D. Barranco, Jesús Campaña, Juan M. Medina, and Olga Pons

Dept. Computer Science and Artificial Intelligence, University of Granada
Periodista Daniel Saucedo Aranda s/n, 18071, Granada, SPAIN
{carlosd,medina,opc}@decsai.ugr.es,jesuscg@fedro.ugr.es

Abstract. The paper describes ImmoSoftWeb, a web based application which takes advantage of fuzzy sets to apply them on the area of real estate management. ImmoSoftWeb is built on a FRDB, initially using a prototype called FSQL Server, which provides application capabilities for fuzzy handling, but ImmoSoftWeb is independent from FRDB by means of XML technologies usage. Moreover, the paper shows the way real estate attributes can be expressed using fuzzy data, and how fuzzy queries can be used to apply typical real estate customer requirements on a fuzzy real estate database.

1 Introduction

There exists several proposals of Fuzzy Relational Database (FRDB) models as well as implementations based on them [1,2,3,4,5,6]. It is important to look for new application fields to find real life problems that can be solved using these models.

ImmoSoftWeb[1] is a real estate management application that takes advantage of different works and research done in the field of FRDB.

We have chosen real estate management as the subject of our research because real estate attributes are suitable of fuzzy treatment, due to the high level of imprecision in their values. Besides, real estate sales agents usually work at this level of imprecision and are used to be flexible in the search process.

ImmoSoftWeb allows flexible storage of some real estate attributes. This application will allow us to define flexible queries that will obtain those real estates that we looked for and those similar at certain degree from the FRDB.

Our application is built on a Fuzzy SQL server [8,9,10,11] based on the GEFRED (a GEneralized model for Fuzzy RElational Databases) model [4]. The used FRDB provides a fuzzy query language, Fuzzy SQL (FSQL), for interaction between the application and the database.

The application has been developed using different technologies, such as JAVA, JSP pages, XML and related technologies.

---

[1] Due to limited paper extension certain application features can not be widely detailed, further information in [7]

J. Favela et al. (Eds.): AWIC 2004, LNAI 3034, pp. 196–206, 2004.

The paper is organized as follows. Section 2 shows how the application represents and handles fuzzy data, attributes suitable of fuzzy treatment and the conditions that can be used by users. Section 3 depicts application's architecture. Section 4 describes the steps, since the user defines a condition until results are obtained. Finally, Sect. 5 exposes conclusions and future lines of research.

2   Fuzzy Data Handling in the Application

Elements related to fuzzy data handling can have different representations. We use the representation defined in [5], which describes the following data types:

1. *Precise data.* It uses the data representation provided by the host RDBMS, allowing fuzzy querying on it. We call this kind of data *"Type 1 data"*.
2. *Imprecise data in an ordered underlying domain.* This kind of data is associated with a membership function. In this case we represent the membership function as trapezoidal possibility distributions, which let us represent imprecise data such as intervals, with and without margin, approximate values and, of course, precise values. For simplicity, this kind of data is called *"Type 2 data"*.
3. *Data with analogy in a discrete domain.* This type of imprecise data is built in discrete domains on which there are defined proximity relations . This group can represent data as simple scalars or as possibility distributions in discrete domains. We denominate this kind of data *"Type 3 data"*.

We also use the following fuzzy relational operators for these types of data:

1. *Fuzzy Equal (FEQ)*: Based on possibility measures when applied on *Type 1* and *Type 2* data, and based on proximity relations when used on *Type 3* data.
2. *Fuzzy Less Than (FLT), Fuzzy Greater Than (FGT), Fuzzy Greater or Equal (FGEQ) and Fuzzy Less or Equal (FLEQ)*: Those relational operators are based on fuzzy extensions of classical relational operators, and so they are only applicable on *Type 1* and *Type 2* data.

2.1   Suitable Attributes for Fuzzy Handling

We have found some real estate attributes which can be modelled using the fuzzy types described before. Those ones are shown in Table 1.

Type 1 attributes can store precise data only. For instance, attribute *Rooms* stores number of rooms: 2, 5, . . .

Type2 attributes are allowed to store imprecise data, in a trapezoidal representation. For instance, attribute *Price* stores real estate's price range: "between 1000 and 1500" or "exactly 1250".

All *Type 3* attributes have an scalar domain, and an associated proximity relation. This is, for instance, for *Kind* attribute: "Apartment", "Flat", "House",

Table 1. Real estate attributes and fuzzy types associated

Fuzzy Type	Attributes
Type 1	Rooms, Floors
Type 2	Price, Area, Age
Type 3	Kind, Orientation, Illumination, Views, Conservation
Geographic Type	Location

Table 2. Proximity relation for attribute *Kind* domain members

Flat	House	Duplex	Attic	Kind
0.75	0.3	0.2	0.75	*Apartment*
	0.3	0.3	0.75	*Flat*
		0.75	0.1	*House*
			0.1	*Duplex*

"Duplex" and "Attic". The associated proximity relation for attribute *Kind* is shown in Table 2.

Geographic Type attribute is designed to store real estate location as a co-ordinate pair (x, y), which can be queried using fuzzy conditions, as we will see later.

2.2 Flexible Conditions Representation in User Interface

Flexible Numerical Conditions. Flexible Numerical Conditions are user definable conditions that must be applied on *Type 1* and *Type 2* attributes of real estates. We have defined these flexible numerical conditions:

1. *"Flexible between" condition:* This condition is the flexible variant to classical "between" condition, adding a margin. This kind of condition must be defined with a lower (l) and an upper (u) limit and a margin (m), and it is applied using the fuzzy condition $a\ FEQ\ [l - m, l, u, u + m]$, where a, in next references, is the attribute value on which the condition is applied, and $[\alpha, \beta, \gamma, \delta]$ represents a trapezoidal possibility distribution.
2. *"Approximate to" condition:* The condition makes the classical "equal to" condition more flexible. The condition is built by means of a central value (v), to which we want to approximate, together with a margin (m) to define the flexibility of the approximation. Actually, the flexible condition applied is then $a\ FEQ\ [v - m, v, v, v + m]$.
3. *"Flexible greater than" condition:* This condition gives to the classical "greater than" condition more flexibility. The condition has to be defined with a lower limit (l) and a margin (m), and it is applied using the fuzzy condition $a\ FGT\ [l - m, l, l, l]$.

4. *"Flexible lower than" condition:* The condition is the flexible version of classical "lower than" condition. This condition must be defined by an upper limit (u) and a margin (m). The flexible condition is applied using the fuzzy condition $a\ FLT\ [u, u, u, u + m]$.

Nearness Conditions Qualifiers. This user qualifiers group is designed to be applied on nearness conditions on *Type 3* attributes. We employ qualifiers to model the semantic concepts used by "humans" to specify to what extent the result must match the value chosen by the user for a concrete attribute.

Nearness conditions qualifiers works setting a threshold, a minimum nearness level, for the nearness degree between the scalar specified in the user condition and the scalar stored in the attribute on which nearness condition is applied.

These nearness conditions are specified as a fuzzy equality condition like $a\ FEQ\ v\ THOLD\ t$, where a is the attribute, v is the user's desired scalar and t is the threshold value for the chosen qualifier.

Those qualifiers and their associated threshold value, are shown in Table 3.

Table 3. Nearness condition Qualifiers

Qualifier	Only	Very	Fairly	Moderately	Not Much	Any
Nearness degree threshold	1	0.9	0.75	0.5	0.25	0

Context Adaptive Conditions. Context adaptive conditions are a special group of fuzzy numerical conditions with a particularity: they are context sensitive.

We use this kind of conditions to query real estate database with "humans" concepts like "cheap", "moderate" or "expensive" — if we are talking about a house price —, or concepts like "small", "middle-sized" or "big" — if we are talking about house size —.

We say these conditions are adaptable because those "human" concepts are not mathematically constant. Let us analyze it using an example: A *"cheap* detached house in suburbs" does not cost the same as a *"cheap* flat in city centre". Of course both are *"cheap"*, but they are not numerically the same, both prices ranges are mathematically different. As we can see, we must consider the context in which the real estate is involved (i.e. "a flat in city centre" or "detached house in suburbs") to obtain the numerical representation of the range "cheap".

Regardless of the house attribute we are referring to, we have these main abstract degree concepts:

1. *Low:* Includes specific concepts like "cheap" (price) or "small" (size).
2. *Medium:* Includes specific concepts like "moderate" (price) or "middle-sized" (size).
3. *High:* Includes specific concepts like "expensive" (price) or "big" (size).

These main abstract degree concepts let us split the underlying domain in three fuzzy regions. The boundaries of these regions are based themselves on average value (M) of the attribute, calculated based on the "context" of the condition.

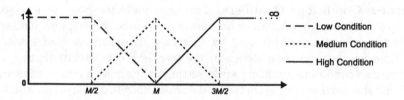

Fig. 1. Partition of underlying domain by context adaptive conditions

To sum up, we follow these steps to obtain a concrete trapezoidal representation, based on the attribute's average value in the context, of that kind of conditions:

1. *Obtaining the context:* Apply all conditions defined in the user query, except context adaptive conditions. The obtained tuples are considered the *context* defined in user query.
2. *Obtaining average value:* Calculate attribute's average value, calculated based on *context* result set, for those attributes which are affected by a context adaptive condition.
3. *Creating trapezoidal representation of context adaptive conditions:* Create the concrete trapezoidal representation of all context adaptive conditions existing in the query, using the average value (M) of the attribute on each condition is applied, as Fig. 1 shows.
4. *Obtaining query result:* Once we have all context adaptive conditions defined as a concrete trapezoid, we apply all conditions present in query to obtain the query result.

Fuzzy Geographical Conditions. We have created these special conditions to allow us to find out the fulfillment degree for a real estate according to a geographic selection area defined by three parameters x, y, *radius* [7].

From these three values a circular area centered in the coordinates (x, y) is defined. The circular area extends around that point with a certain *radius*.

We use the following formula to calculate the membership degree for each real estate inside the area specified in the condition:

$$CDEG((x,y),(x_i,y_i)) = \frac{dist((x,y),(x_i,y_i))}{radius} \ . \tag{1}$$

Where (x, y) are the coordinates of the area's center defined in the condition, (x_i, y_i) are the location coordinates of the real estate evaluated, $dist(a, b)$

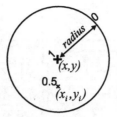

Fig. 2. Membership function for a circular area

computes Euclidean distance between a and b points, and *radius* is the radius of the geographic area defined in the condition.

Real Estate Fulfillment Degree. The Real Estate Fulfillment Degree (REFD) is the value which indicates how well a real estate fits to the query from which it was obtained. This REFD is computed using a weighted average of fulfillment degrees of every condition in the query, using a condition priority order, defined by the user, which determines the weight associated to each condition.

The weights for the average are defined as shown in equations (2) and (3), where t is the number of defined conditions in the query, n the number of conditions included in the priority order, m the number of conditions without a priority requirement, $w_p(i)$ the weight of a condition with a priority level i (considering $i = 1$ the highest priority level, and $i = n$ the lowest priority level) and w_u the weight for conditions without priority user requirement.

$$w_p(i) = \begin{cases} \frac{1}{2^i} & i \neq t \\ \frac{1}{2^{i-1}} & i = t \end{cases} \quad i = 1...n \; . \tag{2}$$

$$w_u = \frac{1}{m2^n} \; . \tag{3}$$

3   Application Architecture

To implement the application we have chosen a layer based architecture in order to ease maintenance and update of components.

3.1   Components

Application is divided in three layers that interact between them as seen in Fig.3. Let us discuss each layer and its functionality.

1. *Presentation Layer:* Generates the user interface in order to provide an easy and comfortable interaction with the application. Main components of this layer are the Web Browser where the interface is visualized, the JSP pages that compose the interface, and the Web Server that processes JSP pages and sends resulting HTML to the user.

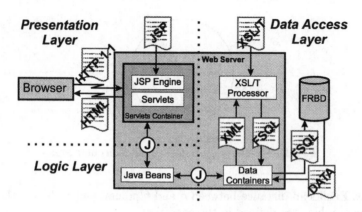

Fig. 3. General application architecture

2. *Logic Layer:* The one that implements functionality and behavior expected from the application and provides methods to access that functionality. This layer receives data from the interface and processes it so that can be used in the following layer. Components of this layer are Java Beans, objects which enclose all application logic.
3. *Data Access Layer:* Allows application logic to access data stored in the FRDB. Data access is managed by data container objects, and it is performed using XML and FRDB fuzzy query syntax. Main components of this layer are the XSLT Parser, that translates user queries expressed in XML to fuzzy queries the FRDB can understand, and the FRDB itself, which executes fuzzy sentences and returns results.

3.2   Fuzzy Database Independence

User queries are expressed in XML and using an XSLT Stylesheet they become fuzzy queries expressed with the syntax used by the FRDB. In case of changes in the syntax used in the FRDB, it would not be necessary to rebuild the application, it would only be necessary to change the XSLT Stylesheet, in order to transform user queries expressed in XML to the new syntax used by the FRDB.

This mechanism provides independence from FRDB syntax which is very important if we consider that we still work with prototypes and that the model evolves continuously, which implies that syntax evolves too, and changes. We need to adapt to this changing environment, and the best way is to become independent from FRDB syntax.

4   Fuzzy Query Process

Our main goal is to communicate a user with a FRDB using fuzzy queries containing imprecise conditions established by the application user. We are going to describe the process followed since a user defines a query until it is executed in the database and the results are given back.

In Fig.4 we can see the route followed by the data and the different transformations that pass along in each stage to transform a fuzzy query into FSQL; now let us comment on them.

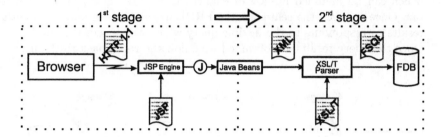

Fig. 4. From the user to the Database

1. The first stage comprehends communication between Web Browser and the Server. The user inserts query parameters in a Web Form as in Fig.5, and sends it. In the server side a JSP page awaits for form data and store it in a Java Object, ready for the next stage. Browser and server communicates using HTTP protocol avoiding incompatibility problems between platforms.

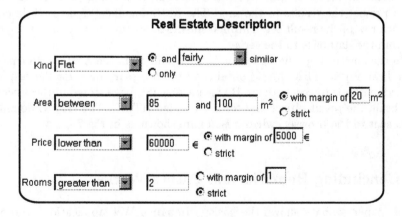

Fig. 5. Web interface query definition

2. The second stage consists of communication between the Web Server and the FRDB. This is an important step, since not only must we find a method to communicate, but we also need to prove the method effective when future changes or updates are performed on the FSQL syntax. To solve this

problem we use XML and related technologies such as XSLT, that allow
the independent interchange of data between elements. Therefore, the Java
object that contains the flexible query definition stated by the user, will generate an XML document describing this flexible query. This XML document
must be transformed in order to obtain valid FSQL sentences to be sent to
the FRDB. The transformation will be made by means of a XSLT Stylesheet,
which can be modified in case of changes in FRDB's query language syntax. Once received the sentences the FRDB executes them and obtains the
results corresponding to the flexible query which was specified initially.
Once the query results are obtained we follow the route back to the user.

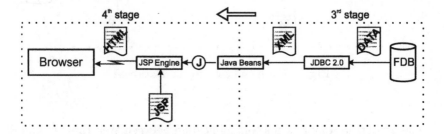

Fig. 6. From the Database to the user

3. In the third stage, we obtain results from the database via JDBC. With these
   results the server creates an XML document, containing the necessary data
   to present the results to the user. The XML document generated describes
   each row of the result set. Through this XML document we transfer the data
   from the database to the server.
4. In the fourth stage the server loads the results from the XML document into
   a Java object. This object contains all the necessary data for the response,
   and methods to access them. By means of a JSP page stored in the server we
   obtain the result object and format it using HTML. The HTML document
   is sent to the browser, where results are shown as in Fig.7.

5   Concluding Remarks and Future Works

In this paper we have shown the basis of ImmoSoftWeb application, whose development permits the achievement of the following goals:

1. Showing that we can solve real life problems using a fuzzy approach, as we
   have done with the real estate management problem, using the capability
   to deal with fuzzy data provided by a Fuzzy SQL Server, and evidence that
   fuzzy approach provides a solution for problems that classical approaches
   can not solve.

Results :: Buy

ID	REFD ▼▲	Kind ▼▲	Price € ▼▲	Area m² ▼▲	Rooms ▼▲
43	100%	Flat	38.000 €	90.0 - 100.0 ±9% m²	3
30	94%	Flat	60.000 €	80.0 ±10% m²	4
1	93%	Flat	65.000 €	90.0 - 120.0 ±9% m²	4
45	92%	Flat	63.000 €	90.0 ±10% m²	4
42	90%	Apartment	40.000 €	85.0 - 90.0 ±9% m²	3
44	90%	Apartment	43.000 €	90.0 - 100.0 ±9% m²	3
29	85%	Attic	63.000 €	100.0 ±10% m²	4
62	82%	Flat	45.000 €	70.0 ±10% m²	5

Fig. 7. Web interface query results

2. Obtaining an application architecture which provides us fully independence from underlying FRDB fuzzy query syntax.

Future works will be guided to make practical use of new features, based on Soft Computing, provided by oncoming FRDB servers, like Data Mining and Knowledge Discovery, applied on real estate management area. By means of these new features, we will obtain new features for ImmoSoftWeb like costumers profiles, shopping profiles, or tendency analysis.

6   Acknowledgments

This work has been partially supported by the Spanish "Ministerio de Ciencia y Tecnología" (MCYT) under grant TIC2002-00480 and TIC2003-08687-C02-02.

References

1. H. Prade, C. Testemale, "Generalizing Database Relational Algebra for the Treatment of Incomplete or Uncertain Information and Vague Queries". Information Sciences 34, 115–143 1984.
2. M. Zemankova-Leech, A. Kandel, "Fuzzy Relational Databases – A Key to Expert Systems". Kln, Germany, TV Rheinland 1984.
3. M. Umano, "Freedom-O: A Fuzzy Database System". Fuzzy Information and Decision Processes. Gupta-Sanchez edit. North-Holand Pub. Comp. 1982.
4. J.M. Medina, O. Pons, M.A. Vila, "GEFRED. A Generalized Model of Fuzzy Relational Data Bases". Information Sciences, 76(1–2), 87–109 (1994).
5. J.M. Medina, M.A. Vila, J.C. Cubero, O. Pons "Towards the Implementation of a Generalized Fuzzy Relational Database Model". Fuzzy Sets and Systems, 75(273–289)1995.
6. S. Fukami, M. Umano, M. Muzimoto, H. Tanaka, "Fuzzy Database Retrieval and Manipulation Language", IEICE Technical Reports, Vol. 78, N° 233, pp. 65–72, AL-78-85 (Automata and Language) 1979.
7. ImmoSoftWeb: http://frontdb.ugr.es/ImmoSoftWeb

206   Carlos D. Barranco et al.

8. J. Galindo, J.M. Medina, O. Pons, J.C. Cubero, "A Server for Fuzzy SQL Queries", in "Flexible Query Answering Systems", eds. T. Andreasen, H. Christiansen and H.L. Larsen, Lecture Notes in Artificial Intelligence (LNAI) 1495, pp. 164–174. Ed. Springer, 1998.
9. J. Galindo, "Tratamiento de la Imprecisión en Bases de Datos Relacionales: Extensión del Modelo y Adaptación de los SGBD Actuales". Ph. Doctoral Thesis, University of Granada (Spain), March 1999 (www.lcc.uma.es).
10. J. Galindo: http://www.lcc.uma.es/~ppgg/FSQL.html
11. I. Blanco, J.M. Martin-Bautista, O. Pons, M.A. Vila, "A Tuple-Oriented Algorithm for Deduction in a Fuzzy Relational Database". Int. Journal of Uncertainty, Fuzzyness and Knowledge-Based Systems vol. 11, pp. 47-66. 2003

Adaptive Watermarking Algorithm for Binary Image Watermarks

Beatriz Corona-Ramirez, Mariko Nakano-Miyatake, and Hector Perez-Meana

SEPI ESIME Culhuacan, National Polytechnic Institute
Av. Santa 1000, 04430 Mexico D. F. Mexico
hmpm@prodigy.net.mx

Abstract. This paper proposes an adaptive watermarking algorithm, in which the watermark is a binary image such as a logotype related directly to the image owner. Obviously the information amount of this type of watermark is much larger than the amount of a pseudorandom pattern generated by secret key. This fact makes it difficult to embed a bi-dimensional watermark code into a given image in an imperceptible way. To achieve this goal, we propose an imperceptible adaptive embedding algorithm using the JND (Just Noticeable Difference) criterion. The evaluation results show the desirable features of proposed algorithm, such as the watermark imperceptibility and its robustness against attacks such as: JPEG compression, filtering, and impulsive noise.

1. Introduction

Recently the inadequate use of the INTERNET, such as illegal reproduction and illegal modification of digital materials such as images, video and sound, has widely increased. Thus, providers of these digital materials are faced with the challenge of how to protect their electronic information. The watermarking is one of the viable solutions to this problem, and because of that, recently many watermarking techniques have been proposed to protect the copyright over these digital materials [1]-[6]. Basically there are two types of watermarks for digital images protection: One of them is the use of a pseudo random sequence and another one is the use of an image or two-dimensional watermarks such as a logotype. In the first case, the pseudo random sequence is generated by using a secret key, which is related to the owner or provider [1], [4]-[6], while in the second one, a two-dimensional watermark represents directly the ownership of the provider as logotype form [7]-[9]. For this reason, the second type of watermarks has a stronger impact than the first one. However, generally the information amount of the second type of watermark is much more than that of the first one. Due to this fact, it is difficult to provide an invisible and robust watermarking system using two-dimensional watermarks. To overcome this problem, one of the more promising approaches is the use of adaptive watermarking systems based on Human Visual System (HVS), in which the insensible area for the HVS is detected using some given criterion [10]-[12], such as the Just Noticeable Difference (JND), which means the minimum difference in luminance, frequency or contrast that the HVS is able to detect.

J. Favela et al. (Eds.): AWIC 2004, LNAI 3034, pp. 207-216, 2004.

Originally the JND criterion has been applied in the image compression field to get high quality compressed images [13], [14]. Taking this fact in account, recently the JND criterion has been introduced as an adaptive watermarking technique to embed pseudo random patterns with maximum energy [11].

This paper proposes an adaptive watermarking algorithm based on the JND criterion to get the maximum strength of a transparent watermark, and the most suitable insertion positions in the DCT domain of a given image. The performance of the proposed algorithm is evaluated since the point of view of the watermark transparency and robustness. Computer simulation results show that proposed algorithm provides a fairly good performance, comparing with other previously proposed algorithms [7]-[9].

2. Proposed Watermarking System

In the proposed watermarking system, a binary image watermark is embedded in a gray scale image using the Just Noticeable Difference (JND) criterion to get robustness against common attacks, specially the JPEG compression. The adaptive quantization process, in the JPEG compression method, has a close relation with the JND values in the luminance and contrast. Thus assuming that $q_{i,j}$ is (i,j)-th element of the quantization matrix, Q, and that $c_{i,j}$ is (i,j)-th DCT image coefficient, and if the modification value in (i,j)-th DCT coefficient, $t_{i,j}$, caused by the watermark embedding satisfies

$$t_{i,j} \geq \frac{q_{i,j}}{2}$$ (1)

we can assure that the embedded watermark will survive after a JPEG compression attack. Taking in account the eq. (1) and the adaptive quantization matrix proposed in [13], the JND value of the k-th DCT block becomes

$$JND_{i,j,k} = \begin{cases} \max\left[t_{i,j,k}, \left|c_{i,j,k}\right|^{\omega_{i,j}} t_{i,j,k}^{1-\omega_{i,j}} \right] & \text{if } \max\left[t_{i,j,k}, \left|c_{i,j,k}\right|^{\omega_{i,j}} t_{i,j,k}^{1-\omega_{i,j}} \right] \leq \left|c_{i,j,k}\right| \\ 0 & \text{in other case} \end{cases},$$ (2)

where $c_{i,j,k}$ is (i,j)-th DCT coefficient in the k-th block, $\omega_{i,j}$ is a constant value equal to 0.7 [13], and $t_{i,j,k}$ is the watermarking embedding energy of the (i,j)-th DCT coefficient in the k-th block, given by

$$t_{i,j,k} = t_{i,j}\left(c_{0,0,k} / \bar{c}_{0,0}\right)^{a^T},$$ (3)

where $t_{i,j}$ is given by eq. (1), considering the equality condition $c_{0,0,k}$ is the DC component of the DCT coefficients, $\tau_{0,0}$ is the mean value of luminance, $\tau_{0,0}=1024$ for 8 bits gray scale image, and a^T is a constant value equal to 0.649 [13], which control the luminance masking effect.

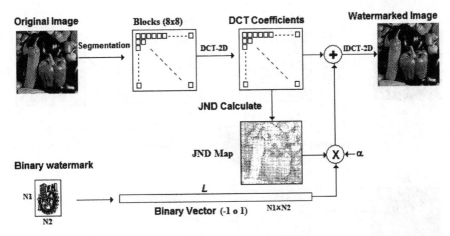

Fig. 1. Proposed watermark embedding process

2.1. Watermark Embedding Process

In the proposed watermark embedding algorithm, shown in Fig. 1, the original image is divided in blocks of 8x8 pixels and subsequently a bi-dimensional DCT is applied to each block to get the DCT coefficients matrix. In the DCT domain, a JND map is generated by estimating the JND values in each block using eq. (2). Next a binary image watermark is transformed into a binary vector with (-1,1) values. Each watermark vector element is then multiplied by the corresponding JND value with a gain α, which is used to control the embedding intensity, and added to the corresponding DCT coefficient. The watermarked image is thus obtained by applying the inverse bi-dimensional DCT to the watermarked DCT coefficients. The eq. (4) shows the embedding process.

$$c_{i,j,k}^{*} = \begin{cases} c_{i,j,k} + \alpha * JND_{i,j,k} * L_l & JND_{i,j,k} \neq 0 \ , (i,j) \neq (1,1) \\ c_{i,j,k} & \text{otherwise} \end{cases} \qquad (4)$$

where $c_{i,j,k}$, $c_{i,j,k}^{*}$ are *(i,j)*-th DCT coefficient in k-th block of an original image and the watermarked image, respectively, α is constant gain factor, $JND_{i,j,k}$ is *(i,j)*-th JND value in k-th block, and L_l is *l*-th element of the watermark vector, given by

$$L = \{L_l\}, \quad l = 1...N1 * N2 \qquad (5)$$

where N1*N2 is total number of elements of the binary watermark. Equation (4) shows that the watermark is not embedded in a DCT coefficient $c_{i,j,k}$, if its corresponding JND value is equal to 0 or if it is a DC component. Because DCT coefficient with null JND value means that JPEG compression operation eliminates the embedded watermark in this DCT coefficient and embedding watermark in the DC component probably cause block artifact in the watermarked image.

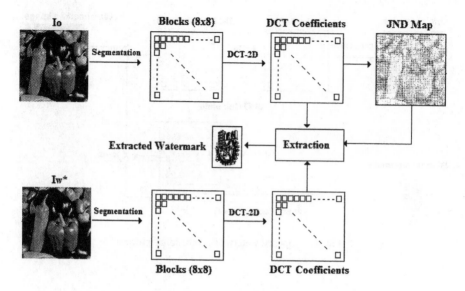

Fig. 2. Watermark detection process in the proposed algorithm.

2.2. Watermark Detection Process.

Figure 2 shows the watermark detection process of proposed algorithm. As we can observe in this figure, in the detection process, both the original image and the watermarked one are required. Firstly, the bi-dimensional DCT is applied to both segmented images to get the original and watermarked images DCT coefficients. Next, from the DCT coefficients of original image, the JND map is calculated using eq. (2), and then it is used by binary image watermark extraction, as show in eq. (6).

$$\tilde{L}_l = \begin{cases} 1 & c_{i,j,k}^* > c_{i,j,k} \quad , JND_{i,j,k} \neq 0, (i,j) \neq (1,1) \\ -1 & c_{i,j,k}^* < c_{i,j,k} \quad , JND_{i,j,k} \neq 0, (i,j) \neq (1,1) \end{cases} \qquad (6)$$

where $\tilde{L}_l$ is l-th element of extracted binary watermark.

3. Evaluation of Proposed Algorithm

The proposed watermarking algorithm is evaluated from the point of view of embedded watermark transparency and robustness against common attacks, such as the JPEG compression, filtering, cropping, etc. The evaluation results are compared with the binary image watermarking Lee algorithm [8].

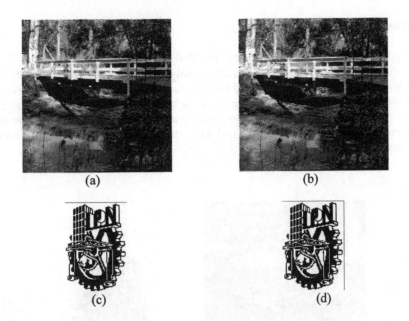

Fig. 3. Imperceptibility provided by the proposed algorithm. (a) original image, (b) watermarked image, (c) original binary image watermark and (d) extracted binary image watermark.

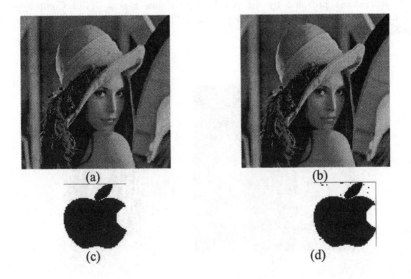

Fig. 4. Imperceptibility provided by the proposed algorithm. (a) original image, (b) watermarked image, (c) original binary image watermark and (d) extracted binary image watermark.

3.1. Transparency

Figures 3 and 4 show the transparency provided by the proposed algorithm. Both figures show (a) the original image, (b) the watermarked image, (c) the original binary image watermark and (d) the extracted binary image watermark. The signal-to-noise ratio (SNR) between the original image and the watermarked one is 42.8 dB in the figure 3 and 39.3 dB in the figure 4. In these figures it is not possible to observe any distortion in the watermarked image and the extracted watermarks don't have any ambiguity.

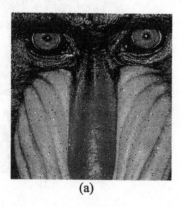

(a)   (b)

Fig. 5. Robustness provided by the proposed algorithm against JPEG Compression. (a) Watermarked and compressed image using JPEG method with quality factor 30, (b) extracted watermark image.

(a)   (b)

Fig. 6. Robustness provided by the proposed algorithm against impulsive noise (a) watermarked image corrupted by impulsive noise with noise density 1%, (b) extracted watermark image.

3.2. Robustness

We evaluated the performance of proposed algorithm from the point of view of robustness against common attacks, such as the JPEG compression, filtering using median filter, noise introduction and cropping. The figure 5 shows the watermarked compressed image by using the JPEG compression method with a quality factor 30 and together with the extracted binary watermark image. Figure 6 shows the watermarked image corrupted by impulsive noise with a noise density of 1%, together the extracted watermark image. Figure 7 shows the watermarked image filtered using a median filter and the extracted watermark, and the figure 8 shows the watermarked and cropped images and the extracted watermark image.

Fig. 7. Robustness provided by the proposed algorithm against median filtering, (a) Watermarked image filtered by median filter, (b) Extracted watermark. (apple image)

Fig. 8. Robustness provided by the proposed algorithm against cropping. (a) watermarked image (b) watermarked and cropping image, (c) extracted watermark image. (IPN logo)

Tables 1 and 2 show a comparison between the performance of proposed and Lee [8] watermarking algorithms [8]. Because both algorithms use an adaptive method according to the original image feature, the performance strongly depends on the image features. Therefore, the table 1 shows the robustness of both algorithms using images with few details, such as, parrot and pepper, while the table 2 shows the robustness using images with much details, such as mandrill and bridge images. From these tables we can observe that the proposed algorithm is more robust regarding the JPEG compression attack as compared with other algorithms proposed in literature [7]-[9], while regarding other kind of attacks such as filtering and cropping, the robustness provided by the proposed algorithm compare favorably with respect to other algorithms.

Table 1. Comparison between the proposed and the algorithm proposed by [8]. Image used for evaluation have few datails.

Attack	Proposed Algorithm	Lee Algorithm [8]
JPEG Compression (quality factor)	20-100	80-100
Impulsive Noise (noise density)	~3 %	~8 %
Median filter	Ok	Ok
Cropping (maximum cropping rate)	~60%	~40%

Table 2. Comparison between the proposed algorithm and the algorithm proposed by [8]. Images used for evaluation have details.

Attack	Proposed Algorithm	Lee Algorithm [8]
JPEG Compression (quality factor)	15-100	70-100
Impulsive Noise (noise density)	~3 %	~3 %
Median filter	Ok	Ok
Cropping (maximum cropping rate)	~66%	~40%

4. Conclusions

In this paper, we proposed an adaptive watermarking algorithm for binary image watermark, because this type of watermark has stronger impact during the copyright reclamation moment, compared with the use of a pseudo random pattern generated by a secret key as watermark code. The proposed algorithm is evaluated from the transparency point of view and the robustness against some common attacks, such as a JPEG compression, filtering, noise corruption and cropping. The evaluation results show the desirable features of proposed algorithm, especially it shows robustness against JPEG compression, in which the embedded watermark can be detected without ambiguity after a JPEG process with high compression rate (quality factor is smaller than 20). The performance of the proposed algorithm is compared with the algorithm proposed by [8], using the same watermarks and images. The comparison results show the advantage of the proposed algorithm over the algorithm by [8].

Acknowledgements

We thanks to the National Science and Technology Council, CONAyT and to The I. P. N. for the support provided during the realization of this research.

References

[1]   G. Langelaar, I. Setywan, R. Lagendijk, "Watermarking digital image and video data", IEEE Signal Processing Magazine, pp. 20-46, Sept. 2000.

[2]   J. Huang, Y. Shi y Y. Shi, "Embedding Image Watermarks in DC Components", IEEE Transaction on Circuits and Systems for Video Technology, vol. 10, no. 6, pp. 974-979, Sept. 2000.

[3]   A. Piva, M. Barni, F. Bartolini, V. Cappellini, "DCT-based Watermark Recorvering without Resirting to the Uncorrunpted Original Image", Proc. of IEEE Int. Conf. of Image Processing, pp. 5210-523, Oct. 1997.

[4]   J. Cox, J. Killian, T. Shamoon, "Secure spread spectrum watermarking for multimedia", IEEE Trans. On Image Processing, vol. 6, no. 12, pp. 1673-1687.

[5]   I. Hernández M. Amado y F. Pérez, "DCT-Domain Watermarking techniques for still images: Detector performance análisis and a new structure", IEEE Trans. Image Processing, vol. 9, pp. 55-68, Jan. 2000.

[6]   J. Shapiro, "Embedded image coding using zerotrees of wavelet coefficients", IEEE Trans. On Signal Processing, vol. 41, no. 12, pp. 3445-3462, 1993.

[7]   C. Hsu, J. Wu, "Hidden Digital Watermarks in Images", IEEE Trans. On Image Processing, vol. 8, no. 1, pp. 58-68, Jan, 1999.

[8]   C. Lee, Y. Lee, "An Adaptive Digital Image Watermarking Technique for Copyright Protection", IEEE Trans. On Consumer Electronics, vol. 45, no. 4, pp. 1005-1015, Nov. 1999.

[9]   S. Lin, C. Chen "A Robust DCT-Based Watermaking for Colpyright Protection", IEEE Trans. On Consumer Electronics, Vol. 46, no. 3, Aug. 2000.

[10] J. Delaigle, C. De Vleeschouewer y B. Macq, "Watermarking algorithm based on a human visual model", Signal Processing, Elsevier, vol. 66, pp. 319-335, 1998.

[11] B. Chitrasert y K. Rao, "Human Visual Weighted Progressive Image Transmission ", IEEE Trans. On Communications, vol. 38, no. 7, Jul. 1990.
[12] S. Westen, R. Lagendijk y J. Biemond, "Perceptual Image Quality Based on a Multiple Channel HVS model", in Proc. IEEE ICASSP, pp. 2351-2354, 1995.
[13] B. Watson, "DCT quiatization matrices visually optimizad for individual images", Human Vision, Visual Processing and Digital Display IV, Proc. Of SPIE 1913-14, 1993.
[14] B. Watson, "Efficiency of a model human image code", Journal of Optics Society of America, vol. 4, no. 12, pp. 2401-2416, Dec. 1987.

Bayesian Methods to Estimate Future Load in Web Farms

José M. Peña[1], Víctor Robles[1], Óscar Marbán[2], and María S. Pérez[1]

[1] DATSI, Universidad Politécnica de Madrid, Madrid, Spain
{jmpena, vrobles, mperez}@fi.upm.es
[2] DLSIS, Universidad Politécnica de Madrid, Madrid, Spain
omarban@fi.upm.es

Abstract. Web Farms are clustered systems designed to provide high availability and high performance web services. A web farm is a group of replicated HTTP servers that reply web requests forwarded by a single point of access to the service. To deal with this task the point of access executes a load balancing algorithm to distribute web request among the group of servers. The present algorithms provides a short-term dynamic configuration for this operation, but some corrective actions (granting different session priorities or distributed WAN forwarding) cannot be achieved without a long-term estimation of the future web load. On this paper we propose a method to forecast web service work load. Our approach also includes an innovative segmentation method for the web pages using EDAs (estimation of distribution algorithms) and the application of semi-naïve Bayes classifiers to predict future web load several minutes before. All our analysis has been performed using real data from a world-wide academic portal.

Keywords. Web farms, web load estimation, naïve Bayes, EDAs

1 Introduction

Today's commerce is, in many cases, fought on the web arena. Form marketing to on-line sales, many tasks are supported by a web architecture. Even several internal procedures of a company are achieved using a web-based application. On this scenario, the quality of the services, or at least the way the user observes how these services are been performed, depends on some characteristics of the web server itself. Subjective values, like page design, are tackled by specific methodologies [16]. But, there are other factors that are also very important in terms of client satisfaction when he/she navigates the site. One of these factors is *web service response time*. There are different strategies to speed-up this response time. Proxy servers and web caches are intermediate storages of the most frequent pages. Another innovative alternative is what has been called **web farms**.

1.1 Web Farms

For high performance services, when it grows beyond the capabilities of a single machine, groups of machines are often employed to provide the service. In the case of web

J. Favela et al. (Eds.): AWIC 2004, LNAI 3034, pp. 217–226, 2004.

servers, this is often referred to a Web Farm. Web farms typically employ both high availability and scalability technologies in order to provide a highly available service spread across multiple machines, with a single point of contact for clients.

The architecture of these systems is divided into three different layers: (i) a first layer, the front-end of the web service, is a single point of access, (ii) a second layer of distributed web servers, which perform the actual HTTP service and (iii) a third layer of a shared data storage, like a back-end database or distributed/replicated file system.

The service provided by a web far is performed as follows. When a request is received by the point of access, this one redirects the request towards the most suitable web server on the second layer. Usually, the response sent by the web server is addressed directly to the client (not using the point of access as a relay).

There are different types of web farms depending on the topology of the architecture itself:

- **Cluster web farms**: All the web servers are inside of the same local area network. In many cases these machines serving on the second layer are connected using a virtual private network (VPN). On this architecture, the point of access selects the most appropriate server depending on short-term load-balancing algorithm. [2]
- **Globally distributed web farms**: In this cases, web servers are connected at different points on a wide area network (like the Internet). On these geographically distributed web farms the point of access decides the server taking into account other aspects like closest web server or interconnection speed. [9]
- **Hybrid approaches**: Sometimes both architectures coexist, a first step of redirection forwards the request to the closest cluster web farm. A second stage is performed inside of the cluster to select the server with less work. A very good example of this approach is Google[3].

1.2   Web Load Balancing

In order to achieve the most important task of this process, *request forwarding*, there have been done many efforts to perform this operation in the most flexible and efficient way. NCSA [19] provides a scalable web server using server-side Round-Robin DNS [6]. LVS (Linux Virtual Server) [3] provides many different methods to redirect request inside of a cluster web farm, like NAT (Network Address Translation), IP Tunneling and Direct Routing. There are also application level solutions, like Reverse-proxy [25] or SWEB [2]. Other techniques available is Load Sharing with NAT (LSNAT) [27].

Although, these are different techniques to forward client requests (at different levels of the IP protocol stack), another open issues is to get the best selection for each of these incoming requests. Cluster web farms and many DNS-based approaches select the next web server are Round-Robin scheduling with additional features like, weighted least-connection correction [30] (also Round-robin DNS). Other approaches select the most responsive web server for a *ping* package. Other approaches consider QoS (quality of service) algorithms to estimate load distribution in replicated web servers [9]. In [14] a client-based approach is presented.

---

[3] http://www.google.com

There are two possible load balancing strategies, depending on how far the status of the system could be forecasted.

- Immediate load balancing: Load balancing decisions take into account present or very near past situations to perform corrective and balancing actions. On this schema cluster web farms forwards messages towards the least overloaded server.
- Long-term load balancing: Although the past strategy is quite efficient and provides dynamic adaptability, there are important limitations due to: (1) a single session from the same user should be forwarded to the same web farm server, since important information held by the server, like session cookies, are stored locally, and (2) high level forwarding technique (like IP Tunneling) performs better if the tunnel that supports the redirection is used several times, or other techniques like DNS-Round Robin once the first message from a user is addressed to one server the next ones will follow the same path.

Since under these circumstances the load balancing algorithms take some actions with a stable application frame of several minutes, the most efficient way to perform these tasks is to estimate the future load of the system, with a time window frame of at least 10-15 minutes.

2   Future Load Estimation Issues

Dealing with future estimation of a web service load has some specific aspect to be taken into account.

First of all is to know what is exactly expected from the estimation. In order to support load balancing algorithms the most important aspect to be known is the future number of requests or the amount of information to be sent. Being able to predict how many bytes should be served in advance provides the possibility to forward clients to other mirror site or discard some requests, in order to provide an acceptable response time for most of the user.

The amount of information requested is a continuous value, but for the objective we are tackling is not necessary to deal with the attribute in the continuous form. A load balancing algorithm uses discrete data input, for most of the algorithms they work with intervals of low, medium or high load. On the other hand, a significant number of classification methods are based on discrete or nominal classes. There are several methods to build these discretization intervals, but, in order to be appropriate with the usage the values are hardware or architecture restrictions from the current system, like network band-width or memory capacity.

Other important issue is to select the appropriate input attributes. The main source of information we have is the server web log. This log records all the connections requested to the web server. For each record we have the requested page, from which page it was accessed, and when it was requested. Very simple methods use the time of the day to predict web load, while others also consider previous load (amount of bytes transferred) to estimate future requests. These approaches (as we will see in section 5.3 are limited and unaccurated). It is very important to have some background knowledge from the application field of these techniques. On our approach an academic portal[4]

---

[4] http://www.universia.es

was used. This portal stores web pages from courses, universities, grants, an so on. The information on this service is addressed both to students, teachers, and people working on the industry. Pages represent news and important notes updated daily. A detailed description of these datasets in commented in section 5.1. These characteristics imply two important hints:

– The patterns from different users or the accesses to different pages on the web site is more intense depending on the contents of the pages. Page subject has an important influence on when this pages is accessed and the range of users interested on it.
– The structure of the web site changes daily. Any page-based analysis using data form several days before will not consider new pages (which are also the most popular visit in the web site).

One important aspect of this method is the segmentation of the pages hosted by the web site, among the different techniques (based on the contents of the page) we have proceeded with this segmentation considering the relationships between the pages (how many times one pages is addressed from other) as discriminant criteria to group similar pages.

According to these assertions we have considered the following method to proceed, (1) the attribute to classify is a discretized value defined over the amount of requested information, (2) accesses to the groups of pages (in a previous time frames) are input data, and (3) only information for few days before the prediction is used in order to support dynamic changes on the contents of the web site.

This method will be compared with simple approaches that only takes into account the time an previous web load.

3   General Process Overview

To be able to estimate the future load in a Web Farm we need to do the following steps (see figure 1):

1. Starting with the log files from *www.universia.es* of four different days (see section 5.1) we create a *Site Navigation Graph*. In this graph, vertices represent Web pages, edges represent links and edges weight represent the number of times the corresponding link was clicked by the users.
2. Partition the *Site Navigation Graph*. We have decided to split the graph in ten different partitions. In this way we will be able to collect users click information for each partition, given us more useful information. This process segmentates web pages based on the relationships among them. Pages visited together will be clustered in the same group.
3. Once data has been partitioned, time windows of 15 minutes have been defined. For each of these windows a new instance is created with the following information:
   – Current time.
   – Clicks and bytes transferred for each of the groups during the las two time frames (15 and 30 minutes before).
   – The amount of information requested to the web site during this period. This is the actual value to be predicted.

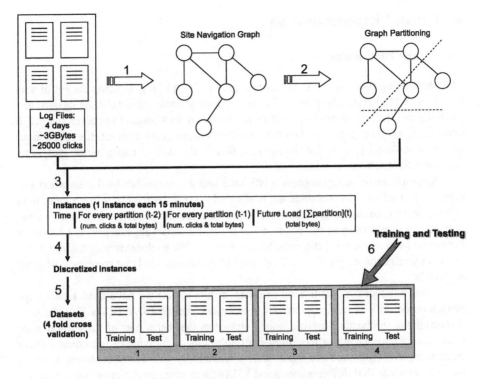

Fig. 1. Overall description of the process

4. Discretization:
   - Class discretization: Rather than the number of bytes, we are interested on the intervals, like idle state, low load, medium load, high load, very high load or similar ranks. As we have said before, these intervals depend on hardware constraints. A discretization method based on probability density with optimal classes definition has been performed, using XLSTAT.
   - Attribute discretization. In order to use the classification methods it is necessary to discretice the instances of the datasets. Thus, a discretization step with the method suggested by [11] has been performed using MLC++ tools. This supervised discretization method is described by Ting in [28] that is a global variant of the method of Fayyad and Irani [12].
5. Once we have created and discretized the instances, they must be splitted in four different datasets, each one including a training set and a testing set. In this way, we are going to make the training with the instances of 3 days, keeping the instances of the last day for validation purposes. This means that we are doing a *4-Fold cross validation*.
6. The last step consist on apply all the classification methods (see section 4.2) to the datasets. Experiment results are in section 5.3.

4 Detailed Experimentation

4.1 Graph Partitioning

The partitioning problem on an undirected graph $G = (V, E)$, V being the set of vertices and E the set of edges arises in many different areas such as VLSI design, test pattern generation, data-mining or efficient storage of data bases. In general, the graph partitioning problem consists of partitioning the vertices into k disjoint subsets of about the same cardinality, such that the *cut size*, that is, the sum of edges whose endpoints are in different subsets, is minimized.

The graph partitioning problem is NP-hard, and it remains NP-hard even when k is equal to 2 or when some unbalancing is allowed [7]. For large graphs (with more than 100 vertices), heuristics algorithms which find suboptimal solutions are the only viable option. Proposed strategies can be classified in combinatorial approaches [13], based on geometric representations [26], multilevel schemes [29], evolutionary optimization [5] and genetic algorithms [8]. We can find also hybrid schemes [4] that combines different approaches.

To solve the graph partitioning problem in this paper, we have used a novel approach based on a heuristic optimization technique named EDA. EDAs [20] are non-deterministic, stochastic heuristic search strategies that form part of the evolutionary computation approaches, where number of solutions or individuals are created every generation, evolving once and again until a satisfactory solution is achieved. In brief, the characteristic that differentiates most EDAs from other evolutionary search strategies such as GAs is that the evolution from a generation to the next one is done by estimating the probability distribution of the fittest individuals, and afterwards by sampling the induced model. This avoids the use of crossing or mutation operators, and the number of parameters that EDAs require is considerably reduced.

To find the best partition we are going to use the next fitness function [5] to evaluate each candidate s,

$$f(s) = \alpha \cdot n_{cuts}(s) + \beta \cdot \sum_{k=1}^{K} 2^{deviation(k)} \tag{1}$$

where, $n_{cuts}(s)$ is the sum of the edges whose endpoints are in different subsets, and $deviation(k)$ is the amount by which the number of nodes in the partition G_k varies from the average number expected.

However, with the objective of partitioning the *Site Navigation Graph* we are going to consider the number of cuts as an objective, while the deviation degree is going to be a restriction. Thus, the fitness function will take the parameters $\alpha = 1$ and $\beta = 0$; with $deviation(k) < 20$ for $k \in [1, K]$. This means that we are allowing a deviation degree of 20% in the partitions.

4.2 Learning Methods

We are using three different types of classification methods.

– **Rule induction methods**.
  - *1R Algorithm*. The 1R procedure [17] for machine learning is a very simple one that proves surprisingly effective. The aim is to infer a rule that predicts the class given the value of the attributes. The 1R algorithm chooses the most informative single attribute and bases the rule on this attribute alone.
  - *NNGE*. NNGE (Non-Nested Generalized Examplers) [21] is a promising machine learning approach that combines nearest neighbor with rule generation.
– **Tree induction methods**.
  - *J48*. J48 is an improved version of C4.5 [23] that is implemented in the Weka toolset [1], an open source machine learning software in Java.
  - *C5.0 with boosting*. C5.0 is quite similar to C4.5 [23] but incorporates several new facilities such as variable misclassification costs, new data types including dates and facilities for defining new attributes as functions of other attributes.

– **Bayesian methods**.
  - *Naïve Bayes*. The naïve Bayes classifier [15] is a probabilistic method for classification. It can be used to determine the probability that an example belongs to a class given the values of the predictor variables. The naïve Bayes classifier guarantees optimal induction given a set of explicit assumptions [10].
  - *Pazzani-EDA*. Pazzani [22] tries to improve the naïve Bayes classifier by searching for dependencies among attributes. He proposes two algorithms for detecting dependencies among attributes: *Forward Sequential Selection and Joining* (FSSJ) and *Backward Sequential Elimination and Joining*. However, Pazzani-EDA [24] makes a heuristic search of the Pazzani structure with the target of maximize the percentage of successful predictions.

The rule induction methods and the tree induction method J48 were run with Weka, an open source machine learning software in Java. The method C5.0 with boosting were run with the See5.0/C5.0 program. For the Bayesian methods we have used our own developed programs.

5 Results

5.1 Data Set

For validating our approach we have used log files from *www.universia.es*. Universia is a community portal about Spanish-speaking higher education that involves 379 universities world-wide. It contains information about education, organized in different groups depending on the user profile.

We have used the log files from four different days. The total size of the logs files is 3 GBytes and they contain a total of 25000 user clicks in approx 5000 different pages.

5.2 Validation Method

As commented before we have used a 4 fold cross validation method. Thus, the learning process is made with 3 days, validating with the remaining day.

Table 1. Experiment results with the simple dataset

Training Days	1, 2, 3	1, 2, 4	1, 3, 4	2, 3, 4	
Tested Day	4	3	2	1	Average
Naive Bayes	70.21	75.00	79.17	79.16	**75.88**
Pazzani-EDA	84.78	89.36	93.61	87.23	88.75
NNGE	64.89	63.54	71.88	71.87	68.05
1R	71.28	72.92	70.83	76.04	72.77
J48	64.89	72.92	73.96	76.04	71.95
C5.0	74.50	72.90	83.30	80.20	**77.72**

Table 2. Experiment results with the enriched dataset

Training Days	1, 2, 3	1, 2, 4	1, 3, 4	2, 3, 4	
Tested Day	4	3	2	1	Average
Naive Bayes	71.28	70.83	76.04	70.83	72.25
Pazzani-EDA	97.82	100.00	97.87	91.49	**96.80**
NNGE	74.47	67.71	78.13	72.91	**73.31**
1R	67.02	73.96	75.00	76.04	**73.01**
J48	72.34	69.79	72.91	76.04	**72.77**
C5.0	70.20	70.83	73.96	75.00	72.50

5.3 Experimental Results

One of the issues tackled by our approach is to evaluate any possible improvement obtained when data are enriched with the segmentation the web pages. On table 1, results based on a simple data input are presented. These simple data are just the number of clicks an bytes requested during the last two time windows (15 and 30 minutes before).

Table 2 shows the results from enriched data including number of clicks and bytes transferred for each of groups of pages clustered by the partitioned graph. On this table we also consider the previous two time windows as in the case before.

We have experimented with simple 1R algorithm with the assumption that just one attribute (either time or the previous requested clicks or bytes) is able to predict web service load.

Induction tree algorithms, like C5.0, performs poorly with the extended input data while complex bayesian classifiers, like Pazzani-EDA, get a significant advantage when more and enriched information is provided. On this case Pazzani-EDA clearly outperforms any other of the classifiers evaluated.

Another interesting result is that 1R selects time as discriminant attribute only in two out of the four experiments. With this we consider that time is not always the best approach to estimate web server load.

6 Conclusion and Further Work

In this paper two innovative techniques have been introduced.

First, a new graph partitioning method has been perform using estimation of distribution algorithms. On this field new open issues arises that could be interesting to explore in a further works.

Second, enriched information has been proved very useful to obtain significant improvements to estimate web service load. The segmentation of the pages using the relationships among them, represented by the number of navigation clicks from one page to the other (site navigation graph) is a very simple way to cluster similar pages without the need to deal with semantic information about the contents of each page. Other similar approaches use information about the subjects or topics related to one page make them difficult to be performed on complex an not well-organized web sites.

Although time is not a discriminant attribute on this kind of analysis, it is very significant. Thus, semi naïve Bayes algorithms like NB-Tree [18] could achieve interesting results as this classifiers is an hybrid method between decision trees and Bayesian classification methods. This approach uses the more discriminant attributes to build a decision tree with leaves that are Bayesian classifiers for solving the more complex relationships.

7 Acknowledgement

We would like to thanks *www.universia.es* for the possibility of working with their log files.

References

[1] Weka 3: Data mining with open source machine learning software in java. http://www.cs.waikato.ac.nz/ml/weka/, 2003.

[2] Daniel Andresen, Tao Yang, and Oscar H. Ibarra. Towards a scalable distributed WWW server on workstation clusters. In *Proc. of 10th IEEE Intl. Symp. Of Parallel Processing (IPPS'96)*, pages 850–856, 1996.

[3] Wensong Zhang andShiyao Jin and Quanyuan Wu. Creating Linux virtual servers. In *LinuxExpo 1999 Conference*, 1999.

[4] R. Baños, C. Gil, J. Ortega, and F.G. Montoya. Multilevel heuristic algorithm for graph partitioning. In *Proceedings of the 3rd European Workshop on Evolutionary Computation in Combinatorial Optimization. LNCS 2611*, pages 143–153, 2003.

[5] R. Baños, C. Gil, J. Ortega, and F.G. Montoya. Partición de grafos mediante optimización evolutiva paralela. In *Proceedings de las XIV Jornadas de Paralelismo*, pages 245–250, 2003.

[6] T. Brisco. RFC 1794: DNS support for load balancing, April 1995. Status: INFORMATIONAL.

[7] T.N. Bui and C. Jones. Finding good approximate vertex and edge partitions is np-hard. *Information Processing Letters*, 42:153–159, 1992.

[8] T.N. Bui and B. Moon. Genetic algorithms and graph partitioning. *IEEE Transactions on Computers*, 45(7):841–855, 1996.

[9] Marco Conti, Enrico Gregori, and Fabio Panzieri. Load distribution among replicated Web servers: A QoS-based approach. In *Proceedings of the Workshop on Internet Server Performance (WISP99)*, 1999.

[10] P. Domingos and M. Pazzani. Beyond independence: conditions for the optimality of the simple Bayesian classifier. In *Proceedings of the 13th International Conference on Machine Learning*, pages 105–112, 1996.

[11] J. Dougherty, R. Kohavi, and M. Sahami. Supervised and unsupervised discretization of continuous features. In *Proceedings of the 12th International Conference on Machine Learning*, pages 194–202, 1995.

[12] U. Fayyad and K. Irani. Multi-interval discretization of continuous-valued attributes for classification learning. In *Proceedings of the 13th International Conference on Artificial Intelligence*, pages 1022–1027, 1993.

[13] C. Fiduccia and R. Mattheyses. A linear time heuristic for improving network partitions. In *Proceedings of the 19th IEEE Design Automation Conference*, pages 175–181, 1982.

[14] Vittorio Ghini, Fabio Panzieri, and Marco Roccetti. Client-centered load distribution: A mechanism for constructing responsive web services. In *HICSS*, 2001.

[15] D.J. Hand and K. Yu. Idiot's Bayes - not so stupid after all? *International Statistical Review*, 69(3):385–398, 2001.

[16] Esther Hochsztain, Socorro Millán, and Ernestina Menasalvas. A granular approach for analyzing the degree of affability of a web site. *Lecture Notes in Computer Science*, 2475:479–486, 2002.

[17] R.C. Holte. Very simple classification rules perform well on most commonly used datasets. *Machine Learning*, 11:63–90, 1993.

[18] R. Kohavi. Scaling up the accuracy of naive-Bayes classifiers: a decision-tree hybrid. In *Proceedings of the 2nd International Conference on Knowledge Discovery and Data Mining*, pages 202–207, 1996.

[19] Thomas T. Kwan, Robert E. McGrath, and Daniel A. Reed. NCSA's World Wide Web server: Design and performance. *IEEE Computer*, pages 68–74, November 1995.

[20] P. Larrañaga and J.A. Lozano. *Estimation of Distribution Algorithms. A New Tool for Evolutionary Computation*. Kluwer Academic Publisher, 2002.

[21] B. Martin. Instance-based learning: Nearest neigbour with generalisation. working paper series 95/18 computer science. Technical report, Hamilton, University of Waikato.

[22] M. Pazzani. Constructive induction of Cartesian product attributes. *Information, Statistics and Induction in Science*, pages 66–77, 1996.

[23] R. Quinlan. *C4.5 Programs for Machine Learning*. Morgan Kauffman, 1993.

[24] V. Robles, P. Larrañaga, J.M. Peña, E. Menasalvas, M.S. Pérez, and V. Herves. Learning semi naïve Bayes structures by estimation of distribution algorithms. In *Lecture Notes in Computer Science (LNAI)*, volume 2902, pages 244–258, 2003.

[25] Ralf S.Engelschall. Load balancing your web site: Practical approaches for distributing HTTP traffic. *Web Techniques Magazine*, 3(5), 1998.

[26] H.D. Simon and S. Teng. How good is recursive bisection? *SIAM Journal of Scientific Computing*, 18(5):1436–1445, 1997.

[27] P. Srisuresh and D. Gan. RFC 2391: Load sharing using IP network address translation (LSNAT), August 1998. Status: INFORMATIONAL.

[28] K.M. Ting. Discretization of continuous-valued attributes and instance-based learning. Technical Report 491, University of Sydney, 1994.

[29] C. Walshaw and M. Cross. Mesh partitioning: a multilevel balancing and refinement algorithm. *SIAM Journal of Science Computation*, 22(1):63–80, 2000.

[30] Wensong Zhang. Linux virtual server for scalable network services. In *Ottawa Linux Symposium*, 2000.

Author Index

Lecture Notes in Artificial Intelligence (LNAI)

Vol. 2700: M.T. Pazienza (Ed.), Extraction in the Web Era. XIII, 163 pages. 2003.

Vol. 2699: M.G. Hinchey, J.L. Rash, W.F. Truszkowski, C.A. Rouff, D.F. Gordon-Spears (Eds.), Formal Approaches to Agent-Based Systems. IX, 297 pages. 2002.

Vol. 2691: V. Mařík, J.P. Müller, M. Pechoucek (Eds.), Multi-Agent Systems and Applications III. XIV, 660 pages. 2003.

Vol. 2684: M.V. Butz, O. Sigaud, P. Gérard (Eds.), Anticipatory Behavior in Adaptive Learning Systems. X, 303 pages. 2003.

Vol. 2671: Y. Xiang, B. Chaib-draa (Eds.), Advances in Artificial Intelligence. XIV, 642 pages. 2003.

Vol. 2663: E. Menasalvas, J. Segovia, P.S. Szczepaniak (Eds.), Advances in Web Intelligence. XII, 350 pages. 2003.

Vol. 2661: P.L. Lanzi, W. Stolzmann, S.W. Wilson (Eds.), Learning Classifier Systems. VII, 231 pages. 2003.

Vol. 2654: U. Schmid, Inductive Synthesis of Functional Programs. XXII, 398 pages. 2003.

Vol. 2650: M.-P. Huget (Ed.), Communications in Multi-agent Systems. VIII, 323 pages. 2003.

Vol. 2645: M.A. Wimmer (Ed.), Knowledge Management in Electronic Government. XI, 320 pages. 2003.

Vol. 2639: G. Wang, Q. Liu, Y. Yao, A. Skowron (Eds.), Rough Sets, Fuzzy Sets, Data Mining, and Granular Computing. XVII, 741 pages. 2003.

Vol. 2637: K.-Y. Whang, J. Jeon, K. Shim, J. Srivastava, Advances in Knowledge Discovery and Data Mining. XVIII, 610 pages. 2003.

Vol. 2636: E. Alonso, D. Kudenko, D. Kazakov (Eds.), Adaptive Agents and Multi-Agent Systems. XIV, 323 pages. 2003.

Vol. 2627: B. O'Sullivan (Ed.), Recent Advances in Constraints. X, 201 pages. 2003.

Vol. 2600: S. Mendelson, A.J. Smola (Eds.), Advanced Lectures on Machine Learning. IX, 259 pages. 2003.

Vol. 2592: R. Kowalczyk, J.P. Müller, H. Tianfield, R. Unland (Eds.), Agent Technologies, Infrastructures, Tools, and Applications for E-Services. XVII, 371 pages. 2003.

Vol. 2586: M. Klusch, S. Bergamaschi, P. Edwards, P. Petta (Eds.), Intelligent Information Agents. VI, 275 pages. 2003.

Vol. 2583: S. Matwin, C. Sammut (Eds.), Inductive Logic Programming. X, 351 pages. 2003.

Vol. 2581: J.S. Sichman, F. Bousquet, P. Davidsson (Eds.), Multi-Agent-Based Simulation. X, 195 pages. 2003.

Vol. 2577: P. Petta, R. Tolksdorf, F. Zambonelli (Eds.), Engineering Societies in the Agents World III. X, 285 pages. 2003.

Vol. 2569: D. Karagiannis, U. Reimer (Eds.), Practical Aspects of Knowledge Management. XIII, 648 pages. 2002.

Vol. 2560: S. Goronzy, Robust Adaptation to Non-Native Accents in Automatic Speech Recognition. XI, 144 pages. 2002.

Vol. 2557: B. McKay, J. Slaney (Eds.), AI 2002: Advances in Artificial Intelligence. XV, 730 pages. 2002.

Vol. 2554: M. Beetz, Plan-Based Control of Robotic Agents. XI, 191 pages. 2002.

Vol. 2543: O. Bartenstein, U. Geske, M. Hannebauer, O. Yoshie (Eds.), Web Knowledge Management and Decision Support. X, 307 pages. 2003.

Vol. 2541: T. Barkowsky, Mental Representation and Processing of Geographic Knowledge. X, 174 pages. 2002.

Vol. 2533: N. Cesa-Bianchi, M. Numao, R. Reischuk (Eds.), Algorithmic Learning Theory. XI, 415 pages. 2002.

Vol. 2531: J. Padget, O. Shehory, D. Parkes, N.M. Sadeh, W.E. Walsh (Eds.), Agent-Mediated Electronic Commerce IV. Designing Mechanisms and Systems. XVII, 341 pages. 2002.

Vol. 2527: F.J. Garijo, J.-C. Riquelme, M. Toro (Eds.), Advances in Artificial Intelligence - IBERAMIA 2002. XVIII, 955 pages. 2002.

Vol. 2522: T. Andreasen, A. Motro, H. Christiansen, H.L. Larsen (Eds.), Flexible Query Answering Systems. X, 383 pages. 2002.

Vol. 2514: M. Baaz, A. Voronkov (Eds.), Logic for Programming, Artificial Intelligence, and Reasoning. XIII, 465 pages. 2002.

Vol. 2507: G. Bittencourt, G.L. Ramalho (Eds.), Advances in Artificial Intelligence. XIII, 417 pages. 2002.

Vol. 2504: M.T. Escrig, F. Toledo, E. Golobardes (Eds.), Topics in Artificial Intelligence. XI, 427 pages. 2002.

Vol. 2499: S.D. Richardson (Ed.), Machine Translation: From Research to Real Users. XXI, 254 pages. 2002.

Vol. 2484: P. Adriaans, H. Fernau, M. van Zaanen (Eds.), Grammatical Inference: Algorithms and Applications. IX, 315 pages. 2002.

Vol. 2479: M. Jarke, J. Koehler, G. Lakemeyer (Eds.), KI 2002: Advances in Artificial Intelligence. XIII, 327 pages. 2002.

Vol. 2475: J.J. Alpigini, J.F. Peters, A. Skowron, N. Zhong (Eds.), Rough Sets and Current Trends in Computing. XV, 640 pages. 2002.

Vol. 2473: A. Gómez-Pérez, V.R. Benjamins (Eds.), Knowledge Engineering and Knowledge Management. Ontologies and the Semantic Web. XI, 402 pages. 2002.

Vol. 2466: M. Beetz, J. Hertzberg, M. Ghallab, M.E. Pollack (Eds.), Advances in Plan-Based Control of Robotic Agents. VIII, 291 pages. 2002.

Vol. 2464: M. O'Neill, R.F.E. Sutcliffe, C. Ryan, M. Eaton, N.J.L. Griffith (Eds.), Artificial Intelligence and Cognitive Science. XI, 247 pages. 2002.

Vol. 2448: P. Sojka, I. Kopecek, K. Pala (Eds.), Text, Speech and Dialogue. XII, 481 pages. 2002.

Vol. 2447: D.J. Hand, N.M. Adams, R.J. Bolton (Eds.), Pattern Detection and Discovery. XII, 227 pages. 2002.

Vol. 2446: M. Klusch, S. Ossowski, O. Shehory (Eds.), Cooperative Information Agents VI. XI, 321 pages. 2002.

Vol. 2445: C. Anagnostopoulou, M. Ferrand, A. Smaill (Eds.), Music and Artificial Intelligence. VIII, 207 pages. 2002.

Vol. 2443: D. Scott (Ed.), Artificial Intelligence: Methodology, Systems, and Applications. X, 279 pages. 2002.

Vol. 2432: R. Bergmann, Experience Management. XXI, 393 pages. 2002.